THE CONCEALED WISDOM
IN WORLD MYTHOLOGY

THE CONCEALED WISDOM
IN WORLD MYTHOLOGY

Illustrated

Geoffrey Hodson

THE THEOSOPHICAL PUBLISHING HOUSE
Adyar Madras 600 020 India

©The Theosophical Publishing House 1983

Photoset and Printed by Offset
At The Vasanta Press
The Theosophical Society, Adyar, Madras 600 020

DEDICATION

THIS WORK IS DEDICATED TO
PHILO JUDAEUS
THE GREAT ALEXANDRIAN SAGE

'Sometimes, when I have come to my work empty, I have suddenly become full, ideas being in an invisible manner showered upon me, and implanted in me from on high; so that through the influence of divine inspiration I have become filled with enthusiam, and have known neither the place in which I was nor those who were present, nor myself, nor what I was saying, nor what I was writing, for then I have been conscious of a richness of interpretation, an enjoyment of light, a most keen-sighted vision, a most distinct view of the objects treated, such as would be given through the eyes from the clearest exhibition'.

— Philo.

Translated by W.R. Inge.

ACKNOWLEDGEMENTS

I acknowledge with gratitude the help in the production of this work received from my wife, Sandra, who at dictation wrote and later prepared the manuscript for the whole of this book. I also thank Mr. and Mrs. Braakenseik of Sydney, Australia, who contributed very greatly, in typed form, original and supporting information from classical literature, especially including that of H.P. Blavatsky, and Mrs. Antoinette Bollard of Auckland, New Zealand, who voluntarily, most skilfully and artistically reproduced with precision from ancient sources — with the exception of the Unicorn — the completely accurate illustrations by which this book is enriched.

My profound gratitude is also felt towards my valued friend and colleague, Mrs. Marie Lovejoy of California, U.S.A. who most generously provided the considerable finance without which this book might not have been published, as she had similarly contributed to the production of my illustrated work, *Music Forms*.

G.H.

CONTENTS

	PAGE
Dedication	v
Acknowledgements	vii
Author's Purpose	xi
Introduction	xiii

CHAPTER

1	Through Fairy Tale and Myth to Theosophia	1
2	The Symbols of the Serpent and the Rod	46
3	The Life, Labours and Ascension of Heracles	68
4	The Argonauts	124
5	The Helios Principle	133
6	The Eros Principle	142
7	The Hephaestus Principle	158
8	The Unicorn	173
9	Prometheus, Imprisoned by Zeus, Freed by Heracles	178
10	Cadmus, The Founder of Thebes	182
	Epilogue	189
	Appendices	197
	Glossary	207
	Scientists' Affirmations	217

AUTHOR'S PURPOSE

The theme of this work is that certain of the Myths of ancient times are far more than mere folk tales. Sages, seers, prophets and inspired authors have, I suggest, added to these material of very great significance. The wisdom attained by the advanced people of ancient times was deliberately concealed as in a tabernacle, was enshrined therein, by the Sages of old. These wise ones on occasion thus embellished the Myths so that they became vehicles for a sublime, but dangerously power-bestowing knowledge. Hence the enveiling.

The purpose for which this book has been conceived and written is to offer for consideration the more immediately applicable and constructive portions of the Wisdom of the Ages learnt primarily from the revelations of H.P. Blavatsky. These have been made available in her truly inspired works, *Isis Unveiled* and *The Secret Doctrine, The Key to Theosophy, The Voice of the Silence,* and *The Theosophical Glossary,* which works I presume strongly to recommend.

Herein, I proffer some of the fruits of my studies in this field.

GEOFFREY HODSON

INTRODUCTION

Why, it may well be asked, should serious consideration—especially philosophic and esoteric—ever be given to the so-often senseless and on occasion even offensive mythological stories of ancient peoples? 'Please look with me beneath the surface', is the answer which the author ventures to offer to readers of this book; 'for thus studied—meaning as parables which both conceal and reveal most important verities—many of the ancient myths can, I have found, prove to be sources of profound wisdom.' Furthermore he believes, truths may be discovered which undoubtedly will prove to be most illuminating, not only in one's spiritual life but also in the conduct of one's daily affairs. Indeed, the incredibilities of certain myths may be regarded as arresting indications of the possible existence of secret meanings deliberately concealed within a number of ancient stories.

Why concealed? Because in those days—as even today—full understanding could lead to knowledge which bestows dangerous powers—*irresistible adverse hypnotism and prematurely aroused physical and superphysical generative forces, for example.*

A friend of the author has very kindly provided a list of exceedingly dangerous powers of Nature which have in these days been made available by Science and gravely misused. These include:

1. *Atomic energy:* Warfare could produce immediate devastation and longer-term radiation sickness and damage to many forms of life on the planet. In the near future, terrorists and other irresponsible groups or even individuals could make their own atomic weapons. Even peaceful uses are attended by the risk of considerable and far-reaching harm to many people over a long period of time by long-lived isotopes.

2. *Conventional Explosives:* In the century that these have been available, a wide range of types of misuse has been witnessed, ranging from guns used by criminals and bombs used by terrorists, to wars both large and small, whatever their 'justification.'

3. *Lasers:* Though not yet fully developed as weapons, these offer the promise of 'death ray' weapons for increasing the power to selectively and instantaneously destroy people and small targets.

4. *Biological 'Weapons':* Knowledge of microbes and body chemistry has been exploited to develop potent poisons such as nerve gases, and virulent disease-producing bacteria. Death by these agents is generally extremely painful and unpleasant.

5. *Drugs:* Though some addictive drugs such as alcohol and marijuana are not new, scientific techniques have added new drugs and placed the means for their extraction in the hands of backyard manufacturers. Drug misuse shows the ends to which some people will go to gain stimulating and exciting psychic experiences, and the utter selfishness of some persons in promoting drugs for gain irrespective of the harm to others.

6. *Psychology:* Motivational research results have been used for some time by advertisers to stimulate desires, existing and new ones, for their products. The results of this so far are not as destructive as are the items above, though they doubtless produce economic and social distortions. A substantial increase of the power to persuade people without their knowing or against their will could be extremely dangerous in the hands of determined and selfish persons or groups. A more extreme case of misuse of psychological knowledge is sophisticated torture and other ways of coercing or breaking down people or 'brainwashing' them.

7. *Harm to others in pursuit of knowledge:* Research on weapons, for example the lasers and nerve gases, is done on animals, sometimes with cruel and extremely unpleasant results. If the primary application were dropped, these secondary misuses would cease.

Animals are frequently subjected to cruel or at least unpleasant procedures for relatively frivolous purposes such as testing of cosmetics and home products. The use of animals for medical experimentation is possibly allowable when carried out kindly and painlessly, but must be classed as a misuse when other satisfactory ways exist of obtaining any information presently obtained by painful methods, and this includes psychological as well as physical pain.

COMMENTS:

Knowledge itself is not harmful or evil, but harm and evil can occur in the misuse of knowledge. The root of this is in the desire of individuals or groups for power or gain irrespective of the harm to other people or life-forms, or to themselves.

Fragmentary occult knowledge is increasingly available in cheap books and magazines. Some of these blatantly appeal to selfish and lower instincts, and frequently no warning is given of the possibility of harm.

From the rate at which science is uncovering new knowledge, it is safe to say that there will be many more discoveries in the future, some of them conferring greater power for harm than anything known at present.

4/4/79, Auckland, New Zealand.   Murray Stentiford, M.Sc.

As this book is being completed, news has appeared of a far more dangerous example, namely the threat of a nuclear disaster at the Harrisburg, Pennsylvania Atomic Power Plant, April, 1979. Fortunately, this disaster was prevented. (Author)

Whilst the scientific discoveries proved harmful, it must also be admitted that they possess value, especially in the advance of civilization, when correctly used. Similarly, more subtle psychological and deeply interior discoveries and powers, whilst in their turn dangerous when misused, nevertheless, rightly used prove to be extremely beneficial. Thus, it is not the knowledge itself which is harmful, but man's misuse thereof.

The veiling of the ways to such capacities is not intended to conceal them from those who would favourably employ them—both personally and for others—but to protect them from discovery and abuse by the unprepared or the unworthy. In consequence, the truths, the powers and the faculties are not to be regarded as evil, since rightly applied they can be extremely beneficent. It is against those who are unworthy or insufficiently evolved and so could misuse them that certain great truths are referred to in the language of allegory and symbol.

If this approach be accepted, the question then arises concerning means whereby enlightening and generally helpful ideas may be both discerned and shared with others. How is one to find out who the great gods Brahma (Hindu), Amun (Egyptian), Zeus (Greek) and Odin (Norse) and all their numerous associates really were and what their often unbelievable activities and adventures may actually mean and even reveal? More important still, it would seem, is the possibility of learning by direct interior experience whether the ancient gods personify the Divine potencies within oneself which, under co-operation may beneficently influence one's thoughts, feelings and so, personal life.

No such knowledge is in these days being more generally, if but partially, revealed and the information can lead to most harmful conduct and experience as I—a consultant in this field for more than fifty years—continue to discover. I have become convinced that both information and safeguards may very usefully be offered. Certain of the myths, not all of them being readily admitted, are, I believe, susceptible of interpretation in terms of direct, *safe*, guidance in one's normal life and development, one's assistance to others and, more especially perhaps, progress upon the spiritual Path.[1]

The story of Daedalus and Icarus may here be cited as a further answer to the last question—why concealed? For although the father was not only himself guarded and controlled concerning the height to which he permitted his wax-adherent wings to carry him—hence the continuance of his own life—but he also warned his son, Icarus, of the danger. His son, on the other hand, as he rose high into the air, not surprisingly became filled with pride—permissibly exalted, one might even say. Unfortunately, he ignored his father's warning and flew so near to the sun that the wax on his shoulders melted. His wings fell off and he descended headlong to his death in the Icarian Sea.

May not this story permissibly be studied—even meditated upon, and so its interior message perceived—as a warning against the harmfulness and great danger indeed of undue pride when beginning to be successful in any walk of life, both material and especially spiritual? Aspirants to the heights of Olympus—the illumined state of consciousness—in their turn may learn much from the tragedy of Icarus; for interior advancement may arouse the desire pridefully to display one's powers and consequent superiority over others—metaphorically to fly too near to the sun. As has been truly said, 'pride goeth before a fall'[2] and indeed, this tendency may justly be regarded as one of

---

[1] The way of hastened spiritual and intellectual unfoldment deliberately entered upon as in the Greater and Lesser Mysteries.

[2] See Proverbs 16:18, for warning that pride can be followed by shame and deterioration.

mankind's 'Achilles' heels'.

Thus, in reply to the further question—how to interpret ancient myths—the Sages[1] of old may answer somewhat as follows: Experiment with the power-bestowing and therefore normally veiled—against misuse—ideas that the supreme deities of India, Egypt, Greece, Central Europe and Scandinavia are personifications of the Divine Principle which is both omnipresent throughout the Universe and also *deeply hidden as a mighty power within every human being*[2]

In due course, one will discover that the truly inspired (only) great dramas included in mythology allegorically portray divinely caused events continually *occurring within* and throughout each of the four kingdoms of Nature—human be it specially noted, animal, plant and mineral and also the four elements, earth, water, air and fire. In addition, it will be found that the adventures of both the supreme deities and their divine relatives—the Olympians of ancient Greece, and their numerous offspring for example—each personify differing procedures occurring throughout the whole of creation.

When duly interpreted, nearly all the interactions between the gods themselves and between the gods and human beings are found to be descriptive of varying relationships. Despite protective veils suggesting the opposite, these are always evolution-quickening, connecting the Godhead within and the familiar normal selves of every dweller upon Earth. This approach is supported by S. De Guaita in *Le Seuil du Mystère*:

> ...To enclose all truth in a spoken language, to express the highest occult mysteries in an abstract style, this would not only be useless, dangerous and sacrilegious, but also impossible. There are truths of a subtle, synthetic and divine order, to express which in all their inviolate completeness, human language is incapable. Only music can sometimes make the soul feel them, only ecstasy can show them in absolute vision, and only esoteric symbolism can reveal them to the spirit in a concrete way.

---

[1] The Greek School of Philosophy had its inception with the seven immortalized thinkers upon whom was first conferred the appellation of *Sophos*, 'the wise'. According to Diogenes Laertius, these sages were: Thales, Solon, Chilon, Pittacus, Bias, Cleobulus, and Periander.

[2] For the author, this is one of the greatest and most profound of all truths and furthermore, *is* capable of being both directly experienced and gravely misused.

If this approach be accepted — especially the last mentioned — and employed, then the god Zeus of Greek mythology was not in truth a profligate deity, continually entering into irregular relationships with the females with whom he fell in love. Quite the contrary; for continuing cohabitation between Zeus, other Olympians and numerous human mistresses may permissibly be interpreted as descriptive of the uplifting influences — such as divine grace — continually brought to bear upon the mortal nature by the God Self within human beings — whether personified as swan with Leda, Zeus and shower of gold with imprisoned Danae, bull with Europa or other mythical unifications. These are allegorically carried out and recorded in order that mythical inamorata (lovers) — actually the mortal selves of every human being — might become spiritually illumined and thus inwardly guided along their varied pathways through life. Indeed, it is taught that the Divine in man — the real Soul — ever seeks the closest possible relationships with the human personality.[1]

One answer which the Sages[2] would possibly offer to the question of how one may thus interpret and effectively apply to one's life the ancient scriptures and mythologies is: "Look within, aspire to knowledge of and union with your own hidden divinity. Render yourself ever more responsive to the wisdom and understanding characteristic of — and so ever available from — the Divine within every human being. Ascend the Mount Olympus — the mythical abode of the Divine within all Nature and every human being — wherein man's spiritual Self perpetually abides. There encounter the favourite child of Zeus, the all-wise Athena Promarchos and Parthenos, who will protect and guide you 'Perseus' that you are — to the decapitation of the most dangerous in-

---

[1] This is revealed in world scriptures. In Hinduism we read that the Lord Shri Krishna affirmed. 'He who seeth Me everywhere, and seeth everything in Me, of Him will I never lose hold, and he shall never lose hold of Me.' *Bhagavad Gita* Sixth Discourse, A. Besant. The Lord Christ similarly affirmed: '...and, lo, I am with you always, even unto the end of the world. Amen.' *(Matt.* 28:20.)

[2] Far-sighted, indeed, were the Sages (Initiates) of antiquity; for they realised that nations come and go, that empires rise and fall, and that the golden ages of art, science, and idealism are succeeded by dark ages of superstition. With the needs of posterity foremost in mind, the sages of old went to inconceivable extremes to make certain that their knowledge should be preserved and humanity guarded from the premature discovery, and so misuse, of the occult powers normally dormant in the body of man.

terior power personified by the serpent-headed "Medusa".[1]

'Thus prepared,' the sages could continue, 'you will be able to free Andromeda (the imprisoned Self) from the dreaded sea-monster—personification of all that is evil in man, when she is "chained" to knowledge of the physical self and world *alone*—the sea-girt Ethiopian rock. Apply to your shoulders the wings invented, constructed and successfully used by Daedalus wherewith to fly from imprisonment by Minos in the Labyrinth—the purely worldly and argumentative mind—up into the heavens above, spiritual awareness, the Olympia within. Be warned, as was his son, Icarus, against the pride, earlier referred to, of ascent dangerously too high and as tragically disastrous.'

THE GORGON, MEDUSA—KUNDALINI-WINGED

Such counsel can in truth be of very great value as I have personally conceived—discovered indeed—whilst engaged on attempted interpretations of the Old and New Testament and world mythologies.

[1] *Medusa*—the only one of the three Gorgons who could be killed, the other two being immortal. Note especially the peculiar and well defined—and I suggest deliberate portrayal—of the 'serpentine hair' rising above the crown of the Gorgon's head, comparing this with the interweaving pathway followed by the Serpent Fire as it arises along the spine of the enfired yogi. See Glossary under *Kundalini* and Appendix.

When these are regarded as revelations of spiritual and philosophic truths which are presented—not infrequently concealed—in the Language of Allegory and Symbols, they can prove to be extremely and very practically enlightening.

May I now refer to—if here permitted to be personal—an arresting experience through which I once passed? As a student of Hinduism, of yoga and hence of the deadly dangerous generative Life-Force known as *Kundalini Shakti* or the Serpent Fire, I was already familiar with the three interlinking pathways or *nadis*[1] within the human body followed by the ascent along the spine into the brain of this great and also Universal, Power.

This Serpent Fire was an ancient symbol of fertility, the sex impulse, and therefore phallic. When either misused or out of control it can prove to be deadly dangerous to both body and mind. Studying Greek Myths, I had perceived that serpentine creatures are therein used as symbols of opposing and destructive agencies such as the Hydra of Lerna, the serpent guarding the 'Golden Fleece and the body and head of the Gorgon Medusa. Perhaps my astonishment may be realised when I also discovered that the form of the Rod in the hands of Hermes was an *exact* reproduction of both the triple *Kundalini* itself and of the three pathways or *nadis*[1] within the body which it follows!

I thereupon remembered the remarkable incident recorded in the Fourth Chapter of the Book of Exodus, of the turning of the Rod of Aaron into a serpent and have offered an interpretation of this incident in Vol.IV *The Hidden Wisdom in the Holy Bible*.[2] Other examples of an apparently identical use of this same symbology are also referred to in this book, together with appropriate illustrations copied with exactitude, notably from ancient Egyptian and Greek sources. Perhaps the most noticeable amongst these works of art consists of the illustration of the Chariot of Triptolemus empowered by winged serpents; for Triptolemus, as the Initiate of the Eleusinian Mysteries, had been both endowed with this Power in order to travel over the world and 'teach agriculture' of the Soul I suggest rather than of the soil: He had evidently also been taught to use the Power with

---

[1] *Nadi* (Sk.) The channel or nerve for the conduction of a current.
[2] Excerpt included in Chapter 2.

INTRODUCTION xxi

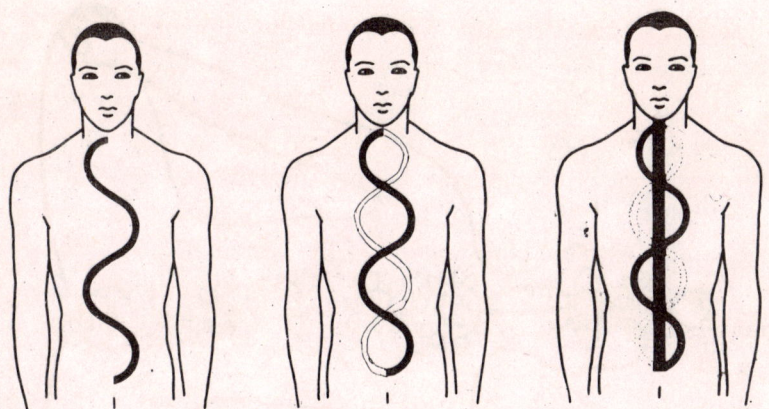

THREE PHASES OF AROUSING *KUNDALINI*

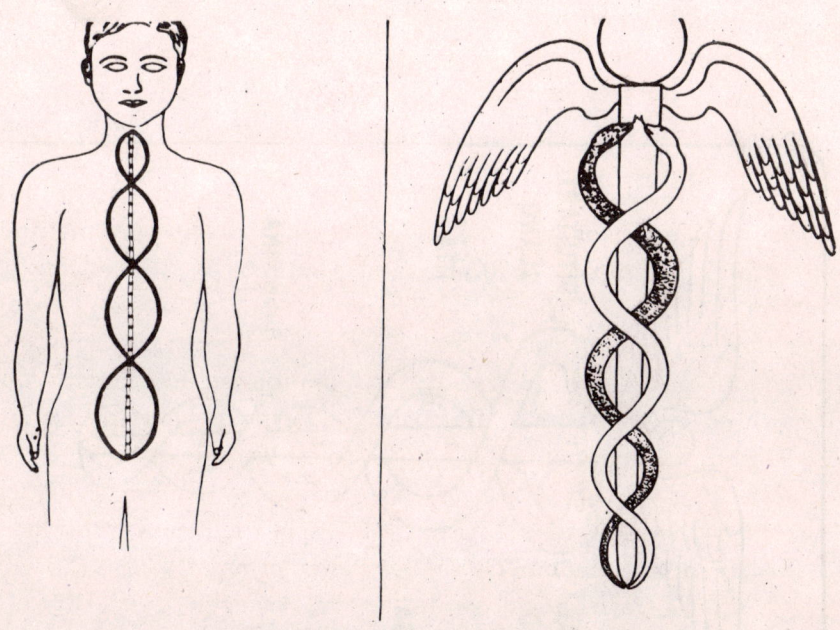

CADUCEUS IN MAN AND CADUCEUS OF HERMES

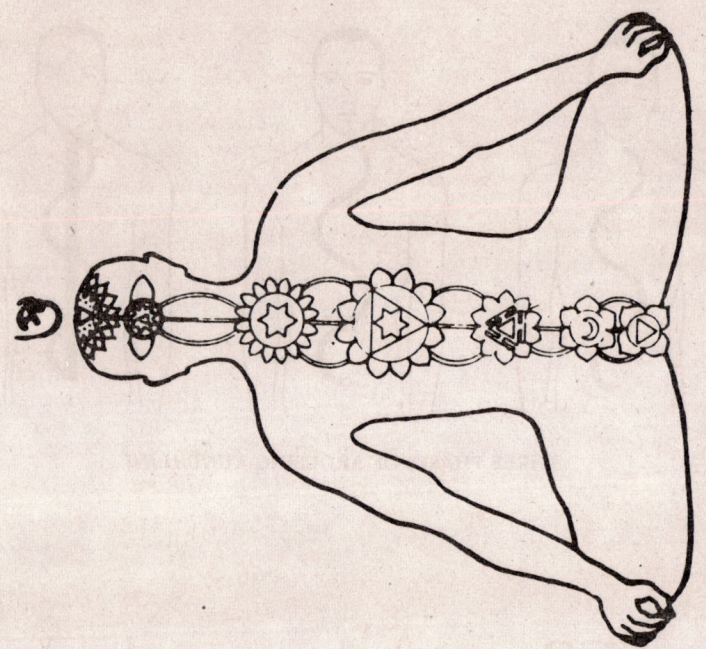

THE CHAKRAS ACCORDING TO TANTRIC PHILOSOPHY
YOGI WITH FULLY AROUSED KUNDALINI.

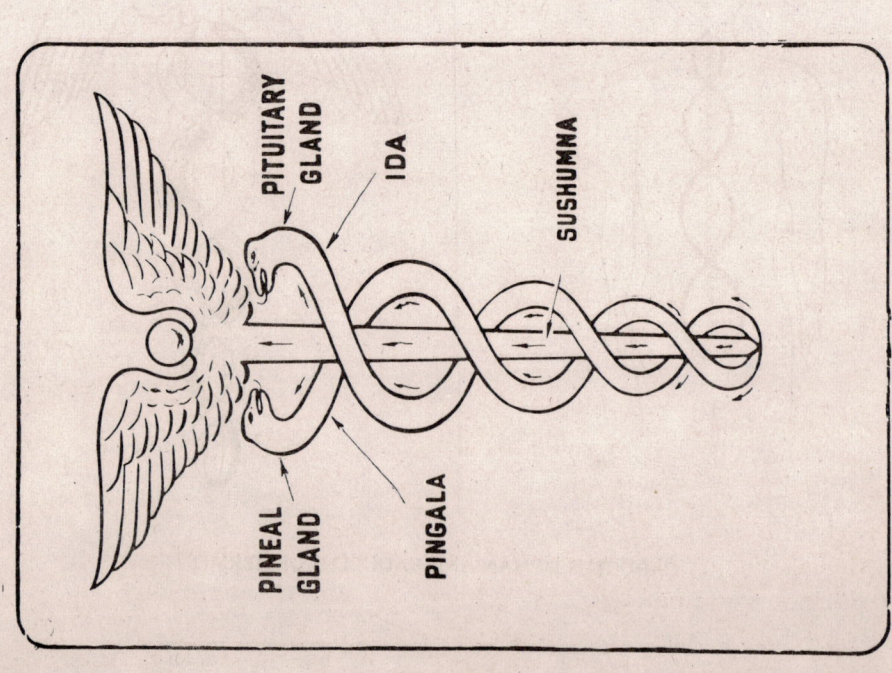

THE THREE CURRENTS OF KUNDALINI SHAKTI IN 'WINGED' MAN.

safety—as is every Initiate—under the direction of the goddess Demeter—who personifies the Initiating Hierophant.[1] When a more serious study had been entered upon, I found—almost with astonishment—as already stated that the design of the Rod of Hermes displayed with remarkable similarity—reproduced indeed—the pattern of the *nadis* in and along which in Hinduism *Kundalini* is said to rise from sacrum to brain.

Interpretations of Greek myths presented themselves to me strictly in accordance with Hindu philosophy, particularly as illustrated in the book, *The Serpent Power,* by Arthur Avalon, with the exactly appropriate Frontispiece. The Third Aspect of the Hindu Trinity—the Lord Shiva—is also pictorially represented as an ascetic whose matted locks are tied in the coils of a serpent which holds its hood above his head whilst another reptile adorns his neck, a third one serving as a 'Sacred Thread'. The production in India of stones upon which the three *nadis* are carved, and their placement in considerable numbers near trees under which women seeking children ceremonially circulate, refers directly to the recognition of the serpent as a symbol of both generative power and esoteric wisdom.

The reader may perhaps imagine and even share my astonishment, when I realised that the selfsame system of channels proved to be the form of the magical Rod of Power which freed the great god Hermes from normal spatial limitations! This Rod in his hand permitted him to ascend to Olympus high in the heavens and to descend into Hades deep below the surface of the Earth.[2]

The Egyptian symbol exoterically representing the union by Pharaoh Menes of Upper and Lower Egypt may reasonably be regarded as a portrayal of the upward-flowing and inter-crossing Serpent Fire which when fully aroused and so employed, reveals by experience to the yogi the truth of the oneness of the Divine Life in the Universe (Olympus-Upper) and man (Hades-lower) Egypt, the yogic culmination of realised unity being exoterically portrayed as a geographical symbol.

Admittedly, the portrayal of the symbol varies in Egyptian art, though all present the same general design. The accompanying illustration is of particular interest both because of the clear indication

---

[1] See *Mythology*, Edith Hamilton, p.53, 60-61.
[2] The Caduceus. See frontispiece.

of the human pelvic bones at the base of the spine and the way in which the spinal column is presented as composed of a number of component vertebrae. These and other Myths will be fully considered throughout this study of symbology especially as so many other equally exact or similar personifications and symbols of the Serpentine Fire are found to be frequently included in them.

As I proceeded to study them with the above and other interpretations dawning in my mind, a whole new world gradually became opened to my consciousness. Into this world I have ever since felt drawn and after the 'door' was 'opened', I have remained an explorer therein, this book being a partial offering of some of my still continuing 'discoveries'; for a close similarity—identity indeed—was found to exist between Indian teachings concerning the Serpent Power and the presentations of the same ideas in symbolic, allegorical and mythical form particularly in ancient Egypt and Greece.

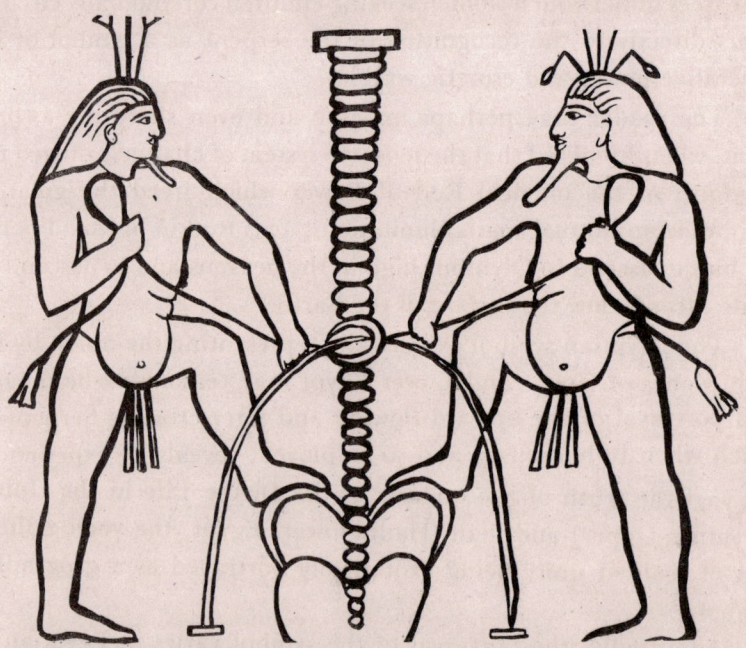

EGYPTIAN SYMBOL OF UNION OF UPPER AND LOWER EGYPT

THE HIDDEN WISDOM AND WHY IT IS CONCEALED

The greatest degree of power which occult science can bestow is to be derived from knowledge of the unity and interaction between the Macrocosm and the microcosm, the Universe and man. "The mystery of the earthly and mortal man is after the mystery of the supernal and immortal One", wrote Eliphas Levi. Lao Tzu also expresses this truth in his words: "The Universe is a man on a large scale."

The whole Universe with all its parts, from the highest plane down to physical nature, is regarded as being interlocked, interwoven to make a single whole—one body, one organism, one power, one life, one consciousness, all cyclically evolving under one law. The 'organs' or parts of the Macrocosm, though apparently separated in space and plane of manifestation, are in fact harmoniously interrelated, intercommunicative and continually interactive.

According to this revelation of occult philosophy the Zodiac, the galaxies and their component systems, and the planets with their kingdoms and planes of Nature, elements, Orders of Beings, radiating forces, colours and notes, are not only parts of a co-ordinated whole and in 'correspondence' or mutual resonance with each other, but also—which is of profound significance—have their representations within man himself. This system of correspondences is in operation throughout the whole of the microcosm, from the Monad to the mortal flesh, including the parts of the mechanism of consciousness, or vehicles and their *chakras*,[1] by means of which the Spirit of man is manifested throughout his whole nature, varying in degree according to the stage of evolutionary development. *The human being who discovers this truth could enter the power aspect of the Universe and tap any one of these forces. He would then become endowed with almost irresistible influence over both Nature and his fellow men.*

The task of safely unveiling a measure of the hidden truth demands some knowledge of Cosmogenesis, of the emanation of the Universe from the Absolute, the finite from the Infinite, and of the successive cycles, major and minor, of involution and evolution. In addition, both knowledge of the symbolical Language, its purposes,

---

[1] *Chakra* (Sk.)— A vortex or 'wheel' in the etheric and superphysical bodies of man. q.v. *The Chakras*, C.W. Leadbeater, and Glossary to this Vol.

methods and classical symbols, and the faculty of analysing and interpreting historical metaphors, are necessary to open the casket containing the treasures of concealed wisdom—the Holy Bible itself.

'Where the Word found that things done according to the history could be adapted to these mystical senses, he made use of them, concealing from the multitude the deeper meaning; but where in the narrative of the development of super-sensual things, there did not follow the performance of those certain events which were already indicated by the mystical meaning, the Scripture interwove in the history the account of some event that did not take place, sometimes what could not have happened; sometimes what could, but did not."

De Principiis, Origen, Christian philosopher and Biblical scholar, famed for his teaching at Alexandria and Caesarea (c.185-c.254 A.D.)

'What man of sense will agree with the statement that the first, second and third days in which the *evening* is named and the *morning,* were without sun, moon and stars, and the first day without a heaven? What man is found such an idiot as to suppose that God planted trees in Paradise, in Eden, like a husbandman, and planted therein the tree of life, perceptible to the eyes and senses, which gave life to the eater thereof; and another tree which gave to the eater thereof a knowledge of good and evil? I believe that every man must hold these things for images, under which the hidden sense lies concealed.'

Origen: Huet., *Origeniana,* 167, Franck, p.142.

'Every time that you find in our books a tale the reality of which seems impossible, a story which is repugnant to both reason and common sense, then be sure that the tale contains a profound allegory veiling a deeply mysterious truth; and the greater the absurdity of the letter, the deeper the wisdom of the spirit.'

Moses Maimonides, Jewish theologian, historian, Talmudist, philosopher and physician (1135-1205 A.D.)

'Woe... to the man who sees in the Torah, i.e. Law, only simple recitals and ordinary words! Because, if in truth it only contained these, we would even today be able to compose a Torah much more worthy of admiration.... The recitals of the Torah are the vestments of the Torah. Woe to him who takes this garment for the Torah itself!... There are some foolish people who, seeing a man covered with a beautiful garment, carry their regard no further, and take the garment for the body, whilst there exists a still more precious thing, which is the soul... The Wise, the servitors of the Supreme King, those who inhabit the heights of Sinai, are occupied only with the soul, which is the basis of all the rest, which is Torah itself; and in the future time they will be prepared to contemplate the Soul of that soul (i.e. the Deity) which breathes in the Torah.'

Zohar III, 152b. (Soncino Ed. Vol. V, p.211).

'Rabbi Simeon said: 'If a man looks upon the Torah as merely a book presenting narratives and everyday matters, alas for him! Such a Torah, one treating with everyday concerns, and indeed a more excellent one, we too, even we, could compile. More than that, in the possession of the rulers of the world there are books of even greater merit, and these we could emulate if we wished to compile some such Torah, But the Torah, in all of its words, holds supernal truths and sublime secrets.' Ibid, 152a.

'Like unto a beautiful woman hidden in the interior of a palace who, when her friend and beloved passes by, opens for a moment a secret window, and is only seen by him: then again retires and disappears for a long time; so the doctrine shows herself only to the elect, but also not even to these always in the same manner. In the beginning, deeply veiled, she only beckons to the one passing, with her hand; it simply depends (on himself) if in his understanding he perceives this gentle hint. Later she approaches him somewhat nearer, and whispers to him a few words, but her countenance is still hidden in the thick veil, which his glances cannot penetrate. Still later she converses with him, her countenance covered with a thinner veil. After he has accustomed himself to her society, she finally shows herself to him face to face, and entrusts him with the innermost secrets of her heart (Sod).'

Zohar II, 99a (Soncino Ed. Vol. III, p.301).

THE TORAH

'Jewish mystics are at one in giving a mystical interpretation to the Torah; the Torah is to them a living organism animated by a secret life which streams and pulsates below the crust of its literal meaning; every one of the innumerable strata of this hidden region corresponds to a new and profound meaning of the Torah. The Torah, in other words, does not consist merely of chapters, phrases and words; rather is it to be regarded as the living incarnation of the divine wisdom which eternally sends out new rays of light. It is not merely the historical law of the Chosen People, although it is that too; it is rather the cosmic law of the Universe, as God's wisdom conceived it. Each configuration of letters in it, whether it makes sense in human speech or not, symbolizes some aspect of God's creative power which is active in the Universe.'

Major Trends in Jewish Mysticism, Gershom G. Scholem.

A SYMBOL

'A symbol retains its original form and its original content. It does not become, so to speak, an empty shell into which another content is poured; in itself, through its own existence, it makes another reality transparent which cannot appear in any other form. A mystical symbol is an expressible representation of something which lies beyond the sphere of expression and communication, something which comes from a sphere whose face is, as it were, turned inward and away from us. A hidden and inexpressible reality finds its expression in the symbol. The symbol "signifies" nothing and communicates nothing, but makes something transparent which is beyond all expression. Where deeper insight into the structure of the allegory uncovers fresh layers of meaning, the symbol is intuitively understood all at once—or not at all. The symbol in which the life of the Creator and that of creation become one, is—to use Creuzer's words—"a beam of light which, from the dark and abysmal depths of existence and cognition, falls into our eye and penetrates our whole being". It is a "momentary totality" which is perceived intuitively in a mystical *now*—the dimension of time proper to the symbol.'

Ibid.

'The shell, the white, and the yolk form the perfect egg. The shell protects the white and the yolk, and the yolk feeds upon the white; and when the white has vanished, the yolk, in the form of the fledged bird, breaks through the shell and presently soars into the air. Thus does the static become the dynamic, the material the spiritual.

'If the shell is the exoteric principle and the yolk the esoteric, what then is the white? The white is the food of the second, the accumulated wisdom of the world centring round the mystery of growth, which each single individual must absorb before he can break the shell. The transmutation of the white, by the yolk, into the fledgling is the secret of secrets of the entire Qabalistic philosophy.'

The Secret Wisdom of the Qabalah, J.F.C. Fuller.

WHY WISDOM IS CONCEALED

'Having taken the Upanishad as the bow, as the great weapon, let him place on it the arrow, sharpened by devotion! Then having drawn it with a thought directed to that which is, hit the mark, O Friend, namely that which is Indestructible! Om[1] is the bow, the Self is the arrow, Brahman[2] is called the aim. It is to be hit by a man who is not thoughtless, and then as the arrow becomes one with the target, he will become one with Brahman.'

Mundaka Upanishad, II

'Know the Self as the Lord of the chariot and the body as, verily, the chariot; know the intellect as the charioteer and the mind as, verily, the reins.

'The senses, they say, are the horses; the objects of sense the paths (they range over); (the self) associated with the body, the senses, and the mind — wise men declare — is the enjoyer.

'He who has no understanding, whose mind is always unrestrained, his senses are out of control, as wicked horses are for a charioteer.

'He, however, who has understanding, whose mind is always restrained, his senses are under control, as good horses are for a charioteer.

'He, however, who has no understanding, who has no control over his mind (and is) ever impure, reaches not that goal but comes back into mundane life.

'He, however, who has understanding, who has control over his mind and (is) ever pure, reaches that goal from which he is not born again.

'He who has the understanding for the driver of the chariot and controls the rein of his mind, he reaches the end of the journey, that supreme abode of the all-pervading.'

The *Kathopanishad* 1·3·3 to 1·3·9, Dr. Radhakrishnan's translation, from *The Principal Upanishads*.

'And the disciples came, and said unto him, Why speakest thou unto them in parables?

'He answered and said unto them, Because it is given unto you to

---

[1] OM or AUM: The name of the triple Deity. A Syllable of affirmation, invocation and divine benediction.

[2] Brahman (Sk.): The impersonal, supreme and incognisable Principle of the Universe, from the Essence of which all emanates and into which all returns.

know the mysteries of the kingdom of heaven, but to them it is not given ...

'But blessed are your eyes, for they see: and your ears, for they hear.'

Matt. 13:10, 11 and 16.

'To enclose all truth in a spoken language, to express the highest occult mysteries in an abstract style, this would not only be useless, dangerous and sacrilegious, but also impossible. There are truths of a subtle, synthetic and divine order, to express which in all their inviolate completeness, human language is incapable. Only music can sometimes make the soul feel them, only ecstasy can show them in absolute vision, and only esoteric symbolism can reveal them to the spirit in a concrete way.'

Le Seuil du Mystere, S. De Guaita

FOUR MAJOR KEYS OF INTERPRETATION

The foregoing enunciation of the principal theme of this work, namely that the inspired portions of world scriptures and myths are allegorical in character, may now be followed by a statement of four of the seven possible keys of interpretation and their Macrocosmic and microcosmic[1] applications to a number of such passages.

ALL HAPPENS WITHIN

The *first key* is that some narratives of supposedly historical events are also descriptive of subjective experiences of races, nations and individuals; in this sense, all happens within. When this key is 'turned', certain stories are found to have at least two possible underlying meanings. One of these refers to the experiences and attainments of those advancing by the normal evolutionary method, and the other to mystics who are treading the Way of Holiness or Path of Swift Unfoldment.

---

[1] Macrocosm and microcosm. All allegories and symbols are susceptible of a threefold interpretation—Macrocosmic or applying to Logoi and Universes, microcosmic or applying to man, and Initiatory or applying to mystical experiences and stages of unfoldment passed through by those treading the path of discipleship and Initiation. (See Glossary.)

KEYS OF INTERPRETATION xxxi

The need for the veiling of magical and occult knowledge in allegory and symbol is especially great in the latter of these two applications of the first key; for, quite early in the approach to and entry upon the Path, an enhancement of will-power and the mental and psychic faculties begins to be apparent. Premature awakening and development of these supernormal powers, and their employment for purely personal, and especially for destructive, purposes could prove extremely harmful both to those who misuse them and to their fellow men.

'CHRIST IN YOU, THE HOPE OF GLORY'[1]

The Apostle Paul would seem to have accepted this first key—the mystical interpretation. For him the Nativity of Christ, for example, was not only a particular event which occurred at a certain time in Bethlehem, but also refers to a universal human experience. The narratives of the Annunciation, the Immaculate Conception and the Nativity of Christ are so written as also to describe allegorically the gradual awakening of Christlike powers of perception within the Soul[2] of advanced man. For St. Paul, evidently, the birth and activities of the Lord Christ were descriptive of the interior awakening and perfecting of the inherent, redemptive Christ-power and nature *within* man. Thus he wrote: '...I travail in birth again until Christ be formed in you'[3] and 'To whom God would make known what is the riches of the glory of this mystery among the Gentiles; which is Christ in you, the hope of glory.'

As the student of the Bible reads the great narratives with this key in his hand, as it were, he may even himself share in the recorded experiences. He may ascend 'the mount' with Abraham, Moses, Elijah and Jesus and, in however slight a measure at first, begin to participate in their exaltation. With the two dejected disciples he may walk the road to Emmaus,[4] and hear the wise words of their temporarily

---

[1] Col. 1:27.
[2] Soul. When spelt with a capital 'S' this word refers to the unfolding, immortal, spiritual Self of man, the true individuality behind the bodily veil. When spelt with a small 's' it is used for the *psyche* or mental, emotional and vital parts of the mortal man. Heb. *Nephesh chaiah*, 'souls of life' or 'living soul'. Gen. 2:7.
[3] Gal. 4:19.
[4] Lk. 24: 13-31.

unknown Companion. At the description of the breaking of the bread he may then become illumined by that inner light which shone when '...their eyes were opened, and they knew him...'. Such indeed is part of the intention of the inspired authors. As one studies the scriptures of the world, therefore, one must read intuitively, sensitively, with one's mind open and responsive to that vaster consciousness which so often seems waiting to burst through. Thus, the first key is that some recorded events also occur interiorly.

PEOPLE PERSONIFY HUMAN QUALITIES

The *second key* is that each of the *dramatis personae* introduced into the stories represents a condition of consciousness and a quality of character. All the actors are personifications of aspects of human nature, of attributes, principles, powers, faculties, limitations, weaknesses and errors of man. When purely human being are the heroes, the life of a person evolving normally is being described. When the hero is semi-divine, however, the accent is upon the hastened progress of the spiritual Self of man, particularly after it has begun to assume preponderant power. When the central figure is an *Avatara*[1] or 'descent' of an Aspect of Deity, the account of His experiences also describes those passed through during the later phases of human evolution to the stature of perfected manhood. Such is the general purpose and such the method of the ancient writers of the world's immortal allegories, parables and myths.

The Deity or Father when introduced into a narrative generally refers to the highest spiritual Essence in man, the Divine Spark, the Monad,[2] as also to the Oversoul of the race. Those who are following the pathway of Initiation seek to hasten this realisation, first of their divine, immortal nature and thereafter of their unbroken unity with the Supreme Lord of All. This full recognition of man's unity with God, of the oneness of man-Spirit with God-Spirit, is the ultimate goal for all mankind. In Hinduism this state is called *moksha* or Liberation; in Buddhism, *nirvana* or conscious absorption; in Christianity, Salvation, Ascension, Christhood.

---

[1] *Avatara* (Sk.). The doctrine of Divine incarnation or 'descent'. See Glossary.
[2] Monad (Gr.)—'Alone.' Other terms are the Immortal Germ, the Logos of the Soul, the Dweller in the Innermost. See Glossary.

In this method of Biblical study the characters—divine, semidivine, patriarchal and human—are thus regarded as personifications of principles and powers of both Nature as the Macrocosm, and of man as the microcosm. Allowances must, however, be made for differing correspondences necessitated by the stories themselves. This reading is supported by St. Paul, who writes: '...all these things happened unto them for ensamples'[1] and '... it is written, that Abraham had two sons, the one by a bond-maid, the other by a freewoman...which things are an allegory...'[2] It is not unreasonable to assume that such a theory may also be true of many other portions of the Bible. One may even go further than this and assert that the practice of studying the scriptures of the world in their literal meaning, and as records of actual historical events alone, can lead to grave error and serious confusion of mind.

Other errors in modern Christianity urgently need to be corrected. Amongst these are: the already mentioned degradation of the concept of the Divine Emanator of the Universe to the level of a tribal god;[3] reliance upon an external (instead of an interior) redemptive power; and the erection of a vast though changing theological edifice founded upon dogmas, some of which are based upon a literal reading of the scriptures.[4]

These difficulties are all avoided, and profound inspiration consistent with reason is gained, by the recognition of a mystical intent and meaning underlying many portions of the scriptures and mythologies of the peoples of old. Thus the humility, the devotion and the selfless love of Mary, the Mother of Jesus; the human frailty and the inherent sainthood of a Magdalene and a Peter; the valuable busyness of Martha and, evidently in the eyes of Jesus, the even more valuable, spiritual, contemplative aspects of human nature and modes of life

---

[1] *I Cor.* 10:11.

[2] *Gal.* 4:22-24.

[3] Exoteric Hebraism, and a literal reading of certain Books of the Old Testament alone present this view of Jehovah; Kabbalism, the theosophy of the Hebrews, their esoteric wisdom, proclaims the unnamed Deity as the self-existent, impersonal Emanator of Cosmos and all that it contains.

[4] Even as this work is in course of preparation, many of these dogmas are being subjected to critical re-examination by the clergy and laity of certain Christian denominations such as, for example, the Roman Catholic, notably at its Ecumenical Councils of recent years.

xxxiv   INTRODUCTION

displayed by her sister Mary[1] all these attributes form part of the character of every individual, the conditions of life drawing out now one and now another. On the surface the remark to Martha, which almost reads like a rebuke, might seem to be somewhat unfair. Apparently, however, Jesus was referring to the fact discovered and taught by every mystic that only in complete quietude of body and mind may the voice of the Master within be heard. Elijah appears to have made this discovery, for after the wind, the earthquake and the fire, a silence fell upon him and in that silence he heard the 'still small voice'.[2] The Psalmist in his turn received similar guidance from the Lord, who said to him: 'Be still, and know that I am God...'[3]

Applying the second key, which is that the *dramatis personae* of many scriptural narratives represent human characteristics, the twelve disciples of Jesus are found to personify attributes and potentialities of man. For example, a twelvefold classification of them as microcosmic manifestations of the qualities given by astrologers to the Zodiacal Signs is discernible. Discipleship, or nearness to the divine Teacher, indicates that the evolution of the disciple has reached an advanced stage. Ultimately all powers of heart, mind and Spirit will be fully developed. Only as the twelve zodiacal qualities in man are 'discipled'—or disciplined and refined—is he able to respond to his own inner spiritual will and to comprehend pure wisdom, both of which are personified by the Master. The Christ Presence and Power—whether asleep as in the ship on Galilee,[4] awakening or being 'born' as in the mystical Nativity,[5] or fully grown to 'the measure of the stature of the fulness of Christ'[6]—must, however, be added to all human attributes in order to present by means of personification a description of the fully 'perfected' man.

The interaction between these various aspects of human nature, the effects they produce upon one another, the waxing or waning of one or more of them at different times and in different lives, and the

---

[1] *Lk.* 10:38-42.
[2] 1 *Kings* 19:12.
[3] *Ps.* 46:10.
[4] *Mk.* 4:38.
[5] *Gal.* 4:19.
[6] *Eph.* 4:13.

gradual, triumphant emergence and predominance of the royal spiritual Self, the Immortal King within, personified by the Saviour and the hero of every saga — all this is allegorically portrayed by the Initiated authors of the inspired portions of the Scriptures of the world. The marriages in which many of these exploits culminate may be interpreted as symbolic references to the unification of the consciousness of the outer and the inner, the mortal and the immortal selves of men. In mystical literature they are not inaptly referred to as 'heavenly marriages'. Thus the narratives themselves describe the experiences — particularly the tests, ordeals, defeats and victories — of one person, who is man himself. Successful exploits describe interior achievements, while partial and complete failures, defeats and surrenders are allegories of temporary victories of the purely human over the divine in man — conquests of matter over Spirit. Thus the second key is that each of the *dramatis personae* represents a condition of consciousness and a quality of character.

STORIES DRAMATISE PHASES OF HUMAN EVOLUTION

The *third key* is that each story may be regarded as a graphic description of the experiences of the human Soul as it passes through the stages, and their intermediate phases, of its evolutionary journey to the Promised Land (cosmic consciousness) — the summit of human attainment. Inspired allegories are always distinguishable from mere novels and biographies by several characteristics, such as the intrusion of the supernatural and the inclusion in the story of angelic and divine beings, even of Deity itself. When these are found, the existence of a hidden revelation may always be suspected. The reader possessed of and applying the keys may then penetrate the veil of symbolism and find that hidden wisdom which it had concealed.

In the main the manifold experiences of the immortal Self of each man on its pathway towards perfection are, as stated above, narrated as the adventures of numbers of persons in any one story. The twelve labours of Hercules, each susceptible of association with one of the twelve Signs of the Zodiac, the voyage of the Argonauts, the experiences of the Israelites, and the lives of the Lord Shri Krishna, the Lord Buddha and the Lord Christ, amongst many others, are all descriptive in the symbolic manner of the journey of the Soul and the psychological, intellectual and spiritual unfoldments which occur on that pilgrimage.

xxxvi   INTRODUCTION

In this third method of interpretation, each story may be studied from at least two points of view. The first of these refers to normal evolutionary progress and the accompanying mental and emotional states, whilst the second reveals the allegories as more especially descriptive of the experiences of those who enter in at the strait gate and pursue the narrow way.[1]

In the Parable of the Sower[2] the different conditions of the ground — as the Christ explained privately to His disciples[3] — represent various evolutionary phases and states of spiritual receptiveness of the race and the individual, from complete unresponsiveness (wayside and rocky ground) to full perception and ratification (fertile ground). In the Parable of the Ten Virgins,[4] the foolish maidens may be regarded as those who are not as yet sufficently evolved to be able to respond to impulses descending from their Higher Self (the bridegroom), and therefore not really to be blamed. The wise virgins, on the other hand, may be interpreted as personifying all those in whom the spiritual Self has attained to a considerable degree of evolutionary unfoldment. The outer, physical nature has then become sufficiently developed to be aware of this fact and to give expression in the conduct of daily life to higher idealism and the fruits of spiritual experiences. This state is, in its turn, followed by the progressive illumination of the mind-brain by the Ego (betrothal), leading to the fusion of the immortal and mortal natures (marriage).

The incidents of the marriage feast of Cana[5] may thus be taken to refer to this interior union achieved by those who have awakened the power of the Christ Presence which is within every man, allegorically indicated by the physical presence of the Master. After this attainment the coarser desires of the emotional nature (water) are transmuted into wisdom and spiritual intuitiveness (wine). Marriages of heroes and heroines in Mythologies and Scriptures, as we have seen, indicate that the all-essential blending of the mortal personality with the immortal Ego, and the further merging of the human individuality with the divine Self and life of the Universe as a whole, 'the Mystic Identity' or

[1] *Matt.* 7:13-14.
[2] *Matt.* 13:1-9.
[3] *Matt.* 13:18-23.
[4] *Matt.* 25:1-13.
[5] *Jn.* 2:1-11.

cosmic consciousness, have both been attained.[1] The presence of the Christ in this story, as in all narratives in which He appears, including those which describe the 'miracles', implies that the phase of the evolutionary journey of the Soul has been entered at which spiritual wisdom, spiritual intuitiveness and a Christlike love and compassion are already well developed and active throughout the personal nature. The changing of water into wine at such 'marriages' is not a miracle, but rather a natural process which occurs when a steadfast aspirant finds and successfully treads the narrow way. The grape and the wine also symbolise knowledge, wisdom and comprehension of the spirit of things. As fermentation gives a certain 'strength' to wine, so the action of the intellect upon accumulated esoteric knowledge turns it into pure wisdom, implicit insight and deeply penetrative intuitiveness. Thus the third key is that many Scriptural stories allegorically describe phases of man's evolutionary journey and their accompanying mystical experiences.

THE SYMBOLISM OF LANGUAGE

The *fourth key* is that some physical objects, as also certain words, have each their own special symbolic meaning. In the cipher of the Bible such words are chiefly used to denote levels of human awareness. Those referring to earthy or physical objects are descriptive of states of consciousness and attributes of character pertaining to the waking state. Water and its association refer macrocosmically to universal space and microcosmically to the emotions. With certain exceptions, air and fire refer to the intuition and the mind respectively. Fire, it should be added, also has reference to the manifested creative life-force of the Logos and that same force as the procreative power in man. This is referred to as the Serpent Fire or *Kundalini*[2] and frequently represented by dragons and serpents. Thus the fourth key is that some physical objects and certain words have each their own symbolic meaning.

[1] The numerous, and in the literal sense scandalous, *amours* of Zeus, the Father of the Gods, are all susceptible of similar interpretation, namely of unions between the Divine and the mortal in human nature. Indeed, each *amour* with its specific symbology (cloud, swan, shower of gold and bull, for example) may be interpreted as descriptive of a descent of the inner spiritual Self into union with the less Divine and also purely mortal levels of human consciousness.

[2] *Kundalini* (Sk.)—. 'The coiled up, universal Life Principle'. A sevenfold, occult power in Universe *(Maha Kundali)* and man *(Kundalini)*. See Glossary.

CHAPTER 1

THROUGH FAIRY TALE AND MYTH TO THEOSOPHIA[1]

Proffered Interpretations of Certain Greek Myths

FROM MYTHOLOGY TO THEOSOPHIA

Admittedly, the myths of ancient peoples may well have begun as folk stories as also have some of the fairy-tales of today. In their transmission down the centuries, certain of these originals have been added to and enriched by sages, seers and inspired poets. Their simplicity and purely imaginary ideas thus became transformed into allegories which, as we will see, were sometimes remarkably exact descriptions of fundamental processes of nature, physical, superphysical and spiritual. Included amongst these were the laws of Being; the origins of universes, suns, planets and their inhabitants, both physically visible and invisible; procedures of evolution; interplay between near and distant worlds; and the presence of an unknowable, incomprehensible deific Power as the basis for all that exists. These were referred to and revealed largely by their personification as gods and goddesses, as semi-divine and supernormally endowed men and women the Races of men upon earth and innumerable and highly complicated relationships between these three products of creation.

Differing peoples gradually evolved their own groups of divinities, adopted those of neighbours and of the inhabitants of conquered lands. A blend was thus formed of wholly fictitious, fairy-tale-like accounts of the creation and evolution of the Universe, of this Planet, and of all known sentient beings. At the centre or heart was the paternal Power who was the postulated Source and Father of All, the closest

---

[1] *Theosophia* (G.K.) Divine Wisdom — a word said to have been coined by Ammonius Saccus of the Neo-Platonic School of Alexandria. (Approximately first three centuries of the Christian era.)

concept of Deity which the originators of the Language of Allegory and Symbol, and so of the myths, considered it both advisable and safe to present. Certain of the customs and household lives of mankind were then attributed to this Father of the gods, his wife and family, even though moral laws and ethical principles were not always regarded as entirely binding upon the deities—Zeus with his many amours for example. Intercourse, normal and sometimes incestuous, within and without the marriage tie, with all its products and results, were included in the original accounts as is indicated by a study of world mythologies.

This may well have been done by sages primarily to explain natural phenomena and secondarily, safely[1] to reveal by personifications and dramatic actions, the interplay of levels of awareness, their forces and their inhabitants. In some cases, however, one or other of Earth's Magi, it may be presumed, and inspired historians, poets and dramatists both re-shaped and enriched various mythological stories. By these means, imaginary accounts were adapted in order to bring them closer to reality as in descriptions of the creation of the Universe and of the moulding of matter by intelligent Beings. The resistance of substance to the will and the formative plan of the Creator was sometimes described as warfare which broke out between the Cyclops, the Titans and the Giants or elder Gods of Greece—Cronus for example—who fought against their divine Father Zeus, and his five brothers and sisters. In Egypt, also, the god Set became the embodiment of the Principle of Evil. He slew and dismembered his brother Osiris, the portions of whose anatomy were later re-assembled and the god re-animated by his wife Isis and her son Horus. In exoteric Hindu Mythology, the Asuras[2] were considered maleficent agents who resisted (actually assisted) the formative procedures of the Supreme Deity.

The Irish poet, James Stephens, sensed and expressed this profoundly occult teaching in his poem, 'The Fullness of Time.[3]

> On a rusty iron throne,
> Past the furthest star of space,

---

[1] See Introduction.
[2] *Asuras* (Sk.) In one aspect only, Demons or Satanic powers.
[3] *Collected Poems*, James Stephens. Macmillan & Co., London, 1931.

INTERPRETATION OF GREEK MYTHS

> I saw Satan sit alone,
> Old and haggard was his face;
> For his work was done, and he
> Rested in eternity.
>
> And to him from out the sun
> Came his father and his friend,
> Saying,—Now the work is done
> Enmity is at an end—
> And He guided Satan to
> Paradises that He knew.
>
> Gabriel, without a frown:
> Uriel, without a spear;
> Raphael, came singing down,
> Welcoming their ancient peer;
> And they seated him beside,
> One who had been crucified.

If read and considered literally and even historically, such enmity within closely related families—particularly those which are said to be Divine—is farcical, even nonsensical, thereby evoking either dismissal with ridicule or a humour-loving reading of a story quite frankly written as a fairy-tale. If, however, certain myths are regarded as allegories concealing power-bestowing truths, then many if not all of such ancient legends may prove to be sources of very valuable information. This view proves to be applicable not only to the procedures of the inception and development of Universes, but also to the beginnings and unfoldments of the human race which forms one branch of their inhabitants. Such a concept especially concerns understanding of philosophical and spiritual truths, knowledge of which, if correctly applied to life, can be of great practical benefit both to the student of philosophy and to all who find themselves in circumstances of stress or strain. Hence this book.

When one reads these stories literally, one can hardly fail to be struck by their 'nonsensicality'—stupidity, one might almost say. The way in which the Rod of Hermes whom the Romans called Mercurius came into being is, for example, difficult if not impossible to believe. The snake-entwined wand called Caduceus, which the god Apollo gave to Hermes was formed when, in order to test its power to reconcile all conflicting elements, Hermes thrust it between two quarrelling [or oppositely polarised] snakes. These became immediately harmonised and wound themselves in friendship around the Rod. Esoterically interpreted, the account of the formation of the Caduceus proves to be a remarkably accurate portrayal of the paths followed by the triple Serpent Fire—*Kundalini Shakti*,[1] the brain-illuminating agent—as it ascends the spinal cord of man, 'the actual Rod itself.' When brought about under Adeptic direction, this ascent can both bestow occult[2] power and increase the capacity directly to perceive harmonising philosophic truths. Thereafter, one's fellow men may be guided along the pathway of self-illumination, being like Hermes free of the limitations of three-dimensional space.

The fall of Icarus may in its turn be esoterically interpreted. His father, Daedalus, made two pairs of wings to enable them to escape from imprisonment within the Labyrinth on the Island of Crete. Before they took flight, Daedalus warned Icarus to keep a middle course over the sea. If he flew too high, the sun might melt the glue and the wings fall off. However, as stories so often show, what elders say youth disregards. As father and son flew lightly and without effort away from Crete, the delight of this new and wonderful power went to the boy's head. He soared exultingly up and up, paying no heed to his father's anguished command; for he had risen higher above the earth than all his fellow men, not one of whom could compete with him as an aeronaut. The inevitable then occurred. The borrowed glue melted. The wings that were not of his *own* making, came off and he fell headlong into the Icarian Sea.

Like the two wings of Icarus, neither the brain nor the intellect of man are of his own personal manufacture. The Father of the human Race (Daedalus)—the Logoic Word[3]—conceived and had them constructed by members of the Elohim.[4] The power to use them both—mind and brain or the two wings—paranormally or beyond the capacity of mankind, may falsely excite a sense of superiority and so of separateness. Whilst a measure of this might possibly be justifiable

---

[1] *Kundalini shakti*—see Glossary.
[2] Occult—see Glossary.
[3] See Glossary under Logos and Logos Doctrine.
[4] Elohim—see Glossary and my *The Hidden Wisdom in the Holy Bible*, Vol.2, pp.92, 93, 94.

under circumstances of very high achievement, nevertheless, to be filled with personal pride is itself a profound and most dangerous mistake especially in the spiritual and occult—winged—life. Strangely, when thus affected, the mind—itself a source of the attainment—can become bedulled. The sense of proportion and dependence upon others for what has been done, then diminishes. Craving for still greater acclaim drives the hitherto brilliant one to motives and conduct that are far, very far indeed, below the ideal of humility *by which alone greatness may be made secure*. Eventually, Alexander-like, seeking still greater prestige (more worlds to conquer), ignoring the guidance of the wise, Icarus—for self-satisfaction—attempts unscalable heights and thus inevitably falls. Personified by Icarus, every egotist 'inevitably falls into the sea' of humiliating failure, whereupon its waters close over him. Thus viewed, the failure of Icarus may well be interpreted and accepted as a very practical warning against both the evil and the danger of excessive pride.

The creative, generative power of the Supreme Deity—personified by the pantheon of the gods and goddesses upon Olympus—and the same creative power in animal and man is in its turn very instructively, and for safety's sake only, referred to in allegorical form. The sex urge is frequently personified by those who seek safely—and so symbolically—to reveal sources of power within mankind—hinted at would perhaps be a more accurate statement—by members of the reptile kingdom, such as hydras, dragons and serpents, essential parts of the Caduceus of Hermes, for example. Other symbols for the procreative agency are the tree and more particularly the tree-trunk, the pillar, the ship-mast, the club and the trident as of Poseidon and also of the Lord Shiva, the Divine Yogi of Hindu Scripture. All such uprights represent both the spinal cord in general and the central, neutrally-polarised currents of the threefold (prongs of the trident) creative Fire, especially when aroused and active in occultly-awakened man. The two other currents which in the Caduceus of Hermes intertwined themselves round the midmost force (the rod itself) and its channel within the spinal cord (Sk. *Sushumna nadi*) were represented by the snakes so frequently and emblematically associated with the various characters—gods, goddesses, heroes and heroines—in the ancient myths.

The successful arousing by man of these forces and their complete domination by his will is portrayed in such allegories as that of the infant Heracles destroying two serpents—holding one in either hand—which attacked him in his cradle; the nine-headed Hydra of Lerna and the dragons guarding the trees of the golden apples of the Hesperides and of the Golden Fleece.[1] Childhood[2] and early youth were not infrequently used to represent the ideal qualities of simplicity and reassumed pre-pubertal purity that are necessary characteristics of the successful Candidate for Initiation. As already advanced, the control of this power is far more directly and accurately portrayed by the Staff of Hermes, known as the Caduceus. The potentially destructive nature of the Serpent Fire—particularly when prematurely aroused by yoga in the absence of a qualified teacher, or over-active in a lustful person, is the principle reason for the veiling in the forms of symbols and allegories of this knowledge in world scriptures and myths. The harm may, however, be both intellectual and physical, as symbolised by such monsters as Cerberus, the Hydra of Lerna and the Gorgon, Medusa with snakes in place of hair, which was beheaded by Perseus under the guidance of Athena.

The capacity of this baleful head of Medusa to petrify those who gazed fully upon it, may be interpreted as a representation of the condition of all who deliberately arouse *Kundalini* with intent to use it for any of the following purposes: the gratification of personal pride: the intellectual domination of others (the snake-covered *head*): the unlawful penetration into certain of Nature's secrets and the misuse of the *Kundalini* power in excessive sexuality and darker forms of magic. To 'gaze upon the head' solely to gain knowledge for itself alone (the Doctrine of the Eye), rather than for increase in capacity to help and to heal (The Doctrine of the Heart), is to experience a complete loss of spiritual idealism, to become a mere power-seeking person restricted to

---

[1] Fuller interpretations of these myths are offered later in this book.
[2] The 'child-state'—the state of evolution and especially of mind in which the condition of complete purity or freedom from the despiritualising and even degrading influences of human life on Earth are contacted. In Egyptian Mythology, the god Horus is sometimes portrayed as a young boy with his finger to his lips. May not this be regarded as a possible reference to the 'youthful' state and to obedience to the vow of silence characteristic of every Initiate of the Lesser and the Greater Mysteries? (See Glossary)

physical awareness and solely pursuing material goals. Symbolically, to engage in such a 'gazing' — or to look upon the head of Medusa — is thus to be 'turned to stone' or to become spiritually 'petrified';[1] for such people are rendered wholly earthbound in their outer, mortal natures.

The Caduceus on the other hand, with its perfect balance and harmony between the three component currents of energy — *Ida* (negative), *Pingala* (positive) and *Sushumna* (neutral) — and the power possessed by Hermes whose Staff it was — fully represents the capacities resulting from the awakened Serpent Fire in purified, sacrificially-serving, selfless, Initiated man, a god, a Hermes indeed!

The resultant treasures of the direct intuitive perception of truth and of intellectually-grasped knowledge of underlying Laws of Being are represented in the myths by the precious metal gold as symbolised by such objects as golden apples growing on trees with golden branches and golden leaves, guarded by the Hesperides,[2] daughters of Atlas, and the Dragon, Ladon. Similarly, the Golden Fleece, guarded by a sleepless dragon night and day at Colchis was the great quest of the Argonauts.[3] The treasure — spiritual wisdom — of which the golden apples and fleece are symbols is obtainable by the quickening and sensitising effects produced by a sufficient measure of sublimated and controlled creative Fire, *Kundalini*, and was therefore appropriately made to be guarded by dangerous reptiles, whether snakes or dragons.

As is later more fully suggested, the accidents and tragedies which befell the crew of the ship Argo allegorically describe the dangers threatening those who ill-advisedly — for selfish reasons, for example — and without due preparation, seek by occult means to obtain the secret Wisdom and the personal power which possession of it bestows. Guardianship of such treasures by terrible serpents may thus be seen as a further allusion to both the dangers when misused and the advantages of the *Kundalini* power when controlled and rightly

---

[1] Lot's wife was said to have been turned into a pillar of salt when she looked back at Sodom and Gomorrah, civic symbols of moral degradation. *Gen.* 19:26. See *The Hidden Wisdom in the Holy Bible*, Vol.2, pp.299-300.

[2] The continuous reference to gold throughout Greek Mythology support, justify give reasons for, the process of delving into them — prospecting indeed! — which I have endeavoured to follow in search of Truth itself. [Author.]

[3] See following Chapter on The Argonauts.

TRIPTOLAMUS IN HIS SERPENT POWERED CHARIOT

used — as under the direction of an Adept, Athena. In these and many other myths one discerns the continual direction of attention to this hidden force, to the dangers associated with its awakening within the body and to the rewards available to those who, wisely instructed and unselfishly motivated, seek the most precious (golden) treasure of all — Divine Wisdom or *Theosophia*.

The capacity for the swift flight of consciousness when free of the physical body and using the superphysical vestures of the hidden Self, are indicated by the winged, serpent-driven chariot of Triptolemus, the Eleusinian.[1] At his Initiation into those Mysteries,[2] he was presumably ordered to spread throughout the world knowledge, not so much of the physical science of agriculture as stated in the Myth, but rather, I suggest, the spiritual 'husbandry' or culture of the Divine Wisdom (wheat) within the 'soul' or substance of the mind-brain of man.

The vase-picture of Triptolemus in his winged, serpent-powered chariot may surely be interpreted as referring to the secret knowledge and intellectual illumination obtainable during the enactment of the Mysteries of Eleusis: for then the *Kundalini* power — the winged serpent force by which the chariot is driven — is safely under wise direction, having been aroused by the goddesses Demeter and Persephone or their Hierophantic representatives within the Holy of Holies, the Anaktoron, the secret Chamber of Initiation at Eleusis. '...Finally, there appeared Triptolemus, Celsus' son and Demeter's pupil, setting out in his car drawn by (winged) serpents to spread the knowledge of agriculture (esoteric or Mystery knowledge) that tells of the 'husbandry' of the Soul of man; for the spiritual Self or 'corn of wheat' is 'planted' (incarnated) by the wise Creator-'Husbandman' in the 'ground' or earth of the mortal bodily nature on the physical plane, where it temporarily 'dies' (abides alone) to its spiritual nature and knowledge. But, by the aid of the Initiations within the Lesser and

---

[1] The Chariot of Triptolemus. See vase depicting his departure on his mission following his Initiation in the Eleusinian Mysteries.
[2] *The Mysteries of Eleusis*, Georges Meautis, Theosophical Publishing House, Madras, India. *Eleusis and the Eleusinian Mysteries*, George E. Milonas. (Routledge and Kegan Paul Ltd. London, England) and *The Secret Doctrine*, H.P. Blavatsky, Vol.V, Adyar Edition.

Greater Mysteries it is 'saved' or rises from the 'grave' of matter into the full illumination and awareness of the temporarily 'lost' Selfhood and so is aided to resurrect the 'dead seed' of the mortal human being raising it into the status and radiance of the perfect Man — or 'it bringeth forth much fruit'. Thereafter the Adept Initiate travels the world on his wonderful mission of the 'husbandry' or Agriculture of the Soul. The Biblical text is as follows: (*St. John* 12:24) 'Verily, verily I say unto you, Except a corn of wheat fall into the ground and die, it abideth alone; but if it die, it bringeth forth much fruit throughout the world.:' — *Forerunners and Rivals of Christianity*, from 330 B.C. to 330 A.D. Francis Legge. (University Books)

The winged-serpent-entwined Rod of Hermes is not dissimilarly indicated. In its turn it bestows like powers of supra and sub-mundane travel upon its possessor. It also is winged and serpent-entwined — both the Chariot and the Rod being symbols for the spatially-liberating force of *Kundalini*. Possession by Hermes of the Rod made such world travel possible; for it gave him access to the deepest densities of matter and its crudest attributes — Hades, the abode of Pluto[1] — and to the highest spiritual levels — Olympus,[2] the home of Zeus. Moses, Law Giver to the Israelites when in bondage in Egypt, was also possessed of a Rod with which he performed magical acts.[3]

The many and varied Mysteries, Lesser and Greater, of ancient times, were centres of the higher learning, of occult instruction and the Initiatory Rites. Capacities were effectively and safely bestowed voluntarily to leave the physical body and to direct awareness both to other parts of the Earth and into the inner worlds whilst fully conscious in astral, mental and Causal[4] superphysical vehicles. In the Greek Myths the attainment of these powers was both concealed and mythologically described as death, resurrection, the acceptance of the hero, heroine or Initiated one amongst the gods of Olympus and in

---

[1] Pluto, King of the Dead. See Myth of the Rescue of persephone.
[2] Olympus. The abode of the gods. A mysterious region far above all mountains of the Earth.
[3] *Ex.* Ch.17:9. This profound subject and these examples of its symbolical references are more fully presented in the succeeding Chapter 2. 'The symbols of the Serpent and the Rod'.
[4] See Glossary under *Causal Body*.

some cases as placement in the heavens either as a Star or as one of the Signs of the Zodiac. The mystical 'flight of the soul'[1] was also represented by aerial journeys on winged horses, such as Pegasus ridden by Bellerophon and those driven by the Sun God, Helios.[2])

In *The Secret Doctrine*[3] H.P. Blavatsky writes as follows: '... One must invoke that divine and great name only in cases of absolute necessity, and when one feels absolutely pure and irreproachable. Not so in the formula of black Magic. Reuvens, speaking of the two rituals of Magic of the Anastasi collection, remarks that they 'undeniably form the most instructive commentary upon the *Egyptian mysteries* attributed to Jamblichus, and the best pendant to that classical work, for understanding the thaumaturgy of the philosophical sects, thaumaturgy based on ancient Egyptian religion. According to Jamblichus, thaumaturgy was exercised by the ministry of secondary genii.' Reuvens closes with a remark which is very suggestive and is very important to the Occultists who defend the antiquity and genuineness of their documents, for he says: 'All that he [Jamblichus] gives out as theology we find as history in our papyri.' But then, how deny the authenticity, the credibility and, beyond all, the trustworthiness of

---

[1] Plotinus described his own inner experience as follows:
'Oftentimes when I awake out of the slumber of the body and come to a realising sense of myself, and retiring from the world outside, give myself up to inward contemplation, I behold a wonderful beauty. I believe then that I verily belong to a higher and better world, and strive to develop within me a glorious life, and become one with the Godhead. And by this means I receive such an energy of life that I rise far above all other things, even the intelligible world...And this therefore is the life of the Gods and of divine and happy men, a liberation from all earthly concerns, a life unaccompanied with human pleasure, and the flight of the Alone to the Alone.' (*Plotinus*, Stephen McKenna.)
Philo Judeus in his turn has written:
'Sometimes, when I have come to my work empty, I have suddenly become full, ideas being in an invisible manner showered upon me, and implanted in me from on high; so that through the influence of divine inspiration I have become filled with enthusiasm, and have known neither the place in which I was nor those who were present, nor myself, nor what I was saying, nor what I was writing, for then I have been conscious of a richness of interpretation, an enjoyment of light, a most keen-sighted vision, a most distinct view of the objects treated, such as would be given through the eyes from the clearest exhibition.'
Philo Judeus translated by W.R. Inge.
[2] *Helios*, the Sun God. See Greek vase.
[3] *The Secret Doctrine*, Vol.5, pp.254-255. Adyar Edition.

those classical writers, who all wrote about Magic and its Mysteries in a most worshipful spirit of admiration and reverence? Listen to...Cicero: "Initiation not only teaches us to feel happy in this life, but also to die with better hope." Plato, Pausanias, Strabo, Diodorus and dozens of others bring their evidence as to the great boon of Initiation; all the great as well as the partially-initiated Adepts share the enthusiasm of Cicero. "Does not Plutarch, thinking of what he had learned in his initiation, console himself for the loss of his wife? Had he not obtained the certitude at the Mysteries of Bacchus that 'the soul [Spirit] remains incorruptible, and that there is a hereafter?"...Aristophanes went even farther: 'All those who participated in the Mysteries, he says, 'led an innocent, calm, and holy life; they died looking for the light of the Eleusinian Fields [Devachan, while the rest could never expect anything but eternal darkness [ignorance?]... and when one thinks about the importance attached by the States to the principle and the correct celebration of the Mysteries, to the stipulations made in their treaties for the security of their celebration, one sees to what degree those Mysteries had so long occupied their first and their last thought. It was the greatest among public as well as private preoccupations, and this is only natural since according to Döllinger, 'the Eleusinian Mysteries were viewed as the efflorescence of all the Greek religion, as the purest essence of all its conceptions.' Not only conspirators were refused admittance therein, but those who had not denounced them; traitors, perjurers, debauchees... so that Prophyry could say that: 'Our soul has to be at the moment of death as it was during the Mysteries, i.e., exempt from any blemishes, passion, envy, hatred, or anger.' Truly, "Magic was considered a Divine Science which led to a participation in the attributes of Divinity itself." Herodotus, Thales, Parmenides, Empedocles, Orpheus, Pythagoras all went, each in his day, in search of the wisdom of Egypt's great Hierophants, in the hope of solving the problems of the Universe.

'Says Philo: "The Mysteries were known to unveil the secret operations of Nature."'

The Author quotes from early authors as follows:
Pindar, Greek Lyric Poet, 522-443, B.C.:
'Happy is he who has seen the Mysteries before being buried underneath the earth; he knows the end of life and he knows its begin-

ning given by Zeus.'

Sophocles, Athenian Dramatist, 495-406. B.C.:

'Thrice happy are the mortals who depart to the abode of Hades after having seen the Mysteries...'

Inscription on the tomb of the Hierophant, Glacus:

'During nine years he initiated mortals into the illuminating ceremonies of Deo (Demeter): in the tenth year he went to the immortals. Beautiful indeed is the mysterious secret which comes to us from the Blessed ones, for the death of mortals is not an evil; it is a blessing.'

Plutarch, Greek Biographer, 46-120 A.D.:

'At first the candidates for initiation jostle each other with shouts and exclamations; but at the moment of the ceremony when the sacred objects are shown, they attend in silence and in fear... At the moment of death the soul experiences the same impressions as those who are initiated into the great Mysteries. They perceive a wonderful light. Purer regions are reached and fields where there is singing and dancing; sacred words and divine visions inspire a holy awe.

'Then the man, perfected and initiated, free and able to move without constraint celebrates the Mysteries with a crown on his head: he lives among pure men and saints; he sees on earth the many who have not been initiated and purified buried in the mire and darkness and through fear of death clinging to their ills, for want of belief in the happiness of the beyond.'[1]

Dionysius Areopagiticus, *De Eccles. Hierarch.* 1. 1-3.:

'We must then, demonstrate that ours is a Hierarchy of inspired, divine and deifying science, of efficacy and of consecration for those initiated with the initiation of the revelation derived from the hierarchical mysteries.

'Head of this Hierarchy is the Fountain of Life, the Essence of Goodness, the one Triad, Cause of things that be...assimilation to and union with Whom, as far as attainable is deification.

'And this is the common goal of every Hierarchy—persistent devotion towards God and divine things divinely and uniformly ministered; prior to which there must be a complete and unswerving

---

[1] *The Mysteries of Eleusis*, George Meautis.

removal of things contrary; a knowledge of things as they are in themselves; the vision and science of sacred truth; the inspired communication of the uniform perfection of the One Itself, as far as attainable; the banquet of contemplation, nourishing intelligibly and deifying every man elevated towards it.'

All quadrupedal creatures, such as the horse, whether wild, tamed or winged as were Pegasus[1] and those drawing the chariot of Helios, God of the Sun, for example, may be regarded as symbols of the combined fourfold mortal bodies of man—mental, emotional, etheric and physical.[2] The obedience of the trained or 'broken' horse portrays the more normal conditions and reactions of these vehicles. Hostile animals, especially the dangerous Nemean lion, the Boar of Erymanthus and the three-headed and dragon-tailed dog Cerberus, guardian of Hades—all of which were overcome by Heracles—represent the outer man, as yet under very little if any, control by the inner Self. When the animal is captured, trained or renders service, evolutionary advancement beyond the usual standard is indicated.

On the Path of Swift Unfoldment, each of these victories must be attained in the form of interior triumphs over the 'disasters' or 'dangers' symbolically portrayed in the Myths. The Ego, Heracles for example, must 'go down' into the Hades of the personality and therein gain mastery over the dangerous self-centredness, egoism, of each of the three mortal vehicles portrayed by the three-headed guardian-dog named Cerberus. This view gains support from the mythical statement that Cerberus was dragon-tailed, a reference, surely, to the Serpent Fire seated in the spinal cord of man and the source of the procreative—but also sensuality-provoking—sexual impulse. An illustration from a Greek vase in which many serpents emerge from the body of Cerberus gives support to this interpretation.

---

[1] Pegasus—a marvellous winged horse which had sprung from the Gorgon's blood when Perseus killed her or eliminated from the personal character and so 'destroyed' the undesirable Soul imprisoning aspect.

[2] The immortal Self consists of manifestations of spiritual Will, Wisdom and abstract Intelligence, whilst as stated above, the mortal man is composed of bodies of mind, emotion, vitality and flesh. See my books, *Basic Theosophy*, Chs. 1-5, and *The Pathway to Perfection*.

The winged horse, Pegasus, is a further example of the mythological portrayal of these evolutionary advances; for it symbolises a totally controlled (hidden), purified (white) and indeed Initiated state in which the mind is freed from the limitations and bondages of matter and so can 'mount into the sky', meaning the 'higher' or superphysical realms of consciousness. The wings themselves, being dual, represent awakened and developed spiritual Will and Wisdom, whilst the rider in his turn personifies the spiritual Intelligence, the immortal Ego, completely in charge. When once the story is recognised as a Myth descriptive of the stages of the evolution of the indwelling Self, Bellerophon[1] mounted upon Pegasus perfectly portrays man in this exalted chimaera — or illusion-conquering condition.

When colour or colourlessness, such as gold[2] or whiteness, is included in the myth, then a white horse or unicorn[3] implies a completely purified and subservient outer mortal nature, a personality which has been 'cleansed' of all self-desire and egoistic separateness and in whom the *Kundalini* is aroused — the spiral horn arising out of the head of the unicorn.

The assumption that much of the mythology of ancient peoples, with its many glyphs and emblems, is Adept inspired for the purpose of preserving for the Race and revealing, while yet concealing, power-bestowing knowledge is supported by the remarkable aptness of the symbology itself.

The unicorn or horned horse, for example, in one of its many possible meanings is an appropriate symbol of the sublimated generative force in man. The horn, emerging from the brain, indicates that the expression of the creative power and desire then occurs

---

[1] Bellerophon — presumed son of Poseidon, a sea divinity.

[2] Intellectually-grasped knowledge of underlying Laws of Being.

[3] White Unicorn. Though not a classical emblem, a possible interpretation of the mythological Unicorn is that it represents a highly developed and successful yogi, Disciple or even Adept. The four legs may refer to the four parts of the human personality and the whiteness of the body to the attainment of complete purity including uttermost selflessness. The up-turned tail and out-thrust horn suggest fully-aroused and upward-flowing *Kundalini*, and the tree-trunk — arising in many pictures from the crown of the head — symbolises the full activity of the Serpent Fire and the resultant freedom of consciousness from the body. See: *A Mythological Investigation*, Robert Brown Jnr., F.S.A. London, 1881; Gould's *Mythological Monsters*, p.3; Excerpts from *The Secret Doctrine*, Adyar Edition, Vol.3, p.222, H.P. Blavatsky.

through the will-inspired intellect and its cranial organ the physical brain and particularly the pituitary gland. The horn is thus occultly phallic whilst the white horse is an oft-used symbol for man's purified lower quarternary—mind, emotion, etheric vehicle for vitality and flesh.[1]

In Greek mythology this is represented by the winged—but not horned—horse, Pegasus, which the hero, Bellerophon, the Initiate-Ego, catches, controls and directs by means of a golden bridle. This harness is a symbol for the developed and wisely-used will-thought by means of which the personal nature of man (Pegasus) has become guided. This winged horse was caught near a fountain. Mounting it, Bellerophon rose into the air and slew the Chimaera, a fire-breathing monster. Whilst riding on Pegasus, Bellerophon had no need to come anywhere near the creature whose breath was flame. He soared above her and killed her with his arrows at no risk to himself.

THE WINGED HORSE PEGASUS

The Chimaera[1] was composed of a lion's head and four legs, a serpentine tail and a goat between the two. It is thus an impossible or unreal conception, a chimaera in the modern meaning of the word, an illusion, only to be 'seen through' (destroyed) when in a superior state of consciousness—mounted on Pegasus. Thereafter, the Initiate Ego, personified by Bellerophon, is no longer limited to the surface of the

---

[1] Chimaera (Gk.) was to be unconquerable, formed of a lion in front, a serpent behind and a goat in between, with breath, which was of unquenchable flame.

earth and the physical body; he ascends as if winged, into the empyrean—the superphysical states of consciousness. Thus elevated, he is beyond the limitations of passionate desires (the fiery breath), the will to dominate (the lion portion) and sensual desires (the serpentine tail).

The unicorn, be it remembered, is a fabulous animal whose spinal cord is presumed to extend beyond the *medulla oblongata,* through the pituitary gland and out between the eyes, after which it becomes hardened into a spiral horn. Occultly interpreted, this refers less to the physical spinal cord than to the interior etheric canal which runs along its length and, as previously stated, is called the *Sushumna Nadi.* The equi-polarised creative fire, Serpent Fire or *Kundalini,* flows along this canal from sacrum to brain and in its progress in man, it is accompanied by the separate positive and negative currents which follow each their own pathways, known as *Pingala* and *Ida* respectively, intertwining the *Sushumna* as they flow.

ASCENT OF THE SERPENT FIRE CREATIVE FORCE

The sublimation of the creative force—the ascent of the Serpentine Creative Fire—occurs as a result of the transmutation of sex-force by means of the continued practice of yoga, aided by passage through valid rites of Initiation. Such knowledge was for a long period of time

MEDUSA WITH PEGASUS

SMALL MEDUSA WITH KUNDALINI SYMBOLS

part of the closely guarded secrets of the Ancient Mysteries, and even now the technique whereby it is thus aroused is kept secret from the world. This reservation is designed not to withhold valuable information, but to protect the profane and the unready from the danger and the strain inseparable from the premature awakening of *Kundalini* and the misuse of occult knowledge.

In Greek Mythology, the author repeats, this human development is represented by the winged—but not horned—horse, **Pegasus**, which the hero Bellerophon, the **Initiate-Ego**, caught at the fountain that sprang from the blood of the Gorgon, Medusa, when her head was struck off by Perseus, typifying the source of life.

Pegasus was controlled and directed by means of a golden bridle. This harness is a symbol for the developed and wisely-used will-thought by means of which the personal nature of man (**Pegasus**) is guided. Medusa, one of the Gorgons, and Poseidon, became the parents of two children who emerged from their mother's body after she had been slain by Perseus. They were Pegasus, the winged horse and Chrysaor, the hero with the golden sword.

The ram and the ram-like head-dresses of Egyptian deities[1] refer to the superabundant formative power of the Creative Logos or Emanator of Universes. In man, however, the ram with its two curved horns indicates an Initiate in whom the twin currents, positive and negative, of the generative Serpent Fire are fully aroused and occultly functioning. This bestows supernormal power to 'butt' against and overcome the resistances of matter, even in its densest states, the physical body, for example.

The actual force involved in the act of 'butting' additionally and very aptly indicates the immense force evoked and turned upon space by the Logos in the Macrocosmic sense. In man, this energy is turned against the mentally and spiritually bedulling effects of both mind and matter, success being attained when *Kundalini shakti* is aroused. The fact that the head is used by animals when fighting as a kind of battering-ram—especially the forehead—gives an added aptness to the

---

[1] Khnemu, for example, who is portrayed as a ram-headed man, 'builder' of Gods and men. *The Gods of the Egyptians*, E.S. Wallis Budge, Vol.II, Ch.3. Also *The Secret Doctrine*, Vol.III, p.217. H.P. Blavatsky, Adyar Edition.

EGYPTIAN RAM-HEADED GOD

symbology since, however wild it may appear to be in an animal, in the Logos and in man the butt is accurately directed and controlled by Logoic thought and by the human mind.

The colour gold, as well as meaning 'great value', 'preciousness', when symbolically applied to animals or objects, as heretofore suggested also indicates the highest and greatest powers of direct perception, penetrative insight, attainable by man. These faculties are acquired when the supra-mental and wholly intuitive capacities of the inner Self are fully developed and employed by the reasoning mind. The Golden Fleece itself, sought and gained by the Argonauts, symbolises this interior enrichment which will quite naturally be acquired by the human race as a whole in future ages, and is developed ahead of the race by those who find and tread the Initiatory pathway — the questing voyage of the Argo.

The application of a colour to an emblem also directs attention to the level of consciousness at which it may best be interpreted. The natural colour of an object used as a glyph generally draws attention to its normal condition. In the case of man, aspects of the mortal, human personality are sometimes emblematically indicated. White or silver refers to the spiritual Will, especially when applied to weapons, spears or swords, for example. Amber, yellow and gold, suggest the spiritual power of implicit insight, intuitive grasp which cannot be either deceived or turned aside from the subject under examination. Red, when used in the ancient myths, tells of a superabundance of energy, an abnormal thrust or drive, a passion or even a lust.

Since the fish, a denizen of water, in its turn frequently appears in world mythology, a special study of this symbol is here enlarged upon. The fishing net may be regarded as a symbol of dual significance concerning the functions of the intellect to which it is applicable according to the level of consciousness referred to. When the use of the net symbolises the Causal Body then catching fish and later 'sorting' them represents the assimilation and intelligent employment of the fruits of life's experience—the fish. All of those circumstances that have in them qualities of spirituality and capacity to endure, are indeed 'caught' in and by the 'netting' procedures of the Higher Self, into which they become permanently incorporated as powers of the Soul.

The net used for fishing or as an enclosing mesh—the mind—which prohibits movement or inhibits the unbiased and impersonal use of the intellect, indicates a certain immaturity or mental limitation preventing the free and unfettered use of the power of thought. When, however, the faculty of intuition becomes sufficiently developed to bestow implicit insight, the limiting or enmeshing attribute of the formal mind is no longer an imprisonment. Thus, Jesus—personifying spiritual intuitiveness—called Simon and Andrew his brother to Discipleship saying "Come ye after me, and I will make you to become fishers of men. And straightway they forsook, [transcended the limitations of the formal mind], their nets, and followed him.' [1] Admittedly, these words could also, and quite well, be granted their purely literal meaning. May not, however, the immediate surrender to a hitherto unknown person of their means of livelihood make of the narrative 'a story which is repugnant to both reason and common sense' and therefore consisting of 'a profound allegory veiling a deeply mysterious truth'?[2]

[1] Mk. 1:16-18. 'straightway'—when the Master 'calls', the Disciple-to-be *immediately* responds.
[2] Moses Maimonides. See quotations earlier.

THE FISH SYMBOL

The fish and the element of water of which it is a denizen are so frequently introduced into world scriptures and myths as to justify detailed study and proffered interpretations. Its importance is underscored in three descriptions of world floods. During His third appearance, Lord Vishnu[1] of Hinduism as the Varaha or boar *avatara*[2] swam fish-like in order to guide the Manu[3] Vaivasvata throughout the period of the flood to safety on dry land. Similarly, Deucalion of Greek mythology, with Pyrrha on board a wooden chest, was guided to dry land (Mt. Parnassus) by his father Prometheus[4] when Zeus with the help of Poseidon had sent torrents of rain to make an end of all mankind by means of a flood. Noah,[5] also, was guided by Jehovah to build an ark as a refuge against the Flood for himself, his family 'and of every living thing of all flesh, two of every sort...male and female'. Athena rescued Hercules from a fish-like sea monster. The prophet Jonah[6] was absorbed into and released unharmed from 'the belly of a whale' after three days and nights therein. Certain of the more immediate followers of the Lord Christ had been fishermen. On acceptance as Disciples they were called "to become as fishers of men".[7] On His reappearance in Galilee after His Resurrection, the Lord Christ asked of His disciples: 'Have ye here any meat? And they gave him a piece of broiled fish, and of an honeycomb. And he took it, and did eat before them'.[8]

Concerning verse 42, the student of the occult sciences would surely find it difficult to believe that an attained Adept would participate in and benefit from the painful slaughter of a sentient creature in order to please his sense of taste and assist in his personal nutrition.

---

[1] *Vishnu. (Sk.)* Second Aspect of the Hindu *Trimurthi*.

[2] Boar *Avatara (Sk.)* Described as 'lacustrine'—a dweller in lakes. *Vayu Purana* and *The Secret Doctrine*, Vol. II. p.84. H.P. Blavatsky, Adyar Edition.

[3] *Manu (Sk.)* 'Father' of the human Race. See Glossary.

[4] Prometheus (Gk.). Offspring of the Titans, 'the Elder Gods' who were for untold ages supreme in the Universe. He was the saviour of mankind in that he guided Deucalion in rescuing his family (all others having perished in the flood). See also Homer, Iliad, Aeschylus and Ovid. See Appendix.

[5] Noah, *Gen.* 6, 7, 8.

[6] *Jonah*, 1:15-17.

[7] *Matt*, 12:40 and *Mk.* 1:17.

[8] *Luke* 24:41-43 and *Jn.* 21:13.

INTERPRETATION OF GREEK MYTHS 23

If, however, the incident be regarded allegorically, then the word 'fish' may well refer to states of consciousness to be achieved by disciples. These would include divine compassion, intuition, implicit insight, purest wisdom and also healing grace for which the fish has been a universally used symbol.

As we have seen, in the more generally quoted sources, the Godhead assumes the function of a fish, a prophet is absorbed into and is ejected from the body of a fish, disciples are to become as spiritual fishermen, and the resurrected Christ requests and partakes of fish as nutriment. In Christian sacerdotal vestments, when worn the Mitre of the bishop resembles an upturned fish's head with opened mouth. Evidently, the fish is of profound symbolic significance. Hence the attempt within admitted limitations here to bestow upon the subject a reasonably full consideration.

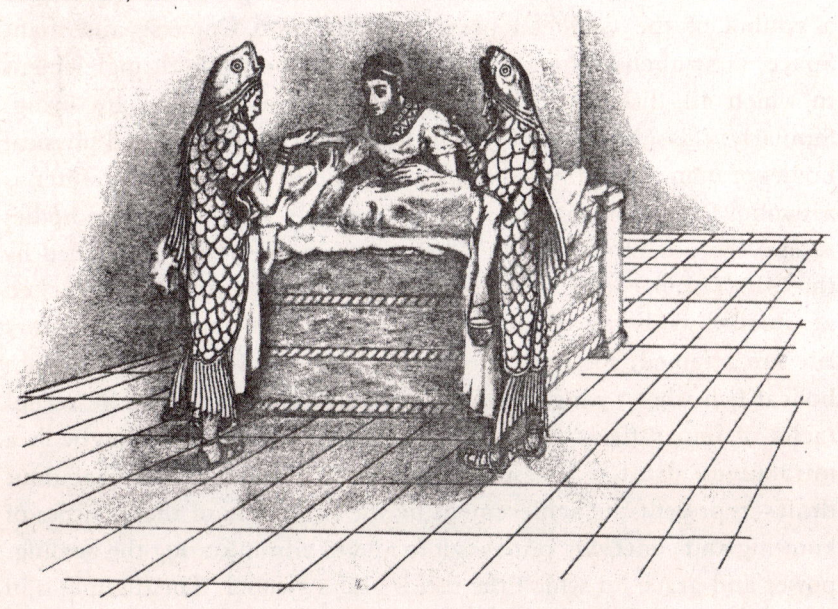

FISH—SYMBOL OF HEALING GRACE

This picture, partly taken from a painting by H.M. Herget, in illustration of an incident of healing during the civilization of Mesopotamia appearing in *Everyday Life in Ancient Times*, published by *The National Geographic Society of America*, portrays two priests—doubtless called in to aid in healing the son of the anxious father—dressed to resemble fishes. This may possibly be in recognition of the fish as a symbol of an aspect of spiritual awareness from which healing grace is derived.

An anxious father stands by the sickbed of his son. Two priests dressed to resemble fishes—for symbolic association with the water god Ea—seek to expel the demons suspected of having caused the malady. One of the priests is seen holding a bowl which, no doubt, contains some magic fluid. The boy's hands are held open, in a gesture of supplication, as are also the right hands of the fish-garbed priests; but the head is hidden by one of the standing figures. This bed scene, incidentally, is partially modelled after a section on a frequently reproduced Assyrian bronze relief which depicts in several registers the exorcism of a female demon.

The fish is frequently used in world mythologies and scriptures as a symbol of the Godhead present within both Universe and man. Space, as symbolised by water, is therefore a perfectly fitting element in which all 'fishes' (including the God-selves of men) are living. Similarly, the substances of which the mental, emotional and physical bodies of man are composed also correspond to the element of water as a symbol for matter or the 'waters of space;'[1] for within these bodies resides the potentiality of the Christ-consciousness, also portrayed by the fish. This becomes actuality when the state of evolution is reached at which discipleship of an Adept and passage through an Initiatory rite are attained; for thereafter, as in the New Testament, the symbolical fish when 'caught' or made manifest are found to be receptacles of imperatively needed 'tribute money'[2] and are caught in a miraculous draft.[3] These two—tribute money and miraculous draft—represent the achievement by the fishermen of the faculties of knowing and conveying pure wisdom and of administering the healing-power and grace for which the fish is also a symbol. The disciple is in *this* sense 'a fisher of men'.

The phenomenon of the tribute money miracle is, in its turn, of profound occult significance. Legally the cash itself refers to the tax,

---

[1] *Gen.* 1:2
[2] *Matt.* 17:24-27
[3] *Luke.* 5:4 to 10.

custom and dues exacted from the Hebrews by their Roman subjugators for the maintenance of the civil authorities, being alluded to by Jesus in the following verse:—

> 'Notwithstanding, lest we should offend them, go then to the sea and cast an hook, and take up the fish that first cometh up, and when thou hast opened his mouth, thou shalt find a piece of money: that take, and give unto them for me and thee.'[1]

Read literally, this verse indicates that very remarkable power was displayed by the great Master in arranging that the first fish caught should contain the necessary coin — perhaps its precipitation therein? The tenth verse of the fifth Chapter of *St. Luke* is of especial interest in that Simon was assured that: ' from henceforth thou shalt catch men '. This gives a deeply philosophic meaning to the procedure of fishing, namely that of seeking, finding and drawing into discipleship and the spiritual way of life, carefully selected acquaintances.

In this incident and especially in this verse, it is submitted, the philosophy and the practice of the art of contemplation are — in terms of the Sacred Language of Allegory and Symbol — very fully described; for the 'sea' is the God-charged substance of man's vehicles of consciousness. To 'cast an hook' is meditatively to turn attention to the divine Presence therein. To ' take up ' the fish is to become aware of and be inspired and illumined by Divine Wisdom. To 'open his mouth...and find a piece of money' is to enter deeply into the heart of the Divinity abiding within both the contemplating mystic and the Universe itself. To take and give this to the officials is to share the fruits of one's meditative life with all mankind.

May we at this point carry our enquiry somewhat further? In the Language of Allegory and Symbol, purely physical objects and activities are used to represent — imply indeed — superphysical human and divine states of awareness and their natural expression when certain corresponding states of consciousness have been attained. Just as in the physical world, the tax money was essential to the maintenance of the State, so the 'tribute money' — meaning the divine power by which Universes and human beings in their turn are maintained by the Logos and His Angelic Hosts — must be realised, consciously received

---

[1] *Matt.* 17:27

and 'paid', or fully expressed, by the occult 'fishermen' (successful yogis) after 'fish-consciousness' or spiritual awareness has been attained. Symbolically, a fish must be 'caught' and 'opened', meaning that meditation must be engaged in and the Divine Presence within revealed (or disclosed) to the soul of the mortal man.

The whole incident occurred, be it noted, in the actual Presence of the Lord Christ or the interiorly realised Christ consciousness.[1] This again suggests, surely, that only in the inspired contemplative condition may the mystical experience be fully entered into. Such a view would seem to be supported by the later textual statement[2] that Peter was not actually in the Presence of his Master when, as prophesied, he thrice denied Him. Symbolically, he was not in the exalted condition wherein Christ consciousness as described in footnote 1, was experienced.

In Cosmogenesis — always necessarily allegorical — water is used as a symbol of Space or virgin substance[3] and in sentient beings, the emotions. Fish represent advanced human beings who have successfully sublimated all coarse desires, have brought them under the control of the will, have intuitively realised unity with all that lives and are in consequence incarnations of divine compassion. As earlier suggested, 'fishermen', when the term is used in the Allegorical Language, are those human beings, who thus moved, become inspirers (catchers) of their fellow men, calling upon them to enter upon the way of the spiritual life and become disciples of a Master. As the fish swims freely with self-mastery in water, so impersonal love, which the fish in part symbolises, finds expression through the higher emotions — pure water — without harm or limitation to other beings — with helpfulness, indeed.

---

[1] Christ consciousness or in Sanskrit, Buddhi. Realised unity, even identity, with the Divine Source of all that exists and therefore with the spiritual life in all beings and things, bestowing direct intuitive insight, fulfilment of every intellectual and psychological necessity, the power to perceive the interior needs of those who are suffering and power to heal diseases whether of mind, body or both. All this is assumed to be implicit in the symbol of the Fish.

[2] *Matt.* 26: 69-75.

[3] Virgin substance. See Glossary under *Prakriti*.

INTERPRETATION OF GREEK MYTHS 27

The fish symbol is also used to indicate both a spiritual 'nutrient'—hence the request of Jesus for fish as food[1]—and a state of interior awareness that one is under divine direction and guidance. As stated, it thereby aptly portrays the function and value of purified and sublimated emotion, especially when expressed as realised oneness and direct intuitive perception. It may here be added, however, that when any attribute of the personal self is de-personalised—*conceived of and employed without reference to loss or gain by the user*—then it can be exercised as a truly spiritual power—pure Wisdom, in truth. Furthermore, the greater the degree of freedom from desire, the loftier the resultant state of consciousness, and therefore the increased capacity for its use.

As is well known, the attainment and expression of Wisdom—symbolised by the fish—is itself found to be dependent upon the achieved ability to render relatively inactive the prideful, argumentative and separative aspects of the concrete mind. This is allegorically portrayed throughout world scriptures and myths by a physically cruel (but, when rightly interpreted, intellectually beneficent) procedure of either cutting open the head or of full decapitation. As the Greek Myth relates in the description of the 'birth' of the goddess of wisdom, Athena[2], who sprang fully-armed from the cloven head of Zeus the Father of the gods, so Wisdom may only be born out of the "head" when self-centred mental attitudes have been outgrown and thus rendered impotent. Otherwise stated, only when the head (the personally-motivated use of thought) of Zeus—or of anyone else, indeed—had been 'cut open' could Athena (Wisdom) be 'born' from within the fully-opened mind. The attached picture portrays Zeus as seated, Athena being born out of his head and Hephaestus armed with his double axe.

The reduction to a minimum of the capacity for formal or concrete thought to prevent the manifestation of intuition is thus allegorically—strangely enough—described in world scriptures and myths either by injury to or the removal of the head. The decapitation

---

[1] *Luke* 24:41-43 and *John* 21:13. See also my book, *The Christ Life from Nativity to Ascension*, pp. 446-7.

[2] See *Mythology*, p.30, Edith Hamilton, **Mentor Books** and Appendix.

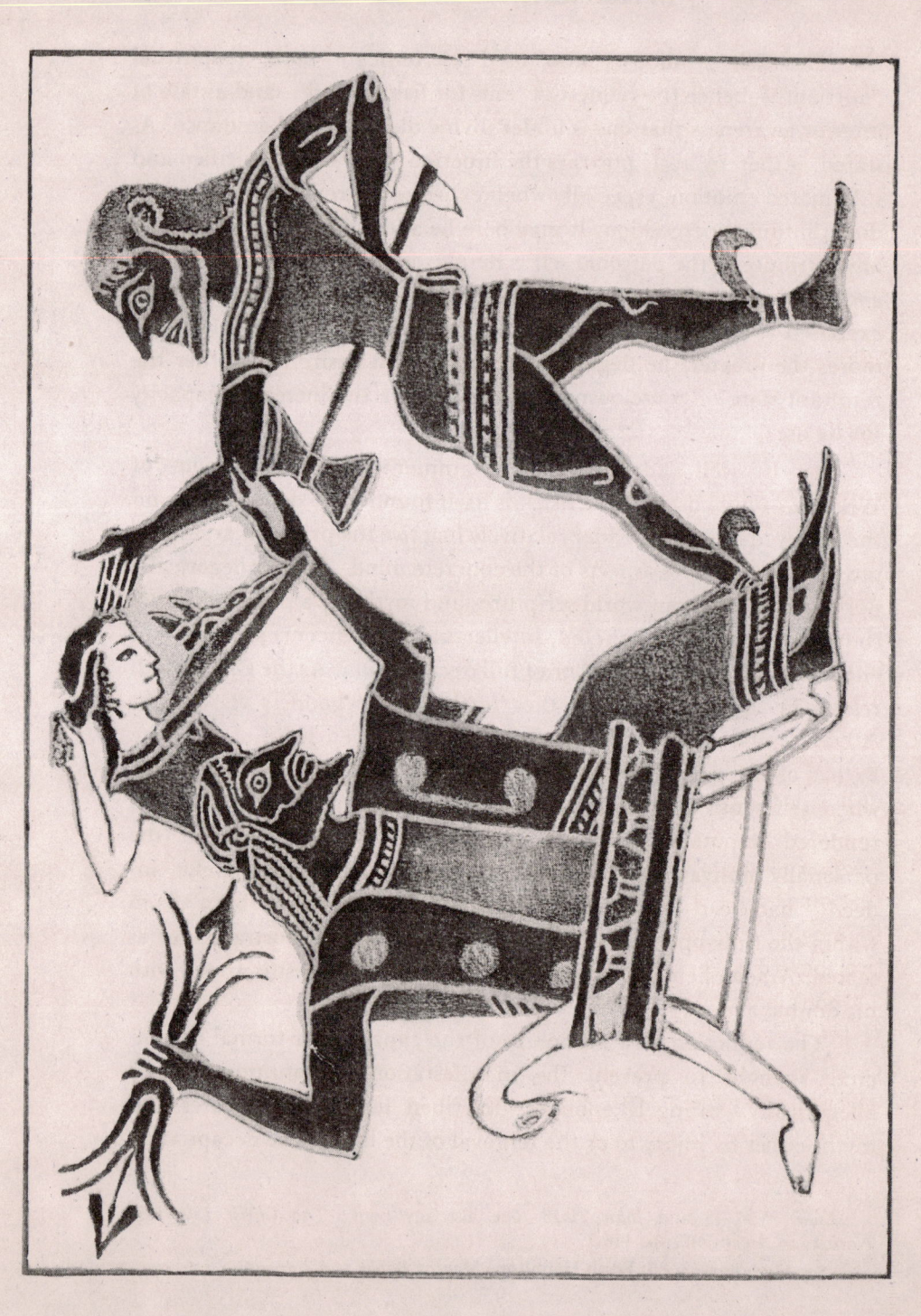

ATHENA BEING BORN FROM THE HEAD OF ZEUS

of Ganesha (the elder son of the Lord Shiva and his consort Parvati) whose head was replaced by that of an elephant (a further symbol of innate Wisdom), is an allegory similarly describing the necessity for the complete subordination of argumentative and so separative thought before the intuition can function. Interestingly, the trunk and two tusks of the elephant may permissibly refer to the awakened threefold *Kundalini shakti*. This interpretation is supported by the alternative name of the god — Ganapati, 'the Lord of the Forces'. These two interpretations are intimately related because once *Kundalini* is *safely* aroused and fully operative, the yogi quite naturally becomes wise.

Similarly, only after he had cut off the head of Goliath[1] (arrogant and cruel mentality) could David move on towards kingship, thereby initiating the lineage[2] of which Jesus the Christ (purest Wisdom) was born. John the Baptist is in his turn made to suffer decapitation before he could be freed from the limitations of personal and mortal existence ('die' to the restrictions of material life). When fully sublimated, physical procreative power (transmuted into mental and intuitional creativeness) links the then enlightened person with the cosmo-generative potency of Deity.[3] This transmutation bestows a high degree — amounting to pure genius — of both intellectual power and practical inventiveness.

Armour — and indeed most of the various kinds of arms — also has its deeply occult significance. Hermes, for example, gave Perseus winged sandals, a sword, a magically adaptable wallet which would always become the right size for whatever was to be carried in it, and a cap that made the wearer invisible and so enabled him to take possession of the single eye of the Gorgons. Thus equipped and with Athena's reflective shield Perseus could then 'fly' to the North and safely cut off the Gorgon's head.[4] If this adventure of Perseus be regarded as a deeply-veiled description of the procedures of the intended use of bodily creative energy and impulse, and also of processes necessary to the control and ultimate transmutation of the sex-force, the three snake-haired Gorgons very aptly symbolise the threefold *Kundalini* with

---

[1] Goliath, 1 *Sam*, 17.
[2] Lineage, *Matt*. 1:1-17.
[3] *Gen*. 1:1-3.
[4] See Appendix.

Medusa as the central current.

Taking each symbol successively, the winged sandals represent the power to elevate consciousness from the physical (they were worn on the feet or lowest part of the body) to superphysical awareness and thereafter to travel on the subtle bodies; the winged helmet in its turn worn on the head (the summit of the body), symbol of the developed appropriate mental power or control of the intellect, so that it can become intuitively illumined; the cap of invisibility, the privacy in which all power-bestowing occult instruction is concealed; the magic wallet which would always become the right size for whatever was to be carried in it, denoting the high degree of adaptability of the personal nature and its intellectual powers, and a preserving capacity for all products of spiritual experience, including genius; the capturing of the single eye to which the three Gorgons were restricted, thereby blinding and rendering defenceless Medusa herself, also indicates the complete mastery, particularly of the limitations of the concrete mind by the spiritual Self represented by the hero, Perseus; the sword of Hermes who is the personification of the fully transmuted triple Serpent Fire also symbolised by his wand (the Caduceus) represents the power attained by the Initiate completely to 'cut off' from personal mind and body, all desire and so wholly to eliminate or kill out sexual lust; the shield itself which protects the body from injury is a symbol of the condition of the reasoning mind that preserves the total man from errors born of unreason; the polished shield may be employed as a mirror enabling its user safely to see or imagine sensual indulgences only indirectly or by reflection, thereby avoiding direct mental gaze upon and thus the danger of physical sexual depravity, and so to be equipped to destroy (behead) the evil of lust.

Thus, the polished shield enabled Perseus, wisely instructed, to avoid a direct gaze upon the Gorgon. With his back towards her and holding the polished shield up before his eyes, he could strike off her head without becoming infected, as it were, by her evil influence. Valuable instruction in the overcoming of sex-desire is here given, namely that desire arises in the mind and it is the mind, therefore, which must refrain from lustful thoughts. Avoidance of the potentially harmful Medusa-like-aspect (evil) of the otherwise beneficent Serpent Fire rising along the spine into the head, may also be indicated. The shield of Athena refers to the blended abstract (polished) and concrete (metal) forms of intellectual power. This blending assures control of the personal nature by the spiritual Self, the Ego being thereafter always in charge.

The goddess of Wisdom—Athena—is a personification of intuitive insight and of the perfect sagacity which its possession bestows, whilst the god Hermes represents the Adept who has fully mastered and wholly transmuted procreative desire into full intellectual and spiritual creativeness. Thus dually developed, every high Initiate is able, Perseus-like, to render harmless (turn into stone as in the incident of the petrification of the sea-monster that was attacking Andromeda) all degrading and disease-producing products of unlicensed sexuality. So endowed, Perseus was enabled safely to see by reflection only and so to destroy the Gorgon Medusa by cutting off her head with its highly symbolical serpentine hair.

The normal, factual mind of mortal man is not by itself sufficient to overcome and eventually transmute the destructive aspects of the aroused *Kundalini* power: for this, mentally indulged in, manifests as lust symbolised as Medusa before decapitation, thereby rendering inactive the intuitive Wisdom, symbolically turning the victim into 'stone' or emblematically an unresponsive, mineral-like state. When, however, the divine Intelligence, Athena, illumines (polishes) the mortal mind (Perseus) the so-called 'shield'[1] becomes mirror-like, reflective, enabling its possessor to destroy *within himself* the deadly or destructive elements and effects of the misused Serpent Fire—the Gorgon's head with its serpentine hair. All the so-called 'gifts' from Deities to human beings may be interpreted as descriptive of the bestowed capacities of the interior god-like attributes of the threefold immortal Self—Divine Will, Wisdom and Intelligence[2]—thereafter made manifest as outward bodily powers.[3]

---

[1] The shield lent by Athena to Perseus enabling him to cut off the Gorgon's head when using indirect vision, thereby avoiding visual entry into his own mind of the evil symbolised by the snake-haired Medusa. Lot's wife turned into a pillar (spine) of salt and brain mineralised, and Prometheus chained to a rock.

[2] See Glossary under Ego.

[3] The Perseus Myth is a precise description in allegorical form of the instruction received and applied by every Initiated member of the Greater Mysteries as he evolves towards Adeptship.

Spears and swords, for example, may be regarded as referring to the inmost willpower in man which, when aroused and active, makes him invincible against those enemies who personify undesirable qualities in man; for, in the Language of Allegory and Symbol, all personified favourable powers as well as all enemies are actually *within* every human individual. Strategical wisdom and perfect planning—Athena and Hermes—which lead to victory portray attributes of the spiritual Self—Zeus—in man, whilst armour and shield are susceptible of interpretation as representing the completely protective higher or abstract Mind. When once these triple powers—Will, Wisdom and Intelligence—of the threefold spiritual Self are sufficiently unfolded and have become active in the conduct of life, the 'enemies' within his lower self, whether monstrous, animal or human, are readily overcome. If this view be accepted, when applied to the microcosm (man), *the mythology of ancient peoples may possibly be viewed as descriptive of phases of evolution through which every human being passes.* Ultimate victories are indications of the triumph of the divine and immortal Self and its powers over the human and mortal man. In cosmogenesis (Macrocosm) also, the enemies of creative deities may personify both the resistance of matter in general and the particular forms which that resistance takes as substances are shaped into Universes and all that they contain.

The Principal Gods

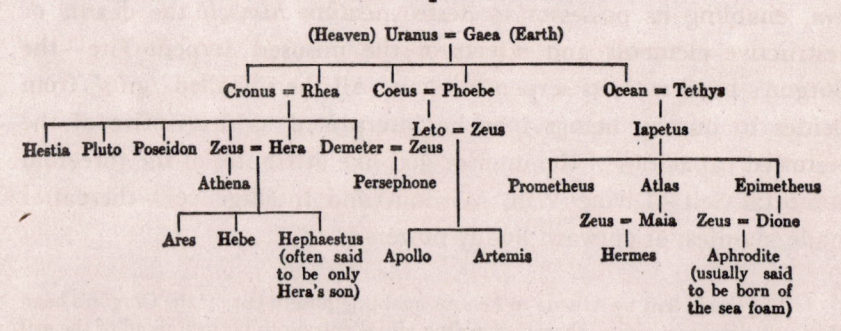

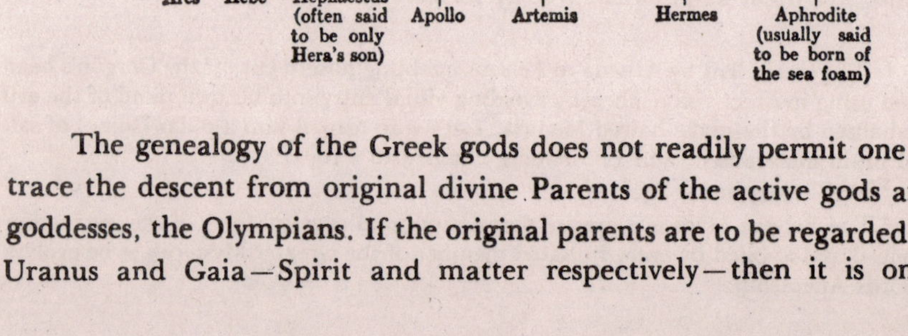

```
                        (Heaven) Uranus = Gaea (Earth)
       ┌────────────────────────┼────────────────────────┐
   Cronus = Rhea          Coeus = Phoebe           Ocean = Tethys
       │                        │                        │
       │                    Leto = Zeus                Iapetus
Hestia Pluto Poseidon Zeus = Hera  Demeter = Zeus        │
              │                        │           ┌─────┼─────────┐
           Athena                  Persephone   Prometheus Atlas  Epimetheus
                                                          │         │
       Ares  Hebe  Hephaestus      Apollo  Artemis    Zeus = Maia  Zeus = Dione
                   (often said                           │         │
                   to be only                          Hermes   Aphrodite
                   Hera's son)                                  (usually said
                                                                to be born of
                                                                the sea foam)
```

The genealogy of the Greek gods does not readily permit one to trace the descent from original divine Parents of the active gods and goddesses, the Olympians. If the original parents are to be regarded as Uranus and Gaia—Spirit and matter respectively—then it is only their *supposed* offspring who came to occupy positions of god-like domination over the four elements and in the case of Earth, its agricultural products (Ceres-Demeter). Thus, after Cronus had dethroned — if the term be permitted — his Father Uranus and so cruelly robbed him of his generative power and organs, the next generation in the divine Family are made to assume their elemental positions of domination — Zeus, sky-air: Pluto, earth: Hepheastus, fire and Poseidon, water, respectively.

The behaviour of each of the gods, goddesses and semi-divine men and women portrays both Macrocosmic and microcosmic activities. As far as Greek Mythology permits — being admittedly quite indefinite concerning origins — the Father of the gods, Uranus, might possibly be equated with both the Logos of the Universe and the inmost Spirit-Self of every human being, the Monad. Olympus, the mythical home of the gods, is therefore an elevated state of human consciousness, including realised immortality, perfect wisdom and irresistible will and, in fact, no Grecian mountain at all. These remarks, however, are not to be regarded — must, please, not be so regarded — as attempts artificially to bring the Greek Pantheon into harmony with that of India and to some extent Egypt. Rather are they ideas proffered to those who may be interested in this aspect of the subjects of both Greek mythology and mythology in general.

The Ageless Wisdom, Theosophia, includes the affirmation that each human being is a miniature Cosmos. In consequence — at varying stages of development — everyone receives and contains within themselves potentially the effects produced by all manifested Logoic Powers and Presences (Zeus) upon both the progressive Monadic[1] evolutionary stature and the mortal personality (Danaë, Leda, Europa. Leto, Semele),[2] These influences included the irresistible inherent Will of the whole of Nature continuously to evolve to ever more highly developed states.

Interior Presences are ceaselessly at work (the divine amours) upon everyone, even in such processes of Nature as the gradual but

---

[1] *Monad* (Gk. "alone"). See Glossary.
[2] To these should be added Dione, Maia, Io, Demeter, Aegina.

unceasing sensitisation of the matter of Universes in general and of human bodies in particular. If so intended, the transformation by the goddess Venus of the hitherto lifeless statue of Galatea, made by Pygmalion, into a living and loving human being[1] may perhaps be interpreted as an illustration of this continuing development. The story is very apt, since the 'quickening' process relates not only to physical matter but also to all superphysical substances. Every atom of the universe is thus being both rendered more responsive to spiritualising agencies, and subjected to a never ceasing interior stimulation to progress through successive degrees of unfoldment. *All personal intrusions by divine Beings upon human minds and lives as portrayed in world mythologies, may permissibly be regarded as allegorical presentations of this hastening procedure—completely impersonal though it is assumed to be.*

Every such relationship between Deities and humans described in world scriptures and mythologies is, I submit, an allegorical statement of the bringing about of increasingly conscious inter-relationships between the divine and the human in mankind — the virgin births for example. The result — and if one may presume to say — the purpose, for this continual Logoic intervention may be described as stated above in one word as 'quickening', meaning *the speeding up of all evolutionary procedures*. Every god, goddess, archangel, angel, demi-god — not even excluding those portrayed as destructive — who have relationships with human beings, represents this activity, frequently with remarkable accuracy and appositeness. *The varying and continuing influence of Spirit upon matter, life upon form and intelligence upon human beings constitutes the significance* — and so 'message' — of those myths, allegories and parables that may justly be described as thus inspired.

THE ANCIENT MYSTERIES

Eventually, the time or period arrives in the evolution — thus quickened — of a particular human Ego[2] when these procedures are discovered, partly by direct experience and partly as a result of

---

[1] Related by Ovid.
[2] Ego. See Glossary.

guidance received from those more evolved. Myth and parable thereupon tend gradually — though sometimes suddenly — to give place to realisation of the truths, laws and processes which they both conceal and reveal. To hasten and, when safely, possibly immediately bring about the interior revelation, was the purpose of the training given in and progress made through the Ancient Mysteries. These culminated in the Rite of Initiation when the head was touched by the *Thyrsus*[1] in order to bring about illumination within the fully conscious mind of the candidate.

At once the most important principle emerges, that knowledge of the nature of Universe, of man and of the purpose for the existence of both, must, as if under omnipotent impulse, by means appropriate to the understanding of recipients, be continually communicated to mankind. This procedure has ever been and still is carried out by such methods as are found to be most effective. They include the portrayal in the form of the partly historical world scriptures and myths — the total mythology of the earth in fact — of the complete 'Saga' descriptive of the meaning and purpose of Cosmic, Solar, Planetary, human and sub-human existence.

THE SACRED LANGUAGE

The fulfilment of this undertaking demanded *a language that would be unaffected by time and the tongues of differing peoples at successive periods—a universal, time-free communication indeed.* In consequence, throughout long Ages, the wise Ones devised and used the Language of Allegory and Symbol as constituting the best and surest channel for the imparting of this Divine Wisdom. Until a certain evolutionary stature has been attained, this means of presenting — to the minds of more primitive people for whom at first the myths were partly written — in personified and dramatic forms, the great truths underlying the existence of all Nature, has proved effective. Furthermore, since the possession of occult knowledge inevitably bestows the power either to bless and to heal, or to curse and to destroy, this preservation and presentation may be presumed to be the only *safe* system of communication that could be invented and used by the Sages of old.

---

[1] The Rod of Power in the hand of the Hierophant.

THE AGELESS WISDOM IS RECEIVED DIRECT

When a certain phase in human evolution is reached, a most dramatic event occurs. This consists of the visible appearance of the Adept Teacher before the sufficiently evolved and responsive candidate for discipleship.[1] The great truths are then presented in increasingly direct and *unsymbolised* form. Ultimately the recipient sees and knows within himself or herself these eternal verities.[2] Thereafter, he or she enters more and more fully into similar activities, finally becoming Adept sage. They themselves will in their turn teach both by parables[3] and directly. This is of immense importance not only to the recipient but also to every member of the human family; for when accepted, understood and effectively applied, these teachings both quicken evolutionary processes and ensure continuing health, happiness and peace of heart and mind. *The search for direct knowledge, the attainment of discipleship of an Adept Master and embarkation upon the task of sharing that knowledge with fellow men has been followed ever since the great epic of human life on earth began.*

This culminates in entry into the states of consciousness named as follows: In Norse mythology, Asgard, the land of the Aesir (the gods of the Scandinavians) which was placed in either the constellation cassiopeia — the Court of Don or Castle of Goydion, the Milky Way! the abode of the Tuatha De Danann (the people of the goddess Dana in Gaelic literature); the homes of the Celtic Pantheon; the Elysian Fields of the ancient Greek; the everlasting Bliss, the *Nirvana*, of the Buddhist; the *Samadhi*-state of the Hindu; the Ascension into the Kingdom of Heaven of the Christian devotee — the culminating experience of the Lord Jesus Christ and the closing Episode in the Gospel story of His appearance on Earth.

An especial purpose of writing this book — in addition to proffering interpretations of World Myths — is to present the exceedingly important idea that *the divine Beings of the Universe are in no sense*

---

[1] See my *The Pathway to Perfection*. Ch.5.
[2] cf. *St. Clement:* 'Here all teaching ends. One sees Nature and all things.'
[3] *Matt.* 13:10 and 11. 'And the disciples came, and said unto Him, why speakest unto them in parables? He answered and said unto them, Because it is given unto you to know the mysteries of the kingdom of heaven, but to them it is not given.'

either separate or different in essence from the divine Principle—Monad—in every man, woman and child. Relationships between gods and men, such as those of Zeus (the supreme Ruler) with mortal women, of Pluto with Persephone (presumed) and of Aphrodite with males may, I again submit, be permissibly and very helpfully read as revelations by means of myth, of degrees of interplay and interrelationship—continuous between the Logos and the Universe on the one hand—and intermittent mystically between the God-Self and the mortal man on the other.

When literally regarded, the '*amours*' of Zeus and of Aphrodite and the sensual desire by which they were assumedly motivated are admittedly distasteful, even abhorrent. They may be further interpreted, however, as descriptive of the continual activity of the Divine Nature in man ever 'seeking' to awaken in the mortal personality an 'adoration' for, and aspiration to be united with, the Godhead *within*. Thus understood, the ultimate objective for all heavenly 'seductions', is to bring about conscious union with the Divine and a liberation of the personal soul from all earthly attachments. *This allegorical rendering cleanses the stories of the undesirable elements of sensuality and sexuality; for the desire to be united with a member of the opposite sex is thus eliminated, greatly to the improvement of a literal or even fairytale reading of ancient myths*. Other examples are the numerous wives of the Hindu *avatara* (Divine Manifestation), the Lord Shri Krishna, the supposed sexual union of the Egyptian goddess Nut with Seb for the creation of a Universe and between Adam and Eve—miraculously created by God—to become the parents of the human Race on Earth.

Just as the physical sun permeates and penetrates the solar system with discharged electro-magnetic energies, so also at all levels above the gaseous, the Solar Logos (Zeus) permeates the Universe and all that it contains with spiritualising radiations. These 'quickening' powers severally affect matter, the bodies or vestures of immortal Souls and the consciousness within them. The effects produced consist of inspiring and illuminating influences—emotional, intellectual, intuition-awakening and will-power enforcing. Such recharging energies and the resultant altruistic motives in those who respond are occultly discernible. Admittedly, meditation is required in order completely to contact and comprehend this inner history of the world at various superphysical levels.

38 THROUGH FAIRY TALE AND MYTH TO THEOSOPHIA

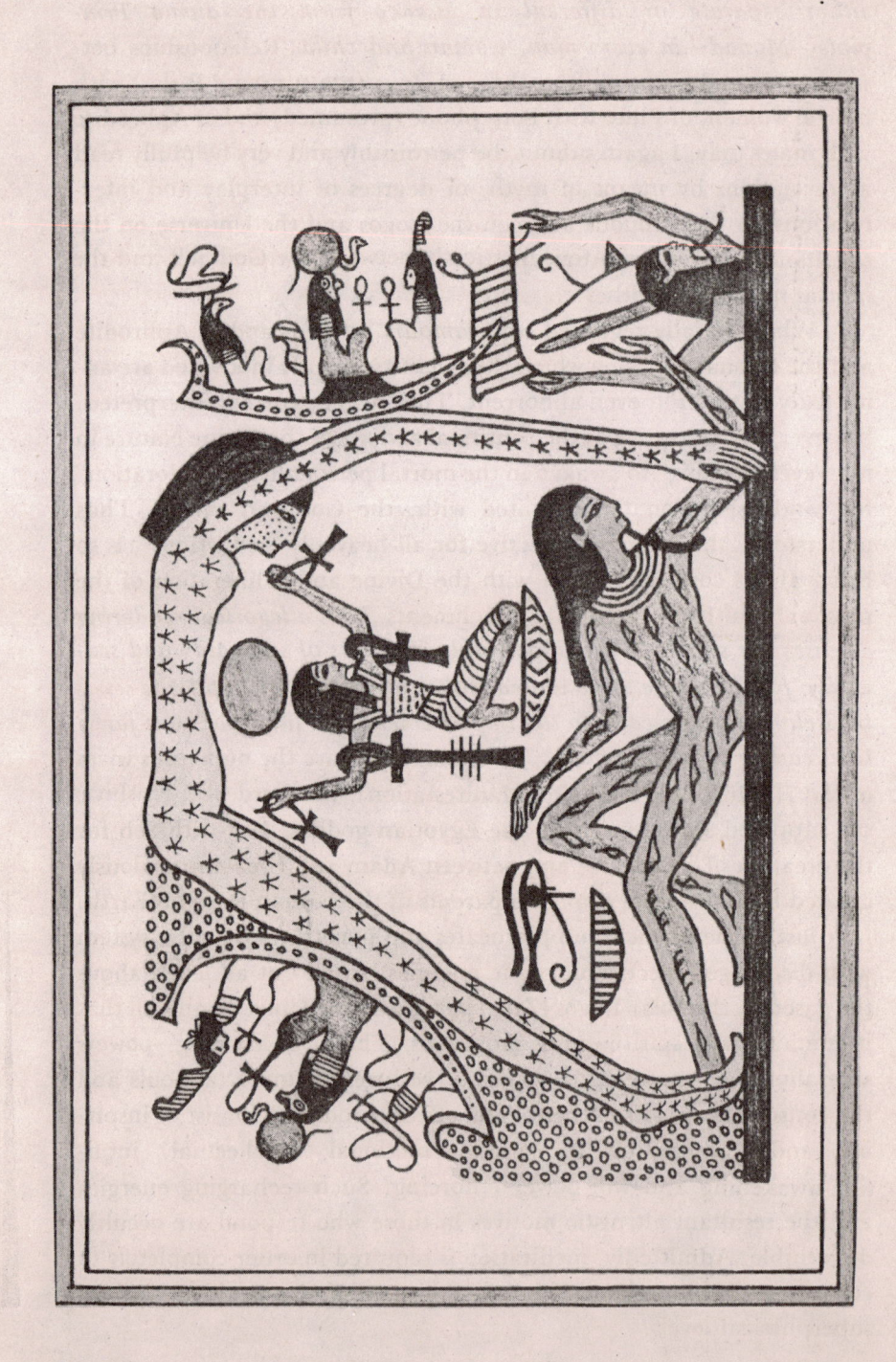

EGYPTIAN COSMOGENESIS

Although the readers of this book may be somewhat prepared to accept the general interpretations offered, they might not be willing to proceed further by such means as extra-sensory investigation. Nevertheless, this subject and the existence of this faculty would seem to be coming increasingly to the fore during the present period of time. The capacity displayed correctly to remember and describe former incarnation,[1] the clairvoyant researches of Edgar Cayce and the capacities for accurately proven mind-reading, are some examples. There are numerous instances of clairvoyance, telepathy, psychometry and other paranormal functions. These phenomena have now been studied for a number of years by the Society for Psychical Research in England and by the Department of Parapsychology at Duke University in the United States under Professor Rhine and in similar societies and institutions of university standing.

The Logos of man's Divine Self[2] (the Zeus within him) produces similar evolution-quickening effects upon his human personality as does the Solar Logos upon the matter and the members of the sub-human kingdoms. These 'descend' as spiritualising, intellectually-enlightening and purificatory influences from Zeus—the human Spirit—into man's mortal nature. If this be acknowledged, then the *amours* of Zeus with human beings—the ladies of ancient Greece—are susceptible of interpretation as descriptive of these selfsame procedures.

Thus viewed, the Lord Zeus was not a personification of a profligate god or an unfaithful husband. Rather was he a very active 'impregnator' of Nature's products with his divine and, at first instinctual, spiritualising influences. Indeed, his nature and powers were impregnated in his offspring Leda, Castor and Pollux, who eventually became stars in the heavens and are still recognised by those names.

As far as can be discovered from varied accounts of the Greek Myths, the *amours* of Zeus with divine and human beings and the resultant offsprings—considered later in this book—were:

---

[1] Dr. Ian Stephenson, author of *Twenty Cases Suggestive of Reincarnation*

[2] *Monad* (Gk) see glossary.

MOTHER	OFFSPRING
Danaë	Perseus
Europa	Rhadamanthus and Minos
Dione	Aphrodite (In the *Iliad*)
Maia	Hermes
Semele	Dionysius
Leto	Apollo and Artemis
Eo	Epaphus
Demeter	Persephone
Aegina	Aeacus
Leda	Helen, Castor and Pollux

At their best the descendants were divine, godlike and when less so they were always heroic as their mythical records reveal.

Perseus—son of Zeus and Danaë—guided by Athena and Hermes, decapitated the evil monster Medusa and then rescued Andromeda from the rock upon which she was chained and from the sea monster.

Rhadamanthus and Minos—sons of Zeus and Europa—were both judges of the dead in Hades.

Aphrodite—daughter of Zeus and Dione—goddess of love and beauty who aided Aeneas to escape from Troy.

Hermes—son of Zeus and Maia—graceful, swift of motion by means of winged sandals, winged hat and magic wand—the Caduceus—Zeus's messenger who 'flies as fleet as thought to do his bidding' and the solemn guide of the dead and rescuer of Persephone and Eurydice from Hades.

Dionysius—son of Zeus and Semele—teacher of the culture of the mystical vine (intuitive wisdom) and the Mysteries of the worship of Dionysius. Defied the power of death to keep his mother from him in the lower world and took her to Olympus where the gods received her as one of themselves.

Apollo and Artemis—children of Zeus and Leto. Apollo, master musician who delighted Olympus as he played on his golden lyre. Healer who first taught men the healing art. God of Light and of Truth. No false word ever fell from his lips. Artemis—twin sister of Apollo—'huntsman-in-chief' to the gods, 'the protectress of dewy youth' everywhere. Never unchaste.

Epaphus—son of Zeus and Io—born on the river Nile. He became king over Egypt and built Memphis and was rumoured to be the sacred bull.

Persephone—daughter of Demeter—radiant maiden of the spring and the summer-time whose footfall made the hillside fresh and blooming.

Castor and Pollux and Helen—children of Zeus and Leda. Castor and Pollux lived half their time on Earth and half in Heaven: special protectors of sailors when 'storm winds rage over the ruthless sea.'

Helen, the fairest woman in the world.

Thus, when the divine in man became unified with the personality, godlike attributes were displayed. When God (Zeus) unifies himself with a human being that person manifests godlike qualities, even if some undesirable attributes may still remain.

THE DIVINE HUNTER

Actually, of course, the time arrives in the course of the evolution of individuals when they are mystically aware that the Inner Self is 'hunting' them and this is the reason why the mystic life is entered upon by whatever means, and eventually the seclusion of the Ashram is sought and established. Then, strangely enough, the story is reversed; for when once the inward Path is sought and entered, it is the outer free world which is the enemy with all its materialising and imprisoning customs. From these, the mystic guards him or herself and seeks monastic or conventual seclusion—safety indeed from this point of view. Meantime, the divine 'Hunter' within, the Monad-Ego, draws nearer and nearer to the climax of the hunt, namely the death of the quadrupedal personality and the absorption into itself of the hitherto ensouling divine Principle.

Thus 'hunting' in this sense truly describes one of the activities of the Logos Who is therefore rightly presented in Mythology by a hunter, huntress, Artemis for example, or bird or animal of prey, hawk or falcon for example, in Egyptian symbology.[1]

[1] A possibly protective function may admittedly also be implied by this relationship.

DEITY-INSPIRED EGYPTIAN PHARAOH, KHEPHREN

The intimate association of the kings of Egypt with falcons as representing Deity suggests both a protective function by the Godhead and a 'preying' upon the royal personage. Indeed, in some statues of the Egyptian kings, they stand between the feet of the falcon, whilst in others the falcon rests behind the head which is enfolded between its wings as shown in the accompanying picture of an Egyptian Pharaoh. This view of either the Godhead or the Higher Self of man as 'preying' upon or 'hunting' the mortal personality is with poetic beauty presented by St. Teresa of Avila in her remarkable spiritual treatise *The Interior Castle*:-

>Struck by the gentle Hunter
>   and overthrown,
>Within the arms of love
>   my soul lay prone.
>Raised to new life at last,
>This contract 'tween us passed,
>That the Beloved should be mine own,
>   I his alone.

All inspired allegories that have emanated from the Greater or Lesser Mysteries — many mythographers of which may be assumed to have been Initiates — were thus designed to preserve through all Ages, to conceal and yet also to convey power-bestowing truths for the ultimate enlightenment of all mankind. Folk tales, as well as epic narratives — some of which did refer to historical events — were retold and embellished by Sages of old in order that they might fulfil these same purposes.

The English poet Francis Thompson pursues this subject in his poem, *The Hound of Heaven*, the word 'hound' being used not in reference to a canine hunter but to the Logos in that 'hunting' aspect of Its activities. The author is privileged to quote here two verses from this wonderful poem:-

>I fled Him, down the nights and down the days;
>I fled Him, down the arches of the years;
>I fled him, down the labyrinthine ways
>   of my own mind; and in the mist of tears
>I fled Him, and under running laughter.
>   Up vistaed hopes I sped;

> And shot, precipitated,
> Adown Titanic glooms of chasmèd fears,
> > From those strong Feet that followed, followed after.
> > But with unhurrying chase,
> > And unperturbed pace,
> > Deliberate speed, majestic instancy,
> > They beat—and a Voice beat
> > More instant than the Feet—
> 'All things betray thee, who betrayest Me.'
>
> > "Now of that long pursuit
> > Comes on at hand the bruit;
> That Voice is round me like a bursting sea;
> > 'And is thy earth so marred,
> > Shattered in shard on shard?
> Lo, all things fly thee for thou fliest Me!
> Strange, piteous, futile thing!
> Wherefore should any set thee love apart?
> Seeing none but I makes much of naught!
> And human love needs human meriting;
> > How hast thou merited—
> Of all man's clotted clay the dingiest clot?
> > Alack, thou knowest not
> How little worthy of any love thou art!
> Whom wilt thou find to love ignoble thee,
> > Save Me, save only Me?
> All of which I took from thee I did but take,
> > Not for thy harms,
> But just that thou might'st seek it in My arms.
> > And which thy child's mistake
> Fancies as lost, I have stored for thee at home;
> > Rise, clasp My hand, and come!"
> > Halts by me that footfall;
> > Is my gloom, after all,
> Shade of His hand, outstretched caressingly?
> > 'Ah, fondest, blindest, weakest,
> > I am He Whom thou seekest!
> Thou dravest love from thee, who dravest Me.' "

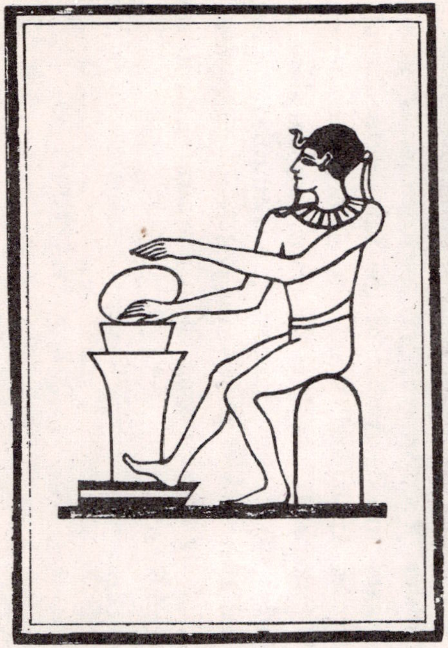

INTERPRETATION OF GREEK MYTHS 45

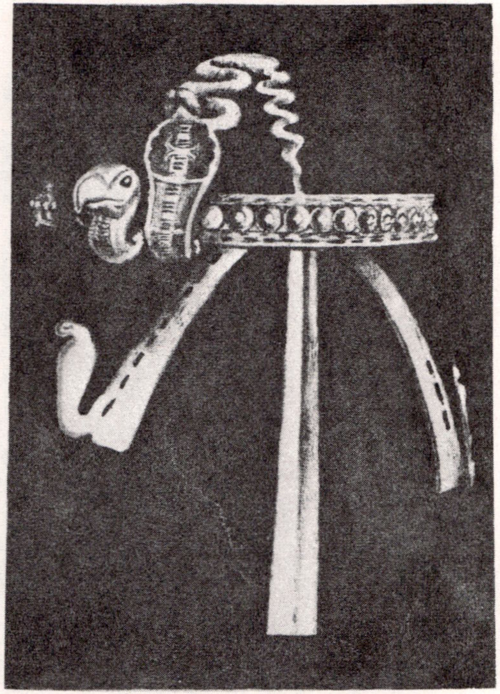

EGYPTIAN UREUS, PORTRAYAL OF TRIPLE *KUNDALINI*

EGYPTIAN SYMBOL OF KUNDALINI PRODUCED EAGLE STATE

PTAH FASHIONING THE EGG OF THE WORLD UPON A POTTER'S WHEEL WHICH HE WORKS WITH HIS FOOT

CHAPTER 2
The Symbols of the Serpent and the Rod
(a) THE ROD OF HERMES

The story of Hermes, and especially of his exercise of the power of free physical and superphysical travel whether to Olympus above or to Hades beneath the earth, reveals the earlier-mentioned identity of the form of the two power-bestowing agencies—*Kundalini* and the Caduceus—the Rod of Hermes. Further similarities between these two and a regular comparison of them led me to perceive that the very same philosophic truths were revealed in them both. When, in due course, I learned that the threefold power delineated by these two symbols is present in every human being, and could be aroused into activity to bestow similar freedom of movement in consciousness and the attainment of extra sensory faculties, my interest naturally was deepened; for I was no longer concerned with two printed symbols, but with the veritable forces which they both portrayed—the Serpent Fire, the *Caduceus* in man. When this energy is awakened into activity, it bestows upon him the power symbolized by the winged helmet, and winged sandals, giving freedom from the limitations of the five physical senses and the exercise of supersensory capacities. No wonder, then, that my interest became acutely aroused—if I may use such a term—and eventually led both to the practice of yoga and to the study of world mythologies.

Delphic Sibyllship, I discovered, was exercised whilst seated upon the three-legged tripod—symbol of the fully aroused triple *Kundalini*. The heroes, Apollo and Heracles, it will be remembered, contended for the tripod at Delphi. Was this really historical alone, it may be asked. Rather was it deeply allegorical, it is affirmed, for the conflict *only* ceased after a *third* power—the god Zeus—intervened, completing the triplicity and bringing about a return of harmony between the two combatants.

ROD OF HERMES   47

Some support for this view may perhaps be gained from the antique bas-relief,[1] illustrating this contest; for also included is the portrayal of a serpent winding its way up the vertical trunk of a closely adjacent tree — possible emblem of man's upright spinal cord. Indeed, as I later learned, effective sibyllship depends upon the harmonised and active presence of the three currents of the Serpent Fire rising directly from sacrum to brain whilst in the Yogi posture.

One is reminded of the serpent associated with the tree of life,[2] tempting Eve to offer its fruit to Adam, and following his acceptance 'the eyes of both of them were opened and they knew they were naked, and they sewed fig-leaves together and made themselves aprons.'[3] Later they became the parents firstly of Cain and secondly of Abel.[4]

May it not well be that whilst fairy-tale-like myths were invented by the people themselves, great sages inspired the introduction of elements, actions and experiences — allegorically portraying spiritual, philosophic and occult truths?

The Greek School of Philosophy is said to have had its inception with the seven immortalized thinkers upon whom was first conferred the appellation of *Sophos*, 'the wise'. According to Diogenes Laertius, these were Thales, Solon, Chilon, Pittacus, Bias, Cleobulus, and Periander.

Far-sighted were the Initiates of antiquity. They realised that nations come and go, that Empires rise and fall, and that the golden ages of art, science, and idealism are succeeded by the dark ages of ignorance and superstition. With the needs of posterity foremost in mind, the sages of old went to inconceivable extremes to make certain that their knowledge should be preserved — when advisable — by using the *Language of Allegory and Symbol*.[5]

Indeed I have become completely assured that for me this is truly so. Actually, these ideas have not only been included in the literature of ancient India and Greece, but are also to be found within world

---

[1] Now in the Louvre.
[2] *Gen.* 2:9
[3] *Gen.* 3:7.
[4] *Gen.* 4:1, 2.
[5] See my book *The Hidden Wisdom in the Holy Bible*, Vol.2, Ch.3. 'Four Major Keys of Interpretation.'

scriptures and mythologies. This proved to be especially true of the Old Testament, concerning which expositions have been published in four volumes entitled *The Hidden Wisdom in the Holy Bible*.

Many years have passed since this discovery was first made, but only in these later years of my life, in pursuance of the Second Object[1] of the Theosophical Society, have I found myself free to present some of the fruits of my studies of Greek and other mythologies for those who may be interested.

The ancient Greek legend tells how the god Hermes came upon two serpents engaged in mortal combat. Placing his magic, winged wand—a gift from his brother Apollo in return for a seven stringed lyre—between the two antagonists, he so charmed them that they returned to harmony, equally intertwining both the rod and each other. And this, it is said, was the origin of the famous Hermetic staff, the Caduceus, symbol today of medical science and the healing art.

Possessed of his famous rod, Hermes became free of the universe from highest heaven to deepest Hades and, therefore, one may assume from the law of correspondences, from the Monad[2] to the physical body of man. Herein lies the secret of much of the power-bestowing knowledge concealed within and revealed both by the myth of Hermes and many of the symbols and allegories of Freemasonry; for the Caduceus displays symbolically but with exactitude the interactive threefold power by means of which man may develop supernormal faculties and win freedom from the confining effects of incarnation in a human body.

The Caduceus itself is found to be a portrayal of the three pathways followed by the triple creative force in man which, when occultly aroused and forced to flow upwards along the spine from sacrum to cranium, bestows extrasensory perception. This sublimation achieved, man ceased to be a prisoner in the flesh, a Hermes in truth.

Allegorically, he is freed from Hades as was Persephone by Hermes, staff in hand. The Caduceus is thus no solid wand, but a symbol of the interharmonized and interactive creative powers in nature and in man.

[1] To encourage the study of Comparative Religion, Philosophy and Science.
[2] The divine Spirit in Man.

ROD OF HERMES 49

HERMES, CADUCEUS EMPOWERED

Ancient Hindu sages gave to this form of the manifestation of the triple, divine energy the name of *Kundalini,* meaning 'the coiled up, universal Life principle.' They described it as a sevenfold, superphysical, occult power functioning in developed man by means of a spiral or coiling action, within and round the spinal cord but also throughout the nervous systems. When supernormally aroused as by yogic practices, this fiery force ascends into and through the brain by a serpentine path, hence its other name, 'The Serpent Fire.' The ability is then attained to leave the body at will and to exercise other supernormal powers.

Much more may be learned by a study of the old Greek legend. Hermes is known, for example, as herald and messenger of Zeus in whose service he traverses without obstruction the regions of the air, the earth and the subterranean kingdom ruled by the god Pluto.

He thus personifies the matured Initiate, the fully-endowed Adept. The winged cap, also possessed by Hermes, may be interpreted as a symbol of both his complete freedom from terrestrial limitations and his realized oneness with the all-pervading, all-directive Universal Intelligence, the deific principle at the heart of Cosmos, of planetary life and of man. The winged sandals both support this interpretation and add the element of swiftness of foot in the service of the Godhead. In this also Hermes represents perfected man, self-freed from all limitations of time and space, actively engaged in assisting evolutionary procedures and even at times hastening their completion.

The god is thus seen not only as messenger of the Supreme Deity but as Hierophant of the Mysteries, prototype of those illumined Teachers who, age by age, visit mankind.

Hermes may thus be regarded as a model for all who aspire to Hermes-like stature and his supernormal powers. Very appropriately did the mythographers of old, desiring thus to inspire and inform mankind, make of Hermes a favourite of gods and men despite his various peccadillos,[1] for he stole the cattle of his brother, Apollo, the girdle of Aphrodite, the arrows of Artemis, and the spear of Ares. He was always forgiven, however, being loved by all the gods and goddesses of the Greek Pantheon.

MODERN MAN SEEKS AGELESS TRUTHS

Extended vision, the organs in the brain through which it functions and the subtle forces by which it is supposedly called into operation are becoming of increasing interest to modern man. Books and also articles in the daily press, the more serious types of magazines, scientific journals, and the latest developments in medicine and

---

[1] Each doubtless with its group of recondite meanings.

psychology indicate that a change may at this time seem to be occurring in the attitude towards supernormal faculties. Clairvoyance, clairaudience, awareness of events happening at a distance, premonitions of things to come which prove to be true, intuitive warnings against life-endangering courses of conduct—not to take particular train, boat or aeroplane, for example—flashes of direct mental perception which solve mechanical, inventive, chemical and other scientific problems—these are reported to be experienced by certain people nowadays. Children who are proving to be hypersensitive in some of these ways present problems to parents and teachers. A study of these phenomena and the application to them of theosophical teachings are thus not only of interest but are in harmony with the Third Object of the Theosophical Society and may be of much practical value.

These supernormal experiences are partly explained by theosophical teachings concerning evolution and the resultant changes which continue to occur in the human brain and nervous system. One of the five senses is said to be developed by each of the successive main or root races of men, five having already appeared so that man now possesses five senses. A sixth race is at this time being born, and in consequence a sixth sense (ESP) now seems to be more generally evident than in former times.

Some (not all) men of science of today would appear to be thinking along these lines, for the supernormal faculties of man have for some time been undergoing careful investigation. The modern phase of experimental work into telepathy and other faculties may be regarded as starting with the work of H.J.F.W. Brugmans at Groningen (1920), Miss Jephson (1924) in England, and J.B. Rhine at Duke University, North Carolina (1930 onwards). Dr. Rhine, Professor of Psychology at Duke, whose contribution to the subject has been very considerable, published in 1934 a book entitled *Extra-Sensory Perception*, which described experiments in telepathy and telaesthesia and aroused considerable controversy.

G.N.M. Tyrrell, in England (1934-6) developed an electrical apparatus in which the percipient had to cognize in which of five closed boxes the agent had caused a lamp to be lit. An ingenious 'scrambling' device insured that the agent himself did not know which lamp he had lit by turning his selector switch, so that any signalling code, conscious or unconscious, would have been stultified. The conditions were virtually those of telaesthesia rather than telepathy, since no mind was aware which lamp was lit until after the choice had been made. Highly significant results were reported with one subject who was tested. At the same time Dr. S.G. Soal, Lecturer in Mathematics at the University of London, began to carry out an extensive repetition of Rhine's experiments with Zener cards, and during the next five years he gave individual tests to 160 persons and recorded 128,350 guesses. The results appeared to be in close accordance with chance expectation, and they were put aside.

A STRANGE PHENOMENON

However, in the autumn of 1939 Whately Carington, as a result of observations he had made while doing some telepathy experiments with drawings, persuaded Soal to re-examine his records in order to ascertain whether any of the percipients had scored hits, not on the cards focused by the agent but on the immediately preceding or following cards. The search revealed that two persons had shown highly significant scores on the preceding (precognitive) and following (postcognitive) cards, while their score on the actual target card was insignificant, suggesting a kind of displacement effect. This, of course, had to be confirmed, and these two percipients were retested. The first of them, Basil Shackleton, a well-known London photographer, was tested by Soal and Goldney over a period of two and a half years, and this displacement effect was confirmed. The most elaborate precautions were taken to guard against fraud and sensory leakage, such as unconscious whispering. In addition, a further curious discovery was made. If the rate of calling was speeded up from one every three seconds to one every one and one-half seconds, Shackleton scored insignificantly on the target card and on the card one ahead, but began to score significantly on the card two ahead. Soal's and Goldney's original paper, which describes in detail the plethora of precautionary measures taken to guard against sensory leakage and fraud, should be studied by all interested in telepathy.

A CALL TO MANKIND

In a statement on the purpose and the philosophy of UNESCO, Professor Julian Huxley, then its Director-General, wrote:

'In general, education should pay special attention to seeing that borderline fields, especially those neglected by orthodox or organized science, are properly explored. As one example, we may take what is now generally called parapsychology—the study of unusual and at the moment scientifically inexplicable properties of the mind, such as extra-sensory perception of various kinds. The painstaking researches of one or two recent workers in this unpopular field seem to have established the reality of some degree not only of extra-sensory knowledge, but also of precognition. It is urgent that these phenomena should be thoroughly investigated, so that a new and more comprehensive scientific frame-work of knowledge can be erected.

'Or take a somewhat different example, that of the astonishing control which, by virtue of elaborate techniques and exercises, Hindu yogis and other mystics are able to exert both over their bodily functions and their mental states. The general facts are undoubted, but neither the physiological and psychological mechanisms involved, nor the general scientific implications, are understood.

'It would seem desirable to have careful studies made of the phenomena by trained physiologists and psychologists, including some who would be willing to undergo the training themselves. Not everyone would be suitable for this long ordeal; but the results ought to be of the greatest importance, not only in enlarging our scientific knowledge but in making the attainment of the spiritual satisfaction of so called mystical experience more widely available to men and women of all countries.'

INTUITIVE PERCEPTION—THE NEW FACULTY

The mystical experience to which Professor Huxley refers is less objective in terms of extra-sensory perception and far more subjective than are clairvoyance and clairaudience. Intuition is defined as the immediate and complete cognition or tacit understanding of any object or truth—perception without reasoning; the connecting link between ancient and modern philosophical knowledge. Other forms of intuition will become manifest as evolution proceeds. These will consist of extensions of such fairly common experiences as the spontaneous arising in one's mind without reasoning of illuminating ideas in general and the discovery of the solution of particular problems with which one has been preoccupied. Though intuition has hitherto been regarded as not to be acquired by training, this view seems likely to undergo a change; for means are already being devised in American schools — and doubtless elsewhere — to bring about a development of the faculty, some scholars proving to be thus naturally endowed.

A theosophical view is that intuitions arise in the sixth principle or Christ-Nature in man, the seat of his spiritual wisdom and his consciousness of oneness with the inherent, intrinsic life in all beings and all forms. This vehicle appears at this time to be undergoing a development which is likely to render it increasingly effective as an instrument of cognition and research. The slow processess of physical observation and classification, mental analysis, deduction and induction will then become less and less necessary for the attainment of knowledge; for those in whom intuition is sufficiently developed will be endowed with an instantaneous implicit insight into every first truth. In later races, these clairvoyant and intuitive faculties will be as consciously used and as fully controlled as are now the five senses and the mind.

THE NEW POWER — THE SERPENT FIRE

The hitherto relatively latent force in the physical body of man intimately associated with this development, would seem also to be awakening into activity at this time. This, as we have seen, is referred to in Hindu literature by the Sanskrit name of *Kundalini*, the power that moves in a serpentine path, also known as 'The Serpent Fire.'

The evolution of man is thus intimately associated with the awakening and action within him of this occult power; for as the sixth and seventh races of men appear on earth, *Kundalini* will naturally and gradually awaken, vitalize and render hypersensitive appropriate cranial organs, chiefly the pituitary and pineal glands, but also the whole of the brain. The sixth and seventh senses, clairvoyance and clairaudience, will then be added to the present five. Some of the resultant faculties will be: positive clairvoyance in time, distance, magnitude; geometric or 'all-sides' vision over-riding perspective; clairaudience and superphysical travel. To these will be added the power to perceive intuitively and then to pass through 'the gateway of stillness' into oneness with the hidden life within all of nature's forms and to comprehend its mysterious activities. This will bring serenity, happiness, and supreme bliss. The union of time and space will be experienced as implicit and all will be known as here and now in the 'ever-present moment.' Man's basic delusion of himself as other than the universe will be dispelled since each human being will be known as embracing the cosmos in its totality. The all-important motive for living will then be 'for others' or 'for everyone'. The universe will come to be experienced as absolute, undifferentiated Reality, an interdependent whole.

A WARNING AND SOME GUIDANCE CONCERNING MOTIVES

All students are here seriously warned against attempts to arouse the Serpent Fire in the absence of a spiritual Teacher. They are, however, reminded of the occult maxim, 'When the pupil is ready, the Teacher appears.' Other conditions under which such occult development may be safely undertaken are: a selfless motive—to know more in order to serve more effectively; signs of a natural gift; guidance from a Teacher; a strong and healthy body, controlled emotions; a stable mind and physical circumstances, especially obligations, which both permit and point the way. Without these safeguards, such dangers could be encountered as self-deceit, pride, and the lust for place and power—perhaps the gravest danger—accentuated sensuality, grave indiscretion, nervous breakdown and distraction from the true highest goal in the spiritual life, which is direct experience of the oneness of the life in all beings and all things.

These dangers avoided, the development of supersensory powers may be safely brought about by regular meditation, the refinement of the body, particularly by a vegetarian diet and the abstention from alcohol and narcotics. All occult experiences and discoveries should, however, be severely tested against the demands of logic and established fact and according to the scientific method of rechecked observations and experiments objectively recorded with absolute honesty and without fear or favour.

THE TRUE VISION

The attainment of supersensory powers alone should on no account be made an end in itself, for seership is but incidental to spirituality. The highest vision is of unity, the highest motive is to serve, and the greatest power attainable by man is effectively to uplift, illumine, teach, heal, and serve one's fellow men. Nevertheless, the way of direct knowledge does exist. *Kundalini* can be awakened and can bestow supernormal powers upon man which can then valuably be used in search of direct experience. There *is* a way of escape from the net of the transient into the freedom of life eternal. There *is* a life in which the fluctuations of terrestrial affairs are of less importance than a passing breeze. There *is* a light by which all things may be perceived according to true values and in perfect perspective, bestowing an unshakable peace and happiness which no adversity can destroy.

Fulfilment, self-unfoldment, enlightenment, power to uplift and to heal, and above all a magnificent purpose in life — all these await the determined man of unprejudiced mind and selfless heart who seeks the truth and aspires to serve. It is indeed true that mighty powers lie latent in man and that they continually, if gradually, awaken from latency to potency and that the evolutionary possibilities and future of man are entirely without limit, as Wordsworth, speaking very theosophically, said:

> Our destiny, our being's heart and home
> Is with infinitude and only there.

Harold Begbie wrote: 'The advance of mankind is not towards mastery of mechanism and the elements, but towards self-mastery. The field of enquiry is consciousness, the destiny of the race is spiritual, and the only happiness possible to the sons of men is a happiness of the heart.'

Compassion is indeed the outstanding characteristic of the advanced human being and this idea is beautifully expressed in the following poem:

> The true citizen of the New Age,
> Will let compassion control even the
>   details of his daily life.
> He will shrink from harming anything that
>   breathes, because he will accept the Law of
> Kinship of all that lives.

ROD OF MOSES

(b) THE ROD OF MOSES TURNED INTO A SERPENT[1]

Exodus 4:1. And Moses answered and said, But, behold, they will not believe me, nor hearken unto my voice: for they will say, the LORD hath not appeared unto thee.

2. And the LORD said unto him, What *is* that in thine hand? And he said, A rod.

3. And He said, Cast it on the ground. And he cast it on the ground, and it became a serpent; and Moses fled from before it.

4. And the LORD said unto Moses, Put forth thine hand, and take it by the tail. And he put forth his hand, and caught it, and it became a rod in his hand.

In this Chapter the symbol of the serpent is once more introduced into the narrative, in which it is made to play an entirely 'supernatural' part. A rod in the hand of Moses is made by the Lord to turn into a serpent, and back again into a rod. A most deeply occult revelation, in those days completely confined to the Sanctuaries, is made in this Chapter; for the actual means is revealed whereby the soul or noumenon of both Universe and man is extricated from enmeshment in matter.

The symbol of the serpent is susceptible of many interpretations — exoteric, esoteric and occult. In general, it is the symbol both of Wisdom and of the Wise, who in the Sacred Language are frequently referred to as serpents. The *Nagas* of Hindu literature are none other than the ancient *Rishis*, liberated yogis, or Adepts. The serpent is chosen as the symbol of Wisdom for various reasons. It glides secretly, and for the most part unseen, on the surface of the globe, just as Wisdom — whether revealed from on High or inborn — is a concealed Power potent either to illumine, if rightly employed, or to destroy if misused. The smooth sinuosity of the snake and of its movements not inaptly portrays the harmonious and rhythmic self-expression of Wisdom in both the Universe and the man in whom it is awake and moving. He is enlightened from within, or secretly.

---

[1] Extract from *The Hidden Wisdom in the Holy Bible*, Vol.IV. Hodson.

The serpent regularly sloughs its skin Despite this seasonal change the reptile itself is unchanged, but appears in a new and glistening covering. So Wisdom, whilst remaining ever the same in essence, is self-manifest in ever new forms, none being able to hold it permanently. The serpent's tongue is forked or bi-polar. So also is Wisdom, being susceptible of degradation into low cunning employed for meanest motives, or of elevation into lofty intuition according to unselfish ideals. Snake venom can destroy or heal according to its use and dosage. So also Wisdom, which when degraded poisons the soul but which, when rightly used, is an antidote for many ills.

The eyes of the serpent are compelling, even hypnotic. Wisdom, once awake in an individual, brooks no resistance, breaks all bonds, and ultimately rules with impelling power. The Wise, also, are irresistible in their might, even though appearing to be lowly and making no claim to high regard. Nevertheless they live near to the Source of Life, just as the serpent lives near to the roots and seeds of living things.

When the serpent's tail is in its mouth an endless circle is made, implying the eternity of Wisdom, and even Eternity itself. Esoterically, however, processes of cosmogenesis are indicated by the union of a symbolised positive and negative, or the entry of the tail into the mouth. All generative processes are, indeed, indicated in that form, which leads to the deeply occult significance of the serpent — namely as a symbol of the universal, divine, creative, ever-active life-force. This is *Fohat* in its dual polarity, sometimes symbolised not as one serpent with tail in mouth, but as two mutually intertwined. Here the laws of electricity, under which all formative processes occur, are indicated.

The driving force from within which leads to inceptive activity in organic forms, and to chemical affinity in inorganic ones, is indeed bipolar. The aptness of the choice of the serpent as a symbol for this power would seem to be supported by the fact that its tongue is forked. A reference is thus made to the positive and negative currents of the Great Breath,[1] continually breathed forth as *Fohat* into and through every atom of every world, to become omnipresent and perpetually active throughout the whole Universe. This fact was both concealed and

---

[1] Great Breath—see Glossary under *Brahma's Night*.

revealed in ancient allegories, in which Jupiter and other male creative deities changed themselves into snakes for the purpose of seducing goddesses, their progeny being the demi-gods, many of whom later attained to full deification.

A serpent with tail in mouth, two serpents intertwined, or one encircling a rod, staff or pillar, all symbolise the electric energy of *Fohat* in action in the material Universe and therefore in man, the microcosmic temple of the Universe.

In man the rod refers both to the spinal cord and to an etheric and super-physical canal or channel in its centre, passing from the root of the cord in the sacrum, along its whole length and into the *medulla oblongata* and brain. This canal is the vehicle for the primordial life-force, a measure of which plays down from above in the generative act. The current is uni-polar, or even of neutral polarity, since it plays upon and produces its effects in both the male and female organism. The historic occult name for this canal is *Sushumna*,[1] but generally that name is only used when by occult means the same neutral force is made to play not downwards, but upwards along the spinal cord. Before such reversal of the flow of originative energy can be achieved, the positive and negative currents must be aroused and themselves, like twin serpents, flow upwards, intertwining as they flow to induce an ascent of the accompanying neutral energy.

Entering the brain, this triple power so illumines the mind of man that he becomes, as it were a god possessed of theurgic powers. This fact is revealed in *Genesis*, Chapters Two and Three, where a man and woman, Adam and Eve, represent the oppositely polarised currents, the tree of knowledge of good and evil (especially the trunk) corresponding to the rod, and the tempting serpent to *Sushumna*. Thus Adam and Eve are forbidden to eat of the fruit of this tree, since by so doing they would become as gods. The intensely heightened vibrations of the brain, the glands, the cells and aerial substance in the ventricles, cause the brain and cranium to become responsive to egoic and monadic life and consciousness. Spirit then predominates in the individual; matter loses its power. Symbolically, through the agency of an interchangeable serpent and rod, the Israelites are freed from bondage in Egypt.

---

[1] *Sushumna*—see Glossary under *Kundalini Shakti*.

In verse three of the Fourth Chapter of the Book of Exodus the order was given to cast the rod upon the ground, after which it became a serpent. The shaft of *Atmic* fire which forms the core of the force which plays along the *Sushumna* is brought down to the densest physical level, or symbolically is cast upon the ground. When that occurs the relatively dormant, positive-negative life-force resident in the sacrum is awakened into activitiy. Each polarity then pursues a mutually intertwining, serpentine path around the *Sushumna* canal. Symbolically stated, the rod becomes the serpent.

This process is not unproductive of a certain shock and some pain. The Initiate momentarily shrinks therefrom, but still persists. Moses is therefore made to flee before the serpent. When, however, he unites his own will with that of the Hierophant Himself and sublimates the creative force, compelling it to flow upwards from the pelvis, it becomes in his hand the magician's wand of power. Symbolically, as in verse four, Moses takes the serpent by the tail and it becomes a rod in his hand.

As portrayed in Egyptian art in which serpents are intertwined round rods or pillars, the tail is at the foot of the pillar, meaning in the sacrum. The head of the serpent is at the upper end, where frequently a lotus flower is blooming. This, too, is a universally used symbol. The opening of the force-centres in the **super-physical** bodies, consequent upon the arousing and the upward flow of the Serpent Power, is depicted by such emblems. The historic occult names for the positive and negative currents are *Pingala* and *Ida*,[1] *and the triple upward flow is most perfectly revealed by the Greek symbol of the Caduceus.*[2]

The Egyptian *Ureus*[3] worn on the head of deities and Pharaohs and the two goddesses Uachit and Nekhebit here portrayed are significant examples of the Egyptian revelation and yet concealment of the Serpent Fire ascending the spinal cord.

In *The Secret Wisdom of the Qabbalah*, pp. 72-73, J.F.C. Fuller writes:

"To the student of the occult it will be apparent that these two trees (the Tree of Knowledge of Good and Evil and the Tree of Life) closely resemble the letter *Shin,* also the **Caduceus of Hermes** with its

---

[1] *Pingala* and *Ida*—see Glossary under *Kundalini.*
[2] Caduceus—see Glossary under *Kundalini.*
[3] See illustration on p.45.

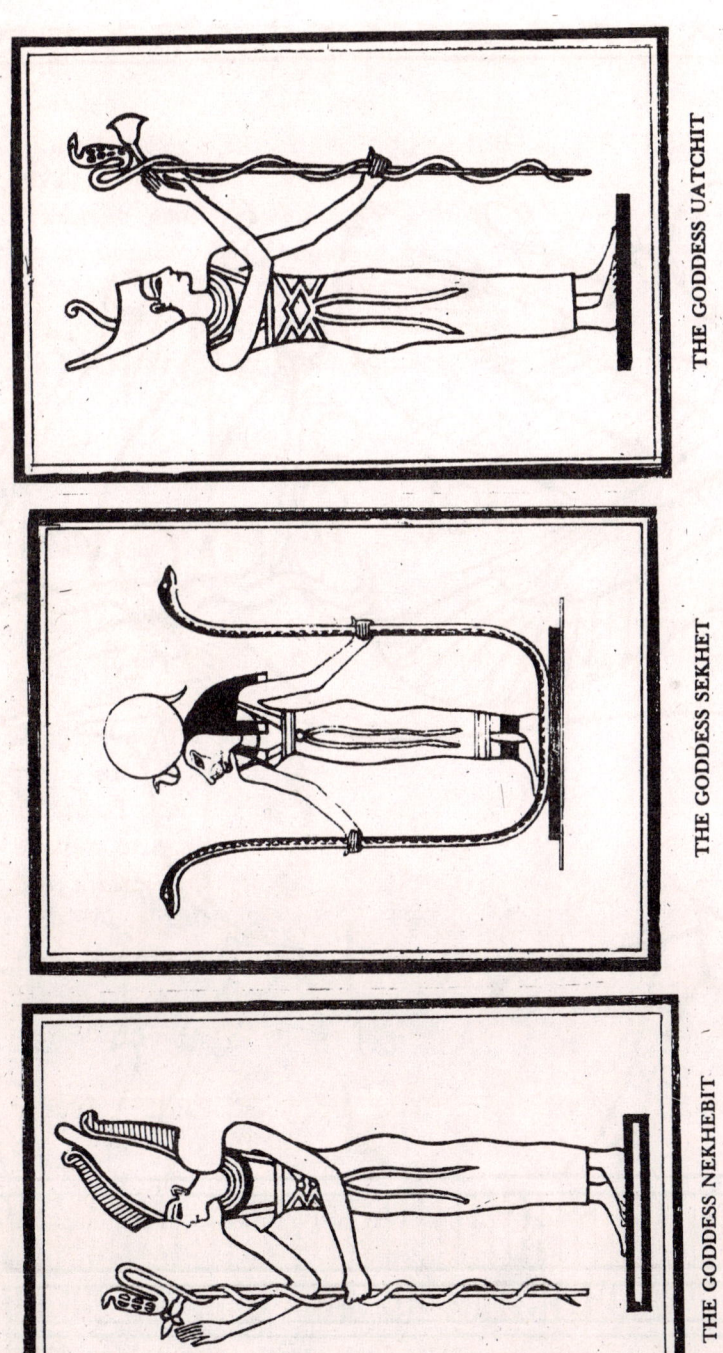

ROD OF MOSES 61

THE GODDESS UATCHIT

THE GODDESS SEKHET

THE GODDESS NEKHEBIT

62 SYMBOLS OF SERPENT AND ROD

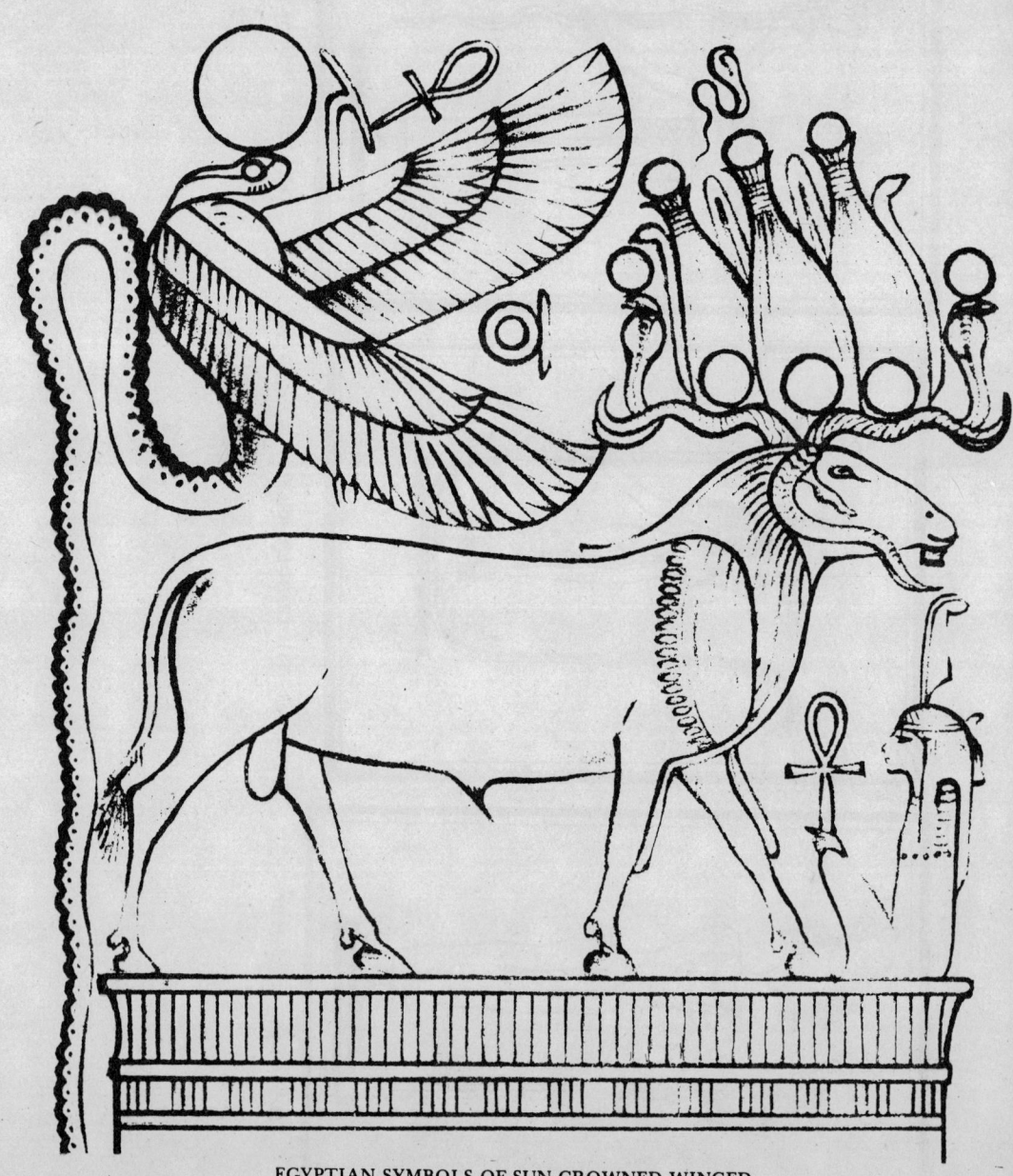

EGYPTIAN SYMBOLS OF SUN-CROWNED WINGED SERPENT AND *KUNDALINI*—ANTLERED RAM

EGYPTIAN GODDESS ISIS

central rod and its two entwined serpents, and also the *Ida, Pingala,* and central *Sushumna* of Hindu Yoga. The whole scheme is symbolised in the Temple of Solomon, the temple itself being the central pillar, whilst its two pylons, Yakhin and Boaz, the white and the black, the right and the left, represent the Tree of the Knowledge of Good and Evil—the eternal complementary forces in life without which nothing can be. This symbolism is an excessively ancient one; thus in Norse mythology we find the mystic tree Yggdrasil, the roots of which are in the material world and the branches of which reach up to Asgard, the happy dwelling of the gods. Again, amongst the Akkadians, Chaldeans, and Babylonians we find the World Tree, or Tree of Life, which 'stood mid-way between the Deep and Zikum'—the primordial heaven above. In Hindu mythology there is also a World Tree—the Asvatta—and in Buddhism the Bodhi Tree, or Tree of Wisdom under which Buddha sat in meditation.

Hermes is the Moses of the Greeks, in that he is both messenger from God to man by virtue of holding in his hand the Caduceus—just as Moses held in his hand the rod—and deliverer of Persephone from Hades, just as Moses delivered Israel from bondage in Egypt. The holding of the Caduceus (or rod or serpent) in the hand is itself a symbol implying mastery of a power, and the possession of knowledge and skill in its employment.

The transmutation of rod into serpent, be it noted, could only occur at the command of the Deity and by His magical power. Actually, the descent of the Monadic *Atma* through all the vehicles and down the spinal cord into the sacrum is essential to the premature[1] full awakening of the triple creative Fire, and its successful sublimation and use as a magical tool. To bring this power of *Atma* down is one part of the office of the Hierophant of the Greater Mysteries. Since thereafter a new life is begun, the act has ever been correctly termed Initiation. The Initiate is one in whom has been aroused the power to liberate himself from the limitations of matter, desire, and self-separateness into the freedom of universal consciousness, life and power. Such is part of the inner meaning of the strange story of the magical power by which Moses overcame the resistance of Pharaoh to the departure of the Israelites.

---

[1] As far as normal evolutionary time is concerned

In the first three-and-a-half phases of all cycles this power drives life and consciousness downward into matter, into generation, and in organic life, to generative activity. It is therefore presented as evil, or contrary to the highest good. Temporarily it is so, since pure spirit, unsullied life and innocent consciousness become stained and aware of passion as a result of the serpent-inspired descent. Ultimately, however, the self-same force liberates spirit, life and consciousness, individualised as man, from the grip and stain of material life and physical generative processes.

In the Garden of Eden, representing the period of the downward arc, the serpent is the devil and his temptations lead to the generative act, and to loss of innocence and banishment from Eden. In the Initiate and the Adept (typified by Moses and Christ) the serpent-force, transmuted and spiritually employed, becomes the redeeming power. This, in part, is the revelation of the serpent symbol in the Book of Exodus. It represents both the creative and the redeeming agencies (the dark and the light serpents of the Caduceus) in Nature and in man.

An incursion into occult physiology is necessary for an exposition of this subject, as symbolised by the mutually interchangeable serpent and rod; for the rod, in its turn, has its own specific meaning in the Sacred Language. In the Universe it is the *fohatic* pillar or current of formative power by which the Universe is created and sustained. It is a pillar less in its shape than in its supporting function of a rod or staff breaking into leaf or flower, as portrayed on the Tarot Cards and in the allegory of Tannhauser. When this process has been fully accomplished, the lower nature is subject to the higher; the vehicles of consciousness acknowledge the rule of the Higher Self. This is stated symbolically in *Exodus* 7:5, wherein is promised the recognition by the Israelites that Moses is divinely inspired.

> *Ex:* 7:10   And Moses and Aaron went in unto Pharaoh, and they did so as the LORD had commanded: and Aaron cast down his rod before Pharaoh, and before his servants, and it became a serpent.

As always, mastery of the creative force and doubt-free, utterly faithful fulfillment of the commands of the God within constitute both the test and the mark of truly illumined manhood. Sublimation of the generative energy[1] in the spinal cord or 'rod', and faithful fulfilment of duty—these are the two pillars of that portal through which every Initiate must pass ere he receives and is able to ratify his initiate powers. When these two are conjoined in any man then, indeed, is he stable before every storm and rocklike in his strong and immovable adherence to spiritual law.

> *Ex.* 7:11 Then Pharaoh also called the wise men and the sorcerers: now the magicians of Egypt, they also did in like manner with their enchantments.

As the devil quotes the scriptures to his own end,[2] so the world and the flesh, represented by Pharaoh, produce a *maya* with which to resist and entrap the ambassador of Truth with his message of liberation.

> *Ex.* 7:12. For they cast down every man his rod, and they became serpents. but Aaron's rod swallowed up their rods.

The body itself performs a magical act every time the creative power[3] is exercised. The spinal cord is the vehicle for that power, and thus may be said temporarily to become a serpent. Sublimated, however, as by Moses-Aaron, representing the Initiated ego-personality, the procreative expression of the power is renounced and the force itself turned upwards for spiritual purposes, chiefly that of self-liberation from the delusion of self-separateness and the appetites of the flesh. Desire dies when transmutation occurs. Procreation ceases for the magician who employs the self-same creative force, and its cerebro-spinal vehicle as the agent thereof, for occult and spiritual purposes.

'*Daemon Deus inversus est.*'[4] The one energy is susceptible of both misuse and right use, but in the latter the former is renounced or 'swallowed up'. The lower worlds and the lower man respectively reflect the higher worlds and the ego of man, quite faithfully as far as their general constitution is concerned. When, however, the human mind is active, distortion becomes possible and can constitute a veritable danger to the soul. It is this distortion and debasement of the

---

[1] See Glossary under *Kundalini Shakti*.
[2] *Matt.* 4:6.
[3] Creative power—see Glossary under *Kundalini*.
[4] The Devil is God inverted.

Divine in Nature and in man which is the so-called and miscalled 'unforgivable sin', and particularly as it concerns the life-force—the cosmic, creative Serpent Fire. This is the true and only 'fall' of man, not the natural and inevitable descent of spirit into matter. Neither is it the advance of child humanity into adult knowledge of so-called good and evil, which are relative terms, especially when applied to evolutionary processes and experiences on the way to Wisdom. The real 'fall' is the *deliberate, self-chosen, and continuing debasement and degradation* to grossly animalistic and Satanic purposes of that which is divine and sacred. As stated, this especially applies to the life-force, and it is an error into which humanity has grievously fallen, greatly to its detriment.

CHAPTER 3

THE LIFE, LABOURS, AND ASCENSION OF HERACLES

(a) Introduction
(b) The Cradle State.
(c) The Twelve Labours of Heracles —

    The Killing of the Nemean Lion.
    The Slaughter of the Hydra of Lerna.
    The Capture of the Ceryneian Hind.
    The Capture of the Erymanthian Boar.
    The Cleansing of the Augean Stables.
    The Destruction of The Stymphalian Birds.
    The Capture of the Cretan Bull.
    The Mares of King Diomedes.
    The Golden Girdle of Hippolyte.
    The Oxen of Geryon.
    The Golden Apples of the Hesperides.
    Bringing Cerberus From Hades to Eurystheus.

(d) The Rescue of Theseus.
(e) Allegorical Elements in the Life-Story of Heracles.
(f) Flaming Death and Ascension to Olympus.

INTRODUCTION TO THE TWELVE LABOURS

The narratives of each of the Labours of Heracles here interpreted are somewhat simplified since various sources contain differing statements. The chief events — particularly those possessing veiled references to occult wisdom — are recorded as accurately as possible.

The invincibility, invulnerability and extreme muscular strength of Heracles and especially his control and strangulation of the serpents which attacked him in his cradle, together with his other heroic attributes — humility, for example — indicate that he represents a human

INTRODUCTION TO THE LABOURS

being in some respects, but not all, who is already considerably advanced along the path of hastened unfoldment. His weaknesses, however, in their turn demonstrate that the great 'Goal' of perfected manhood had not yet been attained.

If this approach be acceptable, then his Labours, other heroic deeds and experiences through which he must pass as he further ascends the 'ladder' of human development from man to Adept may well be approached as containing and conveying valuable guidance to every individual who has vowed to reach the occult and spiritual heights as quickly as possible and Heracles-like is prepared to pay whatever price will in consequence be demanded. Heracles will, applying this view, then be regarded as an Initiated member of the Ancient Mysteries which were founded by Adepts for the purpose of providing every sincere aspirant with the support and guidance that will aid them in the fulfilment of their high ideal.

The first and very potent necessity, it is taught, for acceptance into a temple of The Mysteries and for success therein, is *above all other qualities, the motive by which the aspirant is moved. Without exception, this must always be the welfare of the human race on behalf of which the Initiate is selflessly committed.*

Of interest, therefore, does one find that each of the Labours of Heracles was undertaken not only as an act of penance with its mystical significance, *but in every case for the welfare of others even at the risk—very grave in each case—of the loss of his own life,* save perhaps in the 5th Labour, The Cleansing of the Augean Stables.

Each of the Twelve Labours, or at least nearly all of them, may thus be regarded as allegorical descriptions of the experiences through which—largely interiorly—every Initiate must pass as they tread the ancient Pathway to Perfection or, in Buddhist terms, seek 'to Enter the Stream and reach the Further Shore'.

Eurystheus, then, may well be regarded as portraying the Hierophant who both guides the aspirant into and through each phase of development or 'Degree' and bestows upon him the successive Initiations which lead from humanity to superhumanity. Interiorly, however, the King represents the aspirant's Higher Self.

The apparently cruel and viciously jealous action of Hera in driving him insane may perhaps partially be interpreted as personifying both the law of cause and effect or *Karma,* and its operation upon the aspirant who also aspires as quickly as possible to 'pay all debts' in order that the great consummation may be attained.

The imposed insanity or 'bewitched' condition, be it remembered, whilst leading to the most grave crimes, was nevertheless the one condition which decided Heracles—on the guidance of the Priestess at Delphi—to surrender himself to whatever service King Eurystheus might demand of him. Thus though the madness was at first a tragedy indeed, it actually led to deeds of the greatest heroism and welfare to countrysides and populations. May it not be true, furthermore, that with deeply felt remorse, a determination both to sin no more and to ascend to heights where sin would be impossible, the supposed madness (bewitchment) with its tragic immediate results becomes an ultimate blessing in disguise?—for without this the 'Labours' would not have been embarked upon.

Even otherwise regarded, may the 'madness', with the extreme barbarity to which it led, possibly also be read as a warning against carrying even idealism to extremes *beyond* the level of reason, as has and still does happen to human beings—the neglect of existing responsibilities, even to home and family, for example?

THE CRADLE STATE

The life-story of Heracles may be interpreted as a description of the experiences of every neophyte who successfully treads the hastened Pathway to Adeptship. This attainment is allegorically portrayed as a 'flaming death', which for the hero led to the transmutation of all mortal limitations of the human personality, and consequent ascension to Olympus, the home of the gods, the Adeptic state. Much inspiration and many warnings are made available in the classical Myth for all who—Heracles-like—embark upon the great quest or emblematically undertake the Twelve Labours. Preparedness for this is indicated by the remarkable 'Cradle-Experience'; for the child in the cradle symbolises complete purity or a child-like state of consciousness.[1] The story thus appropriately and correctly begins with Heracles in his cradle.

Further signs are included suggesting that occult knowledge is about to be revealed; for when used in the Language of Allegory and

---

[1] *cf.* 'Except ye... become as little children, ye shall not enter into the kingdom of heaven.' *Matt.* 18:3.

THE CRADLE STATE

Symbol, serpents, serpentine beings, dragons and dragon-like creatures represent the most deeply concealed and potentially powerful, and so dangerous (hence the concealment) force in both Nature herself and all sub-human and conscious beings. As suggested throughout this work—particularly in the author's personal remarks—this force is the cosmic generative power by means of which the Universe itself as well as all that it contains, is brought into objective existence or 'created'. In animals and human beings it is manifest in one form as the sex-urge and is named in Sanskrit *Kundalini Shakti*.[1]

Complete mastery of this force is indicated to the student of symbology by the statement that when as a babe in his cradle Heracles was attacked by two serpents, he easily exercised control over them by grasping one in each hand, then destroying them.

The serpent fire or *Kundalini* consists of three currents of energy, two of these winding round the third which is in a vertical relationship to them as in the Rod of Hermes, and the tridents of the Lord Shiva, Poseidon and other deities, and heart of the modern symbol of the medical profession. Thus, Heracles held a serpent in each hand, his spinal column completing the threefold symbology. In consequence, no danger threatened the child as he entered upon a life that would lead through many dramatic experiences to ascension into Olympus, 'heaven' or the immortal Adeptic state.

The Myth of Heracles, it may thus be assumed, is an example of the intrusion by Initiated Sages[2] of occult wisdom into a group of popular imaginings framed into a mythological story telling of the exploits of a completely fabulous heroic figure. The purely human characteristics, especially the grave weaknesses—always followed by repentance, the superhuman heroic powers—allegorically descriptive of phases of development and achievements, and the fantastic adventures in which they found expression—all these constitute the typical fairy-tale by means of which untutored people created and related the stories of which world mythology chiefly consists.

---

[1] See Ch.2.
[2] *Initiated Sages* Seven extremely wise teachers, who according to Diogenes Laertius were Thales, Solon, Chilon, Pittacus, Bias, Cleobulus and Periander.

THE CHILD HERACLES STRANGLES TWO SERPENTS

As earlier suggested, evidences of the use of such creative imaginings as vehicles for the transmission of occult knowledge are however frequently indicated, particularly in exploits wherein, for example, dragon-like and serpentine creatures are made to appear. When —despite possible changes in the long course of time—these are found accurately to reveal by symbol and legend quite *exact* references to certain specific powers in Nature and advanced humanity, then the case for the use of such stories for the transmission of this power-bestowing knowledge would seem to be not only suggested but even established—proven indeed.

The 'infant', the 'child' and the youth-state' are, I venture to repeat, themselves frequently used as symbolic descriptions of the condition of consciousness and degree of evolutionary advancement of those who are found worthy to be entrusted with power-endowing knowledge; for purity, selflessness and the absence of planning for self-benefit must all be characteristics of one fit to be entrusted with superior knowledge and the superhuman power that its possession bestows. Thus the babe Heracles, when attacked by two dangerous serpents, easily and fearlessly grasps and destroys them.

Herein, surely, the dangerous but also beneficent occult power *Kundalini* would seem to be portrayed, especially as one in the child-state is approached by two serpents, indicating the dual current which winds itself round a central path, namely the spinal column. The fearless grasp of each of these and their mastery by Heracles indicates the control of the otherwise dangerous interior force. This view is supported by the ability of Heracles, at will and unharmed, Hermes-like to descend into the underworld, Hades, and return therefrom, bringing to the surface and his royal master the serpent-maned and serpent-tailed guardian dog, Cerberus. This occult development and other unusual attributes have led me to interpret the Labours of Heracles as allegorically descriptive of phases of spiritual unfoldment and the resultant supernormal powers.

THE FIRST LABOUR
The Killing of the Nemean Lion

The first monster which Heracles had to exterminate was the Nemean Lion that had depopulated the neighbourhood—a beast no weapon could wound—the skin of which King Eurystheus ordered him to bring back. Heracles attempted in vain to pierce the beast with his arrows. He then engaged it hand to hand and finally strangled it in his powerful grip. He removed the skin and from it made a garment which rendered him invulnerable. He then returned to Mycenae (Tiryns in some stories) with his trophy.

Some three years after his marriage to his beloved wife, Princess Megara, and she had born him three sons, Heracles lost his reason, having been made mad by the action of the goddess Hera. After his recovery from this insanity, he learned of his dreadful deeds—the killing of his wife and three sons—from Amphitryon and said, 'I myself am the murderer of my dearest ones. I will avenge upon myself these deaths.' Before he could do so, however, his purpose was miraculously changed.

After much suffering, Heracles consulted the Oracle at Delphi, where the Priestess told him that only a terrible penance could wholly purify him. She advised him to visit his cousin, King Eurystheus of

Mycenae,[1] and submit to whatever was demanded of him. The King then advised a series of penances, the tasks themselves being known as the Labours of Heracles. These were twelve in number and each one was regarded as almost impossible to perform.

The lion, be it remembered, has long been regarded as the greatest or king of all animals on earth. Interpreted as an aspect of human nature, it represents the lion within, the Labour itself being an interior conflict. The leonine elements of extreme and normally irresistible ferocity, animal lusts and the complete assumption and royal possession and rulership of the land of its origin and life — these are characteristics which can become built into the personality as the Monad evolves through the animal into the human kingdom.

These attributes in man prove to be the least desirable, and one of the most difficult labours is entirely to conquer, eradicate and transform them into the opposite spiritual qualities of mastery of one's own personal self and the recognition of the rights of others. This concept indicates the heart or central message of all truly inspired myths: namely that *the mythical events actually occur within every individual.* Thus viewed, each of the Twelve Labours of Heracles allegorically describes an interior task or 'labour', which is to hasten spiritual evolution, by gaining victory over and transmuting into power every undesirable quality. Thus, the Heracles *within* transmutes into positive virtues the adverse tendencies that have been eliminated from his or her own personal nature. Step by step the goal of perfected **manhood and womanhood — admission of Olympus is approached.** The Twelve Labours of Heracles, the Voyage of the Argonauts, the missions of Perseus, Theseus, Hermes, Bellerophon and of other inspired heroes and heroines are thereafter allegorically entered upon and successfully accomplished.

---

[1] Mycenae itself, is susceptible of at least two if not more interpretations. One of these is the temple of the Mysteries, Eurystheus representing the Hierophant. The unfolding spiritual self of the aspirant into which all attained qualities are to be built is a further possible interpretation. Throughout this study of Heracles, the author whilst frequently referring to the lofty characteristics of the hero is in no sense unaware of his described failings; for he may be regarded as an aspirant nearing Adeptship but not yet an Adept.

Applied to the First Labour of Heracles, not only the hero himself, but the surrounding countryside of Nemea was by his victory freed from the leonine menace of such animal propensities to which its inhabitants had been subject. The task of self-perfecting in its turn, is never undertaken by the aspirant for self-gain, but solely for the attainment of greater effectiveness in the service of others—the countryside and its inhabitants.

Astronomically observed, the physical lion and its Zodiacal representative, Leo, have long been intimately associated with both the physical sun and so also mythologically, with the Divine Lord of the Sun in His majesty of Solar Kingship. Thus viewed, the simple story of an act of successful bravery proves to be susceptible of interpretation as the revelation of the necessary freeing of human nature from menacing leonine qualities. The divine radiant Presence may thereafter shine forth from within the Monadic or leonine Self of every human being, ever integrally at one with the Solar Logos, the 'King' of the Solar System; for when the undesirable lion-like qualities are outgrown, the Soul of the hero becomes consciously aware of and responsive to its true kingship, its intimate relationship with our Lord the Sun.

Realisation of oneness with the Divine bestows two amongst other valuable attributes. One of these is great personal power and the other, Heraclean invulnerability to all attacks from without. Such qualities were displayed by Heracles who was regarded as the strongest man on earth and wore throughout his Twelve Labours the impenetrable lion's skin with its head as a helmet, symbol of the now illumined and empowered brain, mind and personality. Even as one thus learns of the great adventure—the First Labour of Heracles—and if so moved accepts the interior interpretation here proffered, may not the directions given be deliberately applied to the quickening of one's own evolutionary progress and so the development of Heraclean capacities in the service of fellow men?

The First Labour indicates the underlying trend of all truly inspired myths, namely that every episode occurs *within*, and can be personally applied by the individual who may wish to do so. Indeed, thus viewed, each one of the Twelve Labours of Heracles is allegorically descriptive of an interior 'Labour', *accepted under order* given by King Eurystheus, personification in his highest qualities only of a Hierophant of the Mysteries; for this Official bestows guidance to every hero, aspirant and Initiate-to-be in their embarkation upon the Pathway of Hastened Unfoldment. During this 'journey' the attainment of victory over objectionable qualities and their transmutation into spiritual power is of first importance.

An interior view would seem to be supported by the statements that the Nemean lion was immune to attacks from without, no arrows being able to penetrate the leonine hide. Similarly, one may presume, purification of human nature from unpleasant attributes can neither be brought about by another person nor externally accomplished. On the contrary, the arena is *within* the aspirant and therein alone may victory and sublimation into inward power be achieved. Heracles thus slew the Nemean lion with his own hands[1] since no arrows could penetrate its skin. Having done so, the hero removed the hide from the body—extirpated all animalistic qualities—and thereafter wore it as a cloak with the head as a kind of helmet over his own head. In consequence, spiritually, he possessed the invulnerability from external attack hitherto characteristic of the Nemean lion. So, too, the would-be Heracles—the successful Initiate within the Temple of the Mysteries[2]—preserves and transmutes into positive virtues, the undesirable tendencies that had not yet been eliminated from his or her character.

THE SECOND LABOUR
The Slaughter of the Hydra of Lerna

This Hydra, born of Typhon and Echidna, was an enormous serpent with nine heads, one of which was immortal. Its den was a marsh near Lerna in the Peloponnese, from which it would issue forth to ravage the herds and crops; its breath moreover was so poisonous that whoever felt it fell dead. Accompained by Iolaus, son of Iphicles, Heracles arrived at Lerna, found the monster near the spring of Amymone and forced it to emerge from the marshes by means of flaming arrows. He then tried to overwhelm it by the means of his mighty club, but in vain; for every time he struck off one of the Hydra's nine heads two grew in its place. Then Iolaus set the neighbouring forest on fire and with the help of redhot brands Heracles seared the neck as he

---

[1] Samson also slew a lion—' and had nothing in his hands'. *Judges:* 14:6.
[2] See Epilogue.

SECOND LABOUR—LERNEAN HYDRA

cut each head off so that it could not sprout again. When all had been chopped off he disposed of the one that was immortal by burying it under a great rock.

Lerna was—and still is—a district in the Peloponnesus. When interpreting the story, however, the region is found to symbolise both Nature herself and certain conditions of human life on earth. Needless to say—and as its general characteristics demonstrate—no nine-headed Hydra ever actually existed either there, or at any other place in the world. Why, then, it may be asked, was the creature 'imagined' into existence and what are the possible significances of both its nature and the heroic performance of Heracles? The symbolism of numbers may possibly help us. Nine may be regarded as expressing numerically both death and rebirth, the approaching end of one epoch or decade and the beginning of its successor. Hence the strange capacity of the creature to reproduce a decapitated head, in this case immediately to grow two new ones, thereby preserving its immortality.

The appearance of two heads where only one had heretofore existed may bear reference to the fact that the creative energy, *Kundalini* or the Serpent Fire—the central subject of the myth,[1]—can only be fully expressed by two oppositely polarised currents *(Ida and Pingala)* or in mythology by two people of the opposite polarities or sex. The neck itself would then represent the central, fiery, neutral current, the *Sushumna* of *Kundalini* and of the Rod of the Caduceus.[2] Therefore only by the application of fire to the severed neck, thus sealing it off by a fully developed and effective master of *Kundalini*, Heracles himself, could the appearance of more heads be prevented. As was the Hydra—itself a personification of misused *Kundalini*—so also is *Kundalini* itself both indestructible and unconquerable until the yogi (Heracles) has controlled it. Hence its quality of dangerousness in the wrong hands. This was shown in the myth by the terrible ravages of the Hydra.

Applied to the solution of the problem of the prematurely aroused, and so very dangerous, *Kundalini Shakti* within a student or practising yogi, victory over the 'Hydra' by the method employed indicates that the prevention of continuing renewal of the destroyed

---

[1] The Hydra was a serpent.
[2] See Ch.2.

heads' is not possible until the application to the neck of the Hydra has occurred, of the symbolical burning club — the fiery will. This is true, because fully awakened *Kundalini* flowing along the spine and scientifically applied is the *sole means* by which the very dangerous effects of prematurely aroused *Kundalini* — with its harmful effects — can be rendered completely harmless. Only by the allegorical application of fire — the flaming brands (themselves symbols of the *Kundalini* fire *in control*) — to the severed neck (the spinal cord) of the Hydra, by one who has dominated active *Kundalini*[1] (the hero) could the fiery power be returned in safety to its source at the base of the spine. Thereafter, the renewal of the harmful activity of the dangerous energy becomes impossible — or, symbolically, the nine-headed serpent is slain. In other words, *Kundalini* out of control — and so perilous[2] — which is the Hydra, can only be mastered by the application of the will similarly empowered — the burning club — to the spinal cord. The hitherto uncontrolled fire is then forced down the spine into the sacrum in which it normally, safely and controllably is stored.

Purposely restating this suggested interpretation, the Hero is by the exercise of strong will (the fiery club) and his own consciously used Serpent Fire, enabled to produce the following results: —

1. To prevent in an evil, occultly-powered person (the Hydra) the harmful and deliberate misuse of the awakened force (ravaging), symbolically by beheading.

2. To drive by highly developed will power (the club) *Kundalini* back to its bodily source (the sacrum) where it is harmless.

3. By decapitation, to render impossible the re-awakening and mental misdirection of the fiery power.

4. Thereby to destroy the ravager and bring its ravages to an end by obliterating its ability ever again to evoke and mentally direct *Kundalini Shakti* for any purposes whatsoever.

Strange though it may appear to one who has not studied occult science, may it be said that, deprived of its mythological interpretation, this total procedure has long been and continues to be, both necessarily and effectively carried out? This is solely possible by occultists of the White Order who have been sufficiently instructed by an

---

[1] See Ch. 2.
[2] Hence the envelment in myth, allegory and symbol.

SECOND LABOUR—LERNEAN HYDRA

Adept concerning *Kundalini Shakti* and trained in its safe arousal and constructive use.

This remarkable myth has also a further and deeply occult meaning which recounts the conflict by an Initiated student of the White Order—Heracles—against an embodied black magician (a human being of the Dark Order) in which he must fight for a cause, for his own reason and even for his very life. Such conflicts do actually occur in various forms. Heracles succeeds in conquering and killing the terrible 'Hydra' or 'Enemy of the Light' by the power of his club and its fire. This burning club is as stated, symbol of the strong will, evoked and applied by an accomplished master of *Kundalini Shakti*. When turned in opposition to the destructive will of the black magician, it both conquers and prevents the *continuance* of evil magic or, symbolically, the re-appearance of new 'heads'—human minds using occult forces—Serpent Fire—for destructive purposes.

The fact that Heracles easily, though with inherent knowledge, mastered the two serpents which attacked him when in his cradle[1]—one on either hand, as artists of old have portrayed—indicated that he was born (had developed in a former incarnation)[2] with the ability thus to control the Serpent Fire, and therefore, when grown up, the serpentine symbol, the Hydra of Lerna; for the two serpents represent the *Ida* and *Pingala* of *Kundalini*, *Sushumna* being indicated by the baby's spinal cord and, as already stated in *this* myth, by the neck of the Hydra. Beneficent when rightly understood and applied, this procreative energy—particularly when possessed by a destructive 'beast' a reptile in this myth—could be perilous in the extreme. When misinterpreted and misused, it becomes very dangerous as allegorically indicated by the ravages of the Hydra of Lerna.

THE HYDRA OF LERNA WITHIN

What then would the burial of the hitherto immortal head under a great rock possibly imply? This could be interpreted as the achievement on the Pathway to Perfection of rendering inert and so ineffective the energy by which sexual desire—the Serpent Fire—is aroused.

---

[1] See Ch. 3.
[2] See the author's *Reincarnation, Fact or Fallacy*.

Thereafter, this hitherto controlling force which causes the desire to procreate to be a continuously active influence in human life, is 'deadened' or converted into a rock-like state.[1] Once this power is symbolically interred in a rock-tomb, it can never again be active as a stimulant to sexual desire, no longer as an insistent, 'immortal' impulse; for it was cut off and made 'rock-like'—fully controlled—as the head of the Hydra had been—one of the most difficult of all Labours. Once this is achieved, however, the liver-consuming 'eagle' of the Prometheus myth is permanently mastered by transmutation. Thus, Heracles was enabled to set Prometheus free from the rock on Mt. Caucasus, where for so long he had been caused to suffer from the persistent activity of the 'eagle'.[2]

Each character in an inspired myth may thus be regarded as personifying an aspect of *one person,* the whole performance being enacted by and within that one alone. All individuals are personifications of attributes, powers and experiences of one and the same person—Heracles himself in his Twelve Labours, for example. Furthermore is it true that every person in an occult myth represents an aspect of the sevenfold human being—physical, etheric, emotional, analytically mental, abstract intelligence, intuitional and spiritual. Therefore, all characters are *within* the central figure, but also all events in their turn occur *within* the same person.

In consequence of rendering inert or "burying beneath a rock" the stimulant to procreative desire, *the energy by which it is rendered physically active may be transmuted into intellectual and spiritual creativeness.* Success in this all-important attainment demands that indeed sexual desire is entirely and finally conquered, renounced with absolute rock-like firmness, 'burnt' forever. Failing this, the aspirant to spiritual progress—Olympus—may either 'fall' for the remainder of that life or experience delay. Hence the potent symbolism of finality—the rock-tomb in which the hitherto immortal but now deceased head of the Hydra was buried.

---

[1] Gen. 19:26 *cf.,* The wife of Lot looked back at Sodom and Gomorrah—which they were leaving (excessive sexuality) and is turned into a pillar of salt, symbol of the totally materialised condition.

[2] See Ch.9

The Labours of Heracles may thus be interpreted as descriptions of the 'Steps' or 'Labours' that must be undertaken by every human aspirant for progress upon the Pathway of the Hastened Attainment of Adeptship—superhuman perfection—'Olympus'. The author is tempted to add 'or even beyond' for Zeus is said mythologically to have taken Callisto up to heaven to become the Great Bear and Arcas to become the Little Bear (mother and son). Zeus placed the image of Chiron—the wisest of the centaurs—among the stars as Sagittarius. Ganymede, carried off by Zeus to become his cup-bearer, was placed by him among the stars under the name Aquarius. Zeus rewarded the attachment of the two brothers, Castor and Pollux, by placing them among the stars as Gemini. All the sages knew this, but authors of lesser stature failed to realise it, thereby getting caught up with the fairy tale fascination of the myth itself.

In a spiritually awakened or 'heroic' human being, the Serpent Fire ascends under conscious direction along the spine into the head. This force represents the continuously creative principle in Nature, which therefore cannot be brought to a cessation of its natural function even by the physical death of the person in whom it is awakened. This would seem to be implied and so revealed by the normal immortality of the Hydra even after its head was destroyed.

When consciously used, the Serpent Fire is directed 'upwards' along the spine and neck into the head, thereby enfiring, inspiring and illuminating the brain-mind of the successful *self-deliverer* from the hitherto *uncontrolled* and even destructive function of the creative element. The Hydra itself thus aptly represents that dangerous aspect of this force in Nature and in man, as indicated by the relationship to its surroundings and to their human and sub-human inhabitants.

The Yogi-Hero or Initiate aided by a Teacher personified by Iolaus—charioteer and armour-bearer indeed—learns about the destructive agency by means revealed in the famous myth. These were two-fold, as we have seen, consisting of decapitation or bringing about the cessation of *conscious* evocation of the power, and the application of fire to the neck at the place where the decapitation had been brought about. As already stated, this forces the descent of *Kundalini* back into the sacrum, its natural centre in the body, from which it may be aroused at will by the trained occultist of the White Order for its sane and wise employment—clairvoyance, clairaudience and the intuitive capacity, for example. The deadly poison of the Hydra's breath portrays the intuition-destroying and mind-deadening effects produced upon individuals who unwisely arouse *Kundalini* or give themselves up unduly to sensual over-indulgence in the procreative and sexual expression of the Creative Fire in man.[1]

The flaming arrows by means of which Heracles forced the Hydra to emerge from the marshes may represent the fiery will of the Initiate (or Hero) directed towards the source of the creative power in the human body. This is performed with the determined intent of its 'death' as an enemy of spirituality and its transmutation to the inner immortal Self of man, where it becomes an addition to the faculties of intuitive and abstract creative inspiration. The full achievement of this procedure does indeed demand highly intensive will-force for its fulfilment as appropriately portrayed by the burning club and the flaming arrows. The procedure of transmutation is not as yet complete, however, for although immediately wounded, the Hydra was still alive with all the dangerous significance of its nine heads entirely intact.

Just as the sufferings of Prometheus were daily resumed by the attack upon his liver by the eagle, so sexual indulgence not only fails to bring about the final disappearance of desire but unfortunately establishes a possibly uncontrollable habit or addiction to sex. This inescapable continuing affliction would seem to be symbolised by the fact that whilst Zeus revenged himself on Prometheus by chaining him to a rock on Mt. Caucasus where symbolically an eagle consumed his liver by day—an allegory for the perpetuated sex desire—*this organ was actually restored during each successive night.* So, also, sexual indulgence, instead of curing the sensuality, only leads to a continuance of the established tendency. Interestingly, it was Heracles himself—Initiate from his cradle days—who killed, not as one of his Twelve Labours, the eagle and delivered the sufferer with the consent of the god Zeus, who—significantly—had punished Prometheus *because he stole fire—the Creative Fire—*from heaven in a hollowed tube![2] So also, when struck off by the club of Heracles, the central head

---

[1] The author here ventures personally but very seriously to warn against these potentially harmful errors.

[2] See Ch. 9.

of the Hydra was daily renewed. Only when the neck of the decapitated head was set alight by the fiery club (will) had victory been finally attained over the Hydra, then deceased. Of interest here is the statement that the destructive flaming brands by means of which the necks were burnt were derived from natural sources—namely trees growing in the surrounding forest.

The solution of the problem of undue sexuality and most harmful slavery thereto evidently is to be found not in the treatment or attempted control of the physical body alone wherein the sensual urges and pleasures are experienced. Such attempts of themselves ever failed, as did at first those of Heracles. However, in the final 'burning away' or 'burning out' *of the mental or thought repetitions of memories—natural to all possessed of procreative power*—the resultant re-excitement of desires becomes finally outgrown.

The difficulty does indeed reside within the *head* of the indulgent one. Thought *itself* must therefore be both purified and *strongly endowed*—enfired indeed—with the will (the club) to bring to an end the undesirable attributes and expressions of sexual excesses. Thereafter, one must transmute the fiery energy—of which they are the product—above the purely physical mentality into powers of creative intelligence and implicit insight—the inherent qualities of man's spiritual Self. This achieved, the outer slavery ceases; for the victorious Hero has 'slaughtered' the undesirable aspects by which the creative or Serpent Fire finds expression in non-heroic humanity.

True, the normal expression of the sexual desire is productive of the continuance of the human race. Unfortunately the whole procedure can become degraded and lead to indulgences, excesses or unhappily diseases as symbolised by the Hydra of Lerna and its influence upon the neighbourhood. This can—and unfortunately does in some cases—bring about the decline of all that is creatively noble in mankind. The process of transmutation, admittedly told as a mythical adventure, is thus seen of necessity to occur *within* the human being or Hero who transmutes the interior Serpent Fire into intellectual and spiritual creativeness.

May not the wise advice revealed in the story itself and the success achieved by Heracles, be turned to practical use by those so moved and who find themselves needing the power of control over the sexual impulse? If so, then the account may be interpreted according to the approach of the individual and used to bring about the death of the nine-headed hydra *within*—largely, be it remembered—by the successful control and application of the power of human will-thought. Hence, doubtless, the reference to the Hydra's central head.

Why, then, it may well be asked, is not this solution itself directly presented? Why is it ensheathed within a fabulous fairy-tale? Because, lacking the information proffered in this interpretation of the myth, the possession of such knowledge bestows power and this can be dangerous—Hydra-like—*when it reveals the means by which the Creative Fire in Nature and in man can be supernormally aroused for occult purposes.* Indeed, such danger does exist during the procedure of the transmutation of the sex-force unless an Iolaus (the Adept Teacher) is present to ensure that the abnormal mind-power gained by the successful transmuter may not be very seriously and harmfully misused against others in Hydra-like destructiveness. So also the hidden wisdom in every sage-inspired myth.

Hence the use of the Language of Allegory and Symbol; for as I have earlier quoted: ' To enclose all truth in a spoken language, to express the highest occult mysteries in an abstract style, would not only be useless, dangerous and sacrilegious but also impossible. There are truths of a subtle, synthetic and divine order, to express which in all their inviolate completeness, human language is incapable. Only music can sometimes make the soul feel them, only ecstasy can show them in absolute vision, and only esoteric symbolism can reveal them to the spirit in a concrete way.'[1]

Even in these proffered interpretations as heretofore stated, only the theory of the pathways to superior power, wisdom and intelligence is presented. Nevertheless, the truly selfless and heroic aspirant to both interior attainment and maximum effectiveness in service to fellow men, once embarked upon the procedure, will with assured certainty find his own 'Iolaus' beside him. 'For when the pupil is ready, the Master is ready also.'[2]

---

[1] *Le Seuil du Mystère*, S. De Guaita.
[2] *Light on the Path*, by Mabel Collins, to which all who are seriously interested may very seriously turn, as also: *The Voice of the Silence*, H.P. Blavatsky. See also *The Pathway to Perfection* by Geoffrey Hodson.

SECOND LABOUR—LERNEAN HYDRA

To sum up; the myth is subject to the following interpretations as a revelation of: —

The grave danger for a non-purified yogi of prematurely awakened, uncontrolled *Kundalini Shakti* and its ever-continuous harmful exercise—the Hydra.

The physical locations in the body of man of the awakened force—sacrum, spinal column and brain—the necks and heads of the Hydra.

A grave warning to all against the premature awakening and misuse of the 'ravaging' Serpent Fire—the devastation in the countryside of Lerna.

The only remedy consists of the application of the same fiery force by an individual *who is both pure in motive* and also more powerful than the victim—the successful Labour and the methods mythologically employed.

The relative omnipotence and immortality of one in whom the controlled arousal of *Kundalini* has been achieved in full consciousness—the physical invulnerability and virtual omnipotence of **Heracles**.

An occult Senior (the Hero) is able to drive the Power down to its source in the sacrum and thereby render it inert or 'rock-like', one consequence of this being the cessation of its continuing demand for expression—symbolically, the loss of the immortality of the Hydra.

Well may it here be asked—and indeed has been asked by the author—why such exactly apposite symbols are included in an apparent fairy tale? Their interpretation according to the language of allegory and symbol supports a proffered answer, namely, that the sages either themselves wrote the wisdom-containing myths, or on other occasions introduced the symbols into existing fairy stories in order to add and so convey profound spiritual, philosophic, occult and therefore exceedingly valuable truths.

If it be further asked why the allegorical method of their presentation is used, the reply is advanced that certain of such truths—concerning the Serpent Fire, more especially—reveal power-bestowing and therefore very dangerous information.

THE THIRD LABOUR
Capture of the Ceryneian Hind

In one of two somewhat differing versions, the Third Labour was the capture of the Ceryneian Hind which was brought back alive from Oenoe to Mycenae. The stag had brazen hooves and horns of gold and lived in the forests where it ravaged the countryside. Unwilling either to kill or wound the Hind, Heracles hunted her tirelessly for one whole year. At last, she took refuge on Mt. Artemisium and Heracles pinned her forelegs together with an arrow, which passed between bone and sinew, drawing no blood. He then laid her across his shoulders and carried her to Mycenae.

In this Labour also, Heracles is not only obeying the orders of King Eurystheus, but carrying out a service to the people of a particular region. The famous story thus reveals one of the essentials—an inescapable one indeed—to success in treading the Path[1] of Hastened Attainment of realised oneness with the Godhead or, symbolically, admission to Olympus, the abode of the gods. Actually this was not a physical mountain but an elevated state of consciousness.

The four metallic hooves and horn by which the Hind was distinguished from all others of its species, are susceptible of interpretation as indicating that throughout the great endeavour the 'feet' of the aspirant must be firmly established on the 'ground' of complete material practicability. This applies to the four mortal vehicles of man—mental, emotional, etheric and physical—in which during life the inward Self is incarnated; for throughout the great undertaking, its 'feet' must remain in contact with and be supported upon the earth. The successful aspirant whilst deeply concerned with spiritual and philosophic wisdom is at the same time a completely practical person.

The golden horn, on the other hand, refers to the illumined condition of the mind of the aspirant— the horns are on the head, seat of awareness and thought —who is already developed in intuitive insight of wisdom as depicted by the metal gold. Thus, metaphorically, Heracles, personifying the idealist, must develop these qualities or capture the mythical animal which is supposed to be possessed of them.

---

[1] See author's *The Pathway to Perfection*.

Fortunately, his feet were firmly planted on the ground—hence the resultant success. Furthermore, his consciousness was already well developed intuitively, thus providing him with the degree of wisdom necessary for the chase and capture of the Hind.

This abnormally built animal is allegorically descriptive of the qualities of mature thought necessary for one to become an Initiate of the Mysteries and later an Adept; for Heracles overcame the creature and bore it on his shoulders to Mycenae. Carrying it next to his 'head' (seat of awareness)—if the story may thus be interpreted—indicates the mental attainment of unity, while, as suggested, the characteristics of the predestined prey—brazen 'hooves' and golden 'horns'—imply the acquirement of practicability and intuitive wisdom.

The great care with which the hunt was carried out, the desire to avoid serious injuries—especially loss of blood—and the readiness to continue throughout one whole year, symbolically indicate further essentials to success. These include the inward determination to attain the heights which is in no sense diminished by the passage of either years or successive incarnations.

A mountain is also introduced into the myth. In the language of allegory and symbol, its general interpretation is the intellectual and spiritual 'heights' of Will, Wisdom and illumined Intelligence.[1] Once attained, these capacities make possible the fulfilment of the great Quest which allegorically is to bring the brazen-hooved and golden-horned creature to Mycenae. This region in its turn, is emblematic of the predestined fulfilment of the purpose for human existence—Adeptship or being taken to heaven or Olympus, where Heracles is said to have rested in eternal peace—his great reward.[2]

At this point in the suggested interpretations, whilst Heracles mythically hunted and captured the stag, he actually became identified with the creature; for the symbols used to describe the Hind also refer to the qualities *within* the 'hunter' that are essential to success.[3]

---

[1] *The King James Bible*, partly written in this language, uses the symbol of the 'mount' thus appropriately, e.g. 'whereon the Law was given to Moses.' (*Ex.* 19:20.) 'And Elijah stayed for forty days'. (*Kn.* 19:8.) In *Hinduism*, Mt. Kailasa and Mt. Meru may be similarly interpreted.

[2] See The Flaming Death and Ascension of Heracles.

[3] So also the various other creatures included in the Labours—frequently as objectives. Their desirable qualities are to be acquired and 'built into' the character of the would-be Heracles.

Thus, Heracles followed the Hind to the heights of consciousness — Mt. Artemisium — and there rendered it incapable of escaping him — the *higher qualities* must be immoveably established *within* the aspirant. This necessity is accentuated by the 'rule' that the Hind must lose no blood, symbol of the divine nature, the 'life principle'. Indeed, no blood was shed in this remarkable story.

In addition, whilst still expressive of these qualities, the fourfold personality (the Hind) must be made incapable of straying from — or in this case, escaping from the Inner Ruler Immortal — the Hero himself and the ideal exalted level of consciousness. Hence, the action by Heracles — the two forelegs are pinned together by an arrow — which made further movement away from him impossible and yet brought no loss of blood, meaning the conserving of necessary powers, faculties and abilities for their full expression, even in the physical body. The hunter and the hunted had then **become** as one. Despite its apparent very heavy weight, the Hind was carried on the shoulders of Heracles — unified with him — to Mycenae, the abode of the king. The stag thus borne had been rendered incapable of 'escape' from the higher qualities and yet had not lost the slightest element of the divine nature symbolised by 'blood.'

Thus, again — if this approach be acceptable — an apparently meaningless and even sometimes senseless myth is susceptible of being interpreted as a deeply reasoned and perfectly truthful presentation of the necessities for finding and treading the ancient Pathway. Furthermore, the single-minded and single-hearted motive of service to the people (humanity) by means of the removal of a dangerous agency, is also symbolically presented.

In this view, the region in which the ravaging had been done may be looked upon as representing the personality itself of the aspirant *within which* every element harmful to success must be 'caught' or fully understood and rendered harmless, its adverse qualities being transmuted to spiritual powers and then 'taken to Mycenae' as an offering. The rendering immobile of the four legs of the Hind may represent the elimination of the capacity for undesirable self-chosen direction of movement by the personal nature. Thus, on the Path to Adeptship, self-gratifying choices are entirely surrendered, this restriction eventually producing not loss but immeasurable gain.

THE FOURTH LABOUR
Capture of the Erymanthian Boar

The Fourth Labour imposed on Heracles was to capture alive the Erymanthian Boar, a fierce, enormous beast which haunted the cypress covered slopes of Mt. Erymanthus and ravaged the country around Psophis. Heracles chased the beast from one place to another until it was exhausted. Then he drove it into deep snow and trapped it.

―――――

During his journey through Pholoe to Erymanthus, Heracles was entertained by the Centaur Pholus, who possessed a cask of wine given to him by Dionysius. When this was opened, other Centaurs besieged the cave. Repulsed by Heracles, they eventually fled, though during the combat Heracles accidentally wounded with one of his poisoned arrows the Centaur, Chiron, who was an old friend. Chiron, an immortal, could not die, although he now longed to do so, and was relieved from pain only when he later surrendered his immortality to Prometheus.[1] Heracles continued his pursuit of the Erymanthian boar, a fierce enormous beast which ravaged the countryside. He drove it into a snow-drift, sprang upon its back, bound it with chains, and carried it to Eurystheus at Mycenae.

The boar has come to be classified amongst the lower order of animals—the swine.[2] The Erymanthian boar was particularly deserving of capture, and so reduction to impotence, because of its destructive attacks upon the locality. Thus viewed, it symbolises the coarser, less desirable and even dangerous aspects of the mortal nature of man, in its turn typified by the countryside. Applied to the pathway leading to realised immortality which Heracles was following, the undesirable elements—the boar—of the aspirant's nature, must be completely controlled and eliminated; for the quickening of intellectual and spiritual development may then be more readily brought about. This, Heracles wholly achieves, for he personifies the individual who is treading the Pathway of Hastened Evolutionary Attainment and so every seeker for admission to the Temple of the Mysteries and the receipt of successive Initiations therein.

[1] See Ch.9, Prometheus.
[2] *Matt.* 7:6 and 8:32

The drinking of wine in its turn has been regarded as a symbol of entry into highly elevated states of knowledge, perception and their accompanying ecstasies. *These, it may be presumed, were the real effects produced upon, or rather within, those Initiates who were admitted to the Mysteries of Bacchus-Dionysius,* and certainly not the popularly—even deliberately—supposed physical drunkenness associated with the god Bacchus.

Whilst beneficial for those human beings who hold their 'lower' natures in control, these spiritually stimulating experiences could be very harmful, dangerous indeed. This applies particularly to those who are still unemancipated from those aspects of their mortal nature symbolised by the boar and normally by the centaurs. Chiron, however, was a purely mythical example of an advanced member of this type of being, one moreover who, whilst symbolically retaining his equine mortal vehicle, had evolved beyond the normal level of humanity—was both quadrupedal and human in bodily form.

Chiron, himself, also represents the member of the Mysteries who has thus advanced in overcoming the limitations and attaining the right use of the fourfold mortal nature (the quadruped). In consequence, the more intellectual qualities of the Inner Ruler Immortal or Higher Self become highly developed and the animal instincts increasingly controlled—hence not only human torso and head, but very significantly, *the ability to teach and the appointment as teacher* to the demi-gods;[1] for the legend relates that he was also an instructor of the young men of his time, particularly the heroes who were regarded as semi-divine, being of divine fatherhood and human motherhood. These included the members of the crew of the ocean-going vessel, the Argo, whom Chiron taught, guiding them in both the construction and the navigation of the craft.

The relationship between Heracles and Chiron is somewhat supported by the fact that after delivering the boar of Erymanthus to Eurystheus, Heracles at once departed to join the crew of the Argo with his later unfortunate armour-bearer, Hylas. As he dipped his pitcher in a spring, this young man, very dear to Heracles, was drawn under

---

[1] Jason, Castor and Pollux, Peleus and Achilles. Zeus placed his image among the stars as Sagittarius.

the water by a water-nymph who saw the rosy flush of his beauty, wished to kiss him, threw her arms around his neck and drew him into the depths, whereafter he was seen no more.

The story of Hylas is of particular interest in that he himself, as armour-bearer of Heracles, was associated with dense substances over which he had supposedly achieved mastery—the metals of which armour is made; for if one has conquered the weight of the armour then it would be reasonable to assume that less dense materials—water, for example, would be easily controlled. Nevertheless, even as an **Argonaut**,[1] Hylas fell a prey to a much less resistant element, namely water and the water nymph. Strangely also, it was not Hylas who became a victim to 'illusion' as one form of the Myth records, but that a water-nymph fell in love with him—a reversal—and drew him to his apparent doom. This 'Fall' possibly illustrates the idea that although one may have been victorious over the hazards of dense matter, one has not necessarily acquired complete control of the more subtle element of water (symbol for the emotions in the language of allegory and symbol) and so can become its victim. This, in fact, did occur, with Hylas an apparently helpless victim to both water itself and the water nymph.

If the incident is further studied, the difficulty is increased by the fact that not only water itself brought about his fall, but a conscious elemental dweller therein—a water-nymph. This creature accentuated his lack of mastery of her element by mythically falling in love with him and drawing him to the watery depth wherein she dwelt, thereby destroying, at least for that incarnation, his hope of success in the expedition of the Argonauts—a phase of the Path of Hastened Unfoldment. Thus, though a master of metals, Hylas was almost impotent when faced with the problem and even danger associated with the finer element of water. If one may here apply the traditional symbolic meanings of the two elements, the metals would refer to physical matter and so the physical body, and water to the emotions and their vehicle of expression over which evidently Hylas—although an armour-bearer—had not yet attained mastery.

---

[1] *Argonaut*—one who is presumably evolved enough to know of and aspire to achieving that for which the Golden Fleece was a symbol: evolutionary progress to the phase at which intuitive wisdom has become a natural faculty.

One's sense of logic is further strained by the fact that a water-nymph would presumably be composed of the elements of water and air, and such a being could not possibly have drawn by force a body composed of physical matter, including one of the heavier constituents, namely the bone of the skeleton. On embracing the neck of Hylas, her arms would merely pass through without obtaining the necessary grip.

When, however, in mythical and so presumed allegorical literature, one is confronted with such total **inconsistencies**,[1] it is not unreasonable to assume that the author may well by this means, be encouraging the reader to *look below the surface* of the apparently illogical story and interpret the account in terms of the Sacred **Language**.[2] Again, the necessity with which aspirants to spiritual attainment—the Golden **Fleece**[3]—are faced, of learning to control not only the body, but also the emotions and the mind, is indicated by the strange story of Hylas.

If a normal interpretation be acceptable, then heavy metals indicate the physical body with its appetites and desires, whilst close attention to them—as in armour-bearing, for example—renders the relatively innocent one—Hylas was only a lad—susceptible of response to the physical sensations experienced in love-making. Being quite young, moreover, he was unable to resist their pleasure-giving charms. This view gains some support that—as portrayed by the legend—a water-nymph fell in love with Hylas and drew him out of the earth—physical awareness and control—into surrender to the passions as symbolised by the water-nymph herself. Thereafter he would unfortunately be lost to the great enterprise of gaining the Golden Fleece—spiritual and intuitive awareness. The possibility is not overlooked, however, that this relatively minor episode, added to a

---

[1] As when Joshua makes the sun stand still in order to gain a longer day. See my *The Hidden Wisdom in the Holy Bible*, Vol.1 pp.49-52.

[2] *The Sacred Language*—See my *The Hidden Wisdom in the Holy Bible*, Vol.III pp.XII to XVI. See also in this book 'The Concealed Wisdom in World Symbology.'

[3] *The Golden Fleece:* To save the son of the King Athamas, Phrixus, with his sister, was placed upon an altar in order that he should be destroyed. However, Hermes sent a wondrous ram with a fleece of pure gold which snatched him and his sister up and bore them away through the air. Strangely, Phrixus sacrificed the ram to Zeus although it had saved him—and gave the precious Golden Fleece to King Aeetes of Colchis. See Ch.4.

very dramatic account of successful heroism, may have been born in the mind of an author given to the invention of mere fairy tales. Or in occult terminology, Hylas would lose his status—discipleship of his Initiated Teacher, Heracles, who was unfortunately also lost to the Great Quest of the Golden Fleece. This was only temporarily, of course, for eventually Heracles ascended into Olympus—Cosmic Consciousness.

The fall of Hylas would presumably be but temporary, however, since in a later incarnation the same opportunities would present themselves to him, particularly as his failure occurred whilst serving fellow disciples—the Argonauts—for whom he was collecting water. Applied to the Fourth Labour of Heracles the failure of Hylas as one of the Argonauts draws attention to a test which is applied and must be successfully passed through by all aspirants to occult advancement; for when once the Path of Hastened Unfoldment has been entered, the aspirant—Heracles, engaged in his Fourth Labour—must acquire the capacity to overcome and then transmute the baser animal passions (the boar) from their physical expression to intellectual creativeness, **thereby greatly enhancing the power of the spiritual or 'kingly' Self (Eurystheus).**

The Fourth Labour was however completed, the captured animal—subdued undesirable porcine nature in man—having been overcome and delivered in a helpless state **to Eurystheus**[1]—in this case personifying the Inner Self—that now had conquered it. In consequence, the countryside of Psophis—the mortal man—was freed from its ravages and the Fourth Labour successfully completed.

The great Calydonian Boar Hunt to which the King of Calydonia called upon the noblest in Greece to help him in killing the boar which **was laying waste his country, the author suggests, is susceptible with** appropriate modifications of a similar interpretation.

THE FIFTH LABOUR
The Cleansing of the Augean Stables

Augeas, King of Elis, owned innumerable herds of cattle among which were twelve white bulls sacred to Helios. One of them whose name was Phaethon was privileged to shine like a star. Unhappily these

---

[1] Eurystheus—also the Hierophant in the Temple of the Mysteries.

magnificent animals lived in foul stables, heaped high with manure of many years accumulation. Heracles undertook to clean them out in one day on condition that the king gave him a tenth part of the herd. In order to do this he breached the walls of the building and, altering the course of the rivers Alpheus and Peneus, made them rush through the cowsheds. When the job was done Augeas, under pretext that Heracles was merely executing the orders of Eurystheus, refused to fulfil his part of the bargain. Later the Hero was to punish this dishonesty.

When the Fifth Labour is studied with intent to realise its possible occult significance, one finds that the **myth** applies more especially to the individual, though of course being of universal interest not only to one person, but to the human race as a whole.

The total disinterestedness in self-purification and the coarse in**dulgences that permitted an enormous accumulation of 'filth', may be** read as descriptive of a relatively unevolved, crude-minded and grossly self-indulgent type of person. This refers more especially to the series of incarnations that preceded spiritual awakening and the resultant aspiration to make amends for the past, to be cleansed and to be whole. The cattle as the source of the ensoilment suggest the more animalistic aspects of human nature and the effects of their indulgence.

Since the spiritual Self of every human being is undergoing an irresistible process of evolution towards the stature of perfected humanity, the time eventually comes—as in this story it was made to come—to the owner of the Augean Stables when that high goal begins to be perceived. Former self-indulgences and grossness evoke **repentance** and the decision is made to live worthily and eventually, in purity, by cleansing the personal vehicles, physical, emotional and mental—the stables—and to arise and ascend towards the accepted future ideal.

How may this best be achieved? This is the problem to be solved by every aspirant to the spiritual life, by everyone indeed, who sincerely seeks to find and tread the Pathway of Hastened Evolution to Adeptship aided by admission to Temples of the Lesser and Greater Mysteries. Does the answer consist of *detailed* labour carried out amidst the mire? Definitely no, this particular narrative would seem to reply. What then, must be done? Begin digging out from the stables the accumulated manure? Again, definitely no, as the Fifth Labour answers, however allegorically. On the contrary, instead of sheer and long maintained physical effort, intuitively perceive and carry out the wiser, more strategic plan, as naturally would every 'Hero' or inspired, Initiated servant of humanity. Meditate upon the task to be done and thereby discover and apply the best means for its fulfilment, namely in this case the absolute purification of the whole nature from every trace of preceding impurity.

Otherwise expressed, find the sources of absolute purity—Alpheus and **Peneus** geographically at higher levels—*within the Inner Self*, the threefold, immortal reincarnating ego consisting of spiritual will, intuition and intelligence, or power, wisdom and abstract thought. Tap especially the spiritual will and intuitive wisdom—the rivers Alpheus and **Peneus** within—and by means of Herculean power direct these stainless forces so that they flood the mind, the emotions and the waking consciousness, until these three **become completely cleansed and ennobled**, thus purifying the hitherto ensoiled and degraded bodily life—the stables themselves.

Naturally, when at first undertaken such a task may occupy many years and, for completion, even many successive reincarnations. Eventually, however, the evolutionary stature equals that of a Heracles. The seemingly impossible task will then be swiftly performed or, as Heracles promised, would be completed ' before nightfall ', possibly meaning the closure by death of the particular physical life.

Only a Heracles—meaning a Hero of almost invincible will and irresistible strength—psychological and mental as well as physical—is able successfully to follow the age-old guidance offered to all awakened aspirants to the Inner Life: *Look within* and—evoking the inmost will—wisely, skillfully indeed (taking advantage of the force of gravity) direct the purifying powers—the fresh and clean river waters—of the higher, spiritual Selfhood into and throughout every thought, feeling and action of the 'stable' of the lower mortal personal nature.

Do there not also exist amongst us those who at times find themselves similarly afflicted with regret for the past, repentance for errors and a strong—even Herculean—determination to achieve self-purification and thereafter Self-realisation? For all of these the author suggests that the ensured means of success is clearly if allegorically stated in this Fifth Labour. Indeed, the original author of the Myth, whether one alone or many, would seem to speak directly to those thus moved: 'Embark upon the spiritual life: discover your true Selfhood: awaken and direct its power unwaveringly, but also very wisely as Heracles did, to bring about swiftly—'within twelve hours' as it were—entry upon the purifying and spiritually oriented way of life.'

THE SIXTH LABOUR
To Destroy the Stymphalian Birds

The marshes of Stymphalus in Arcadia were peopled by monstrous birds whose wings, beaks and claws were brazen and who in addition exuded a poisonous excrement which blighted the crops. They fed on human flesh and were so numerous that when they took wing the light of the sun was blotted out. Heracles—helped by Athena—frightened them with brazen cymbals and slew them with arrows.

In the Language of Allegory and Symbol, the bird generally represents both divine and superhuman powers and ministrations—the pelican and the dove, for example. When, however, as in the present story, undesirable attributes are applied, then the opposite is true. The Stymphalian birds are examples of the latter; for they are said to have possessed and displayed at least two evil characteristics. One of these, by far the greatest, was that when they rose from the ground, instead of elevating the mind of the human observer, they obliterated the light of the sun, thereby darkening the day. In addition, their wings, beaks and claws were made of brass, with all the adverse interpretations applicable to that metal—inertness, resistance and unresponsiveness compared with the cellular material of beaks and claws.

The beak is normally beneficent, since it is used for the gaining of nutriment, but when made of gross metal and misused, an opposite influence is implied—the cruel destruction of those who are attacked. The same may be attributed to claws or talons, especially when capable of injury which can be mortal. Furthermore, from such qualities in an individual, the coarse, auric emanations (excrements) would be very lowering both in themselves and their effects upon others who came under their influence.

Wings themselves are generally regarded and used in the Sacred

SIXTH LABOUR—STYMPHALIAN BIRDS

Language as means of ascent from earth—meaning the limitations applied to the mortal personality—to the upper air or state of consciousness in which inspiration is experienced and illumination attained. When, however, wings—as in this case—are made of brass, very serious if not complete *opposition* to these procedures is inferred and stultification is caused of the usual means of elevating the body to aerial heights and the rays of the sun. All of these limitations are, of course, to be regarded as being completely interior or *personal*, particularly when self-applied to the deliberately matter-blinded and self-imprisoned individual.

The country of Stymphalus in its turn is descriptive of this condition—being 'marshy'—whilst the very large numbers of the birds indicate a civilisation which is deliberately materialistic and directed by a majority of its citizens to the gaining of personal advantages—or who were wholly self-centered.

What, then, is the remedy, how is this symbolically portrayed in this Labour, and why with so much misleading secrecy? The answer, naturally, is Heracles himself, meaning in this case a Heraclean effort not only in terms of invaluable sheer strength and courage, but also being invulnerable to the undesirable qualities (clothed in the impenetrable skin of a lion that he had successfully destroyed). In addition, guidance and inspiration must be available (from within or Athena as the spiritual Self), as also weapons of irresistible effectiveness (brazen **cymbals** and poisoned arrows) all employed with entire selflessness—solely in the service of Eurystheus, King of Mycenae.

Thus aided from within and correctly armed, both outer and interior "enemies", although hitherto indestructible, will assuredly be overcome. When confronted by and sufficiently aware of one's own grave deficiencies, these may be rapidly eliminated by heroic efforts inspired by the higher Self (Athena) and effectively carried out with ir**resistible** power of spiritual will—the 'Heracles' that exists within every human being. Then, also, one's outer personality, habits of life and environment (Stymphalus) may with certainty be freed from all that is represented by the Stymphalian birds. Even with these powers, the danger of excess and of the hitherto hidden quality of pride must be guarded against, examples in the life of the Hero being the attempt to steal the Delphic Tripod and the mortal injury resulting from the envy of others as was symbolically recorded by the effect of donning the

Shirt of Nessus.

Whilst these warnings directly apply to daily life, they are even more important for those who have embarked upon the Path of Swift Unfoldment — the Twelve Labours, for example. Privileges granted and 'Steps' taken may dangerously awaken remaining elements of self-conceit and satisfaction in the aspirant. The would-be disciple and accepted disciples are very seriously warned against these errors.

THE SEVENTH LABOUR
To Capture the Cretan Bull

*As his Seventh Labour, Eurystheus, King of Mycenae, ordered Heracles to capture the Cretan Bull. Poseidon had given this bull to Minos, King of Crete, believing that, in his turn, he would offer it in sacrifice to Hera. As Minos refused, Poseidon drove the animal mad. In consequence, the country was terrorised and the king appealed for aid to Heracles who at that time was visiting the Island of Crete. Single-handed, the Hero captured the animal even though it belched scorching flames. He then carried it on his back to the seashore, placed it in a boat and conveyed it completely tamed to Mycenae, where Eurystheus after **dedicating** it to Hera, set it free.*

The Myth tells of the gift of a bull by the god of the sea, Poseidon, to Minos, the King of Crete. In so doing, Poseidon believed that Minos would sacrifice the animal to the goddess Hera — the consort of Zeus. Minos refused to carry out the wish of the god who thereupon 'drove the animal mad.' Heracles captured and tamed the bull and presented it to Eurysthus who dedicated it to the goddess Hera and thereafter set the creature free.

If the flame-belching bull — the masculine creative agent for cattle — be regarded as an emblem of the procreative fire in all Nature — and therefore human beings — then mastery of the same by man demands that it should be controlled and its power transmuted to intellectual and spiritual creativeness. The actions of sacrificing the bull to the goddess Hera and setting it free may well symbolise this

---

[1] See below, The Flaming Death of Heracles.

transmutation; for hitherto the bull had belonged to a numan being—Minos—whilst Eurystheus sacrificed it to a goddess.

Unfortunately, Minos—the first recipient of the gift—refused to comply with Poseidon's request, to sacrifice it to Hera, whereupon it is reported the creature lost its reason. So also if one, either a man or a woman, possessed of hyper-active creative fire, failed in this procedure of control and transmutation, then loss of sanity could well be the result. Thus interpreted, the flame-belching bull symbolises *Kundalini Shakti* and the myth describes allegorically both the danger of failure to control it and the advantages of ability to do so.

Heracles himself represents throughout an advanced occultist who had himself both mastered the *Kundalini* fire and consecrated it to spiritual purposes. He was therefore well able to control, capture, restore to sanity and then convey the bull to his King. Minos, on the other hand, had not thus attained. Symbolically, he therefore refused to sacrifice the bull to Hera. This implies that he was not sufficiently evolved either to 'tame' the creative fire or—in consequence—to dedicate it to spiritual unfoldment and objectives.

The madness of the bull caused by the refusal of Minos to do so aptly describes the danger of the loss of sanity which assails those who prematurely arouse the Serpent Fire and are not moved by the idealism represented by its dedication to the goddess Hera, meaning employment for wholly beneficent purposes. This is especially the case when the fiery power of *Kundalini Shakti* has been awakened and become active, as is suggested by the emission of flames from the mouth of the bull. The solution of such a problem could only be known and applied by one who had himself aroused and totally controlled this selfsame Serpent Fire.

This attainment is affirmed by the story of the victory of Heracles over two snakes which attacked him even as a babe in the cradle. Heracles was thus able to overcome the bull despite its burning flames and carry it on his back—suggestive of the spinal cord of man along which *Kundalini* fire ascends into the brain. Thereafter, sanity was restored to the bull—as would be the case for all those capable of controlling the *Kundalini* aroused *within* the body. The process of transmutation was allegorically completed by the Hero as indicated by the delivery of the bull to his King. Eurystheus in his turn fulfilled the wish of Poseidon, and dedicated the animal to the goddess

Hera—consecrated the function of the creative power to spiritual purposes—thereby symbolically setting free the fire-belching bull which he had both tamed and restored to sanity.

THE EIGHTH LABOUR
To Obtain the Man-Eating Mares of King Diomedes

Diomedes, son of Ares and king of the Bistones, owned mares which he fed on human flesh. Heracles, accompanied by a few volunteers, approached Thrace and captured these terrible mares, having first killed their guardians. The alert was given, the Bistones rushed upon him and the battle began. Heracles at last vanquished his assailants and Diomedes was given to his own mares to eat.

Permission is here requested to be excused from an attempted interpretation of this Labour in terms of the Occult Sciences. Apart from portraying the obedience under orders, courage, skill and strength for which he is famous, Heracles does not appear to have performed actions and passed through experiences that refer to a possible spiritual Wisdom concealed in this story. Otherwise stated, the story may be regarded as one of the numberless fairy-tale legends which do not convey occult instruction. Perhaps other writers entering this field may advance interpretations of it that give weight to an opposite view, in which case the author stands ready for correction.

THE NINTH LABOUR
The Golden Girdle of Hippolyte

Hippolyte, whom some call Melanippe, was the Queen of the Amazons in Cappadocia. As a mark of her sovereignty she possessed a magnificent gidle given to her by Ares. Admete, daughter of Eurystheus, greatly coveted this marvellous adornment, and Heracles was therefore given orders to obtain it for her. Accompanied by several celebrated heroes—Theseus, Telamon, Peleus—he set sail and when at last he reached the country of the Amazons he at first encountered no obstacle; for Hippolyte agreed to bestow the girdle upon him. The goddess Hera was in consequence enraged and, disguising herself as an

Amazon, spread abroad the untrue story that Heracles planned to abduct the Queen herself. The Amazons seized their weapons and attacked Heracles, who believing they had betrayed him slaughtered the Amazons together with their Queen. He then took the girdle and proceeded towards Troy.

This story, with its murder of both the Queen of the Amazons and all her subjects by Heracles in order to gratify the desire of his Master Eurystheus, is repellent in the extreme. Apart from the symbol of the girdle of a Queen it does not appear to contain either stories or symbols used in The Sacred Language of Allegory and Symbol. In consequence like its immediate predecessor, no interpretation of the legend is at this time offered. However, as previously stated, the author stands ready for correction.

THE TENTH LABOUR
To Fetch the Oxen of Geryon

Geryon was the King of Tartessus in Spain and reputedly the strongest man alive. He had been born with three heads, six hands and three bodies joined together at the waist. His cattle of marvellous beauty were guarded by the herdsman Eurytion and the two-headed watchdog Orthrus.

During his passage through Europe, Heracles erected a pair of pillars across the Straits, one in Europe, one in Africa. Helios beamed down upon Heracles who, finding it impossible to work in such heat, strung his bow and let fly an arrow at the god. 'Enough of that,' cried Helios angrily. Heracles apologized for his ill-temper, and unstrung his bow at once. Not to be outdone in courtesy, Helios lent Heracles his golden goblet, shaped like a water-lily, in which he sailed to Erythia, a western island. But the Titan Oceanus, to try him, made the goblet pitch violently upon the waves. Heracles again drew his bow which frightened Oceanus into calming the sea.

Another account is that Heracles sailed to Erythia in a brazen urn, using his lion pelt as a sail. On his arrival, the dog Orthrus rushed barking at him, but Heracles' club struck him lifeless and Eurytion, the herdsman, died in the same manner.

Challenged to battle, Heracles shot Geryon sideways through all three bodies, or in another account, let loose a flight of three arrows. Thus, he won the cattle without either demand or payment, having destroyed their owner. Thereafter he set sail upon the golden goblet.

As Heracles drove Geryon's cattle to the Peloponnese, he became the lover of a strange being, half woman, half serpent whom he kissed three times. He then went on his way, eventually completing this Labour and bringing the cattle to King Eurystheus.

If, despite its fantastic and even nonsensical ingredients, the Tenth Labour be interpreted as a description of the full and safe arousal of the *Kundalini Shakti* then the two pillars erected across the straits of Gibraltar by Heracles would represent the two *nadis, Ida* and *Pingala*, with the passage between them as *Sushumna*. The three-bodied monster, Geryon, personifies a threefold mortal man, Heracles himself—physical, emotional and mental—whilst his cattle could represent the products of the normal exercise of the triple Creative Fire, particularly in this case when controlled and transmuted. Hence their beauty. The dog Orthrus, on the other hand, which rushed barking at Heracles, **alludes allegorically to discordant sub-human qualities.**

The Herdsman, Eurytion—who also guarded the cattle—a humble occupation—signifies the attributes in the Candidate remaining from an earlier evolution. Both the dog and Eurytion were presumably clubbed to death by Heracles or, allegorically, their personal limitations were outgrown in the Hero. To gain possession of the cattle and convey them to King Eurystheus at Mycenae—in this instance representing the Hierophant in the Temple of the Mysteries and the **corresponding state of consciousness, Causal, Buddhic and Atmic** —may well refer to the successful transmutation of the more animalistic attributes of the sex-force into its spiritual expression. Certain otherwise completely strange, if not weird, aspects of the myth, consist of the three bodies of Geryon composing one vehicle of form—above interpreted.

The almost unbearable light of the Sun, the Solar donation of the goblet-shaped ship wherewith to make the transfer across the ocean, and the triple flight of arrows (as in one version) whereby Geryon was rendered helpless, may all permissibly be interpreted as further references to the threefold Solar Serpent Fire itself. The necessity is also stressed for the destruction of the restrictions to the awakening of this force and to its proper use on the Pathway of Swift Unfoldment (the Twelve Labours). These include amongst others materialism, animality and egoistic possessiveness. The author ventures to make such suggestions because without this understanding, aspects or parts of the Myth would seem to be entirely without meaning—fabulous indeed.

The inclusion of the Lord of the Sun gives support for this reading, especially since the Sun—physical and superphysical—is the main source and centre from which *Kundalini Shakti* is projected into the Universe. Thereafter, it becomes available for the fulfilment of the single purpose for the existence of the solar system and the totality of its associated beings or inhabitants. This purpose may be described as the unfoldment of spiritual power, life, consciousness and the creative faculty to the highest possible degree. In mankind this includes the supernormal developments achieved by those who are admitted to the Mystery Tradition or enter upon the Path of Hastened Evolutionary Progress.

The fiery solar energy can induce stress—even causing resentment, in those by whom it is experienced (the anger of Heracles)—Helios having beamed down upon him with great heat. In one sufficiently developed, however, discord is speedily overcome and harmony with the sublime source and its power quickly follows. Also this applies to the surrender of the earlier limitations of human nature—resentment for example. In consequence, the solar power becomes practically available and used, as is emblematically indicated by the solar loan of the means of transport towards the goal. This consisted of either the golden goblet shaped like a water-lily or the brazen urn for which the lion pelt—powerful personal attainments skilfully used—becomes the 'sail' or means for the fulfilment of the whole labour (the transference to the Inner Self of the cattle—the purified and now beautified lower desire nature) as previously suggested.

The Titan Oceanus, to try Heracles, caused the goblet to pitch violently upon the waves. Heracles again drew his bow, which frightened Oceanus into calming the sea. In this procedure, also, a hitherto inexperienced feeling of strain can prove at least an annoyance which in its turn must be harmoniously overcome. Oceanus, Lord of the Ocean, was thus associated with water, itself a recognised symbol of emotion,

This incident provides a useful indication that negative emotions can be rendered harmless by the exercise of a positive power (Heracles armed with his bow) and by perfect mental direction or aim of the arrow (will-power correctly 'aimed' and 'fired').

The introduction of the serpent symbol in however strange a form —(presumably chosen both to conceal and yet to reveal) the person of a weird being, half serpent, half woman—whom he kissed three times, is also of symbolic interest; for the symbols of both femininity and triplicity are employed, possibly indicating by means of a strange woman and three kisses, a deeply occult truth and with special reserve, veiling, on account of the profound importance and value of the knowledge, but also the danger of its misuse. Hence, was both revealed and concealed the attained intimate association (kisses) of the Initiate with the threefold feminine Serpent Fire, the combined half serpent and half woman.

Thus viewed, the inclusion of this apparently meaningless episode gives further evidence of a sage-inspired use of the Sacred Language of Allegory and Symbol in order both to conceal and yet draw attention to a profound power-bestowing truth by means of its partial allegorical concealment. May it not even be possible that the presumed inspired authors bestowed the same significance by mean of the chosen number of the Labours themselves—twelve—which by addition equals three—again referring to the triple *Kundalini Shakti?* Indeed, in one interpretation, Eurystheus—in his highest attributes— himself might be regarded as a heavily veiled personification of the Head or Hierophant, Mycenae being a symbolic reference to the regions and Temples in which the Mysteries were and *are still being performed*[1] and brought to fulfilment in the Initiate or Adept-in-the-becoming.

---

[1] The path of Swift Unfoldment is never closed, continues to be trodden, the aspirant being aided by admission to the Lesser and Greater Mysteries. Fortunately, also, the 'Labours of Heracles' are perpetually being performed, by many successive Personifications of the Hero.

SUMMARY

The complex nature of the descriptions of this Tenth Labour has moved the author here to add to his general interpretations some suggested meanings of the chief incidents. These apply especially to the interior states of consciousness and the developments of the would-be Heracles or Aspirant to hastened progress upon the Pathway to Adeptship. In consequence, each incident which appears to possess occult significance is here briefly repeated and followed by a proffered unveiling in the above-mentioned terms. A particular emphasis is placed upon the interior applications and suggested underlying significances of both the Myth itself and certain of its component parts.

Geryon—the awakened triple *Kundalini* and its bestowal of supernormal powers.

His oxen of marvellous beauty—the animalistic tendencies transmuted into harmonious and inspiring conditions.

The herdsman Eurytion, and two-headed watch-dog, Orthros—a trinity, again referring to the triplicities in both Nature and man, useful for self-guardianship when duly available.

Pillars of Heracles and the Straits—the triple *Kundalini* the awakening of which is essential to the fulfilment of the 'Labour', or the ability to travel to and return successfully from Erythia.

The winning of the cattle without either demand or payment after the destruction of their owner—the complete mastery (killing) of any unnatural and so undesirable elements of *Kundalini* and their transmutation—as cattle of great beauty—into desirable qualities.

The temporary error of anger felt against the Sun-God, the apology and cessation of warlike action—victory over undesirable qualities and recognition of the natural laws by which the Universe is governed.

The test by the Titan Oceanus overcome by the demonstrations of superior power—complete mastery of the emotional nature, and the ability to change 'storms' into peacefulness or a calm sea—the emotions—being completely controlled.

The loan by the Sun God of the golden goblet in which Heracles returned from Erythia—the acquirement of additional occult capacities, including the ability to transcend apparent geographical separation.

The metals and the colour gold—generally used as symbols for intuitive insight and spiritual wisdom, which qualities would also assist Heracles on his voyage and in the fulfilment of his 'Labours'.

Since these are attributes of the immortal Self they may not permissibly be regarded as personal possessions, but rather as having been received from the Inmost Self or 'Sun'. Symbolically, they may legitimately be looked upon as 'loans'. (For those for whom the symbolical language proves to be a method of revelation, the briefly described incident may be seen as a highly informative description of both *Kundalini Shakti* and the means of its awakening into activity—in preparation for a specific undertaking, for example).

This peculiar incident may draw attention to the ever-to-be remembered key to the interpretation of mystical allegories, namely that every presumed external action and experience occurs *within* the subject of the myth.

The weird lady—actually the threefold *Kundalini* within Heracles himself which he is able to awaken into activity by the intimate application—a kiss—of his own three-fold spiritual power, wisdom and intelligence. Interestingly, as the title '*Kundalini*' demonstrates, the Serpent Fire is regarded as a feminine force, as indicated in the Sanskrit Language by its four final letters '*lini*'.

Heracles brings the cattle to Eurystheus—Heracles completes his tenth Labour by bringing to Eurystheus—in this case more especially, his inmost spiritual Self—the marvellously beautiful cattle, signifying the success of the Aspirant who passes through the great Initiations with their interior empowerments, illuminations and perfections leading to the stature of the Adept.

THE ELEVENTH LABOUR
The Golden Apples of the Hesperides

The eleventh Labour was for Heracles to bring back the Golden Apples of the Hesperides and the Hero did not know where to find them. Hera—the owner of the golden apple trees—had entrusted their guardianship to the daughter of Atlas. When Hera discovered that the *daughters of Atlas were stealing the apples, she set the dragon, Ladon, to coil round the tree as its guardian. This was definitely a suitable choice, since Ladon possessed no less than one hundred heads and spoke with divers tongues. Atlas, who bore the Vault of Heaven upon his shoulders, was the father of the Hesperides, so Heracles went to him and asked him to get the apples for him. He offered to take upon himself the burden of the sky while Atlas was away. Atlas, seeing a chance of being relieved forever from his heavy duty, gladly agreed. He came back with the three apples, but he did not give them to Heracles, telling him that he could keep on holding up the sky and Atlas himself would take the apples to Eurystheus. In this dilemma, Heracles had only his wits to assist him; for he had to give all his strength to supporting that mighty load. He seemingly agreed to Atlas' plan, but asked him to take the sky back for just a moment so that he—Heracles—could put a pad on his shoulders to ease the pressure. Atlas did so and Heracles picked up the apples and departed. Heracles was successful because of Atlas' stupidity rather than his own cleverness.*

In the Sacred Language of Allegory and Symbol, each of the colours of the spectrum is given its own specific meaning. In terms of psychology and consciousness, the colour gold, for example, symbolises Wisdom, including the faculties of implicit insight and complete—and generally instant—understanding. As suggested in the interpretation of the myth of Jason and the Argonauts, the Golden Fleece itself was a symbol of these self-same capacities. The Myth allegorically portrayed the means whereby—after many adventures—success may be gained. When thus interpreted, the Eleventh Labour similarly offers guidance in the fulfilment of this purpose—the development of Wisdom.

Heracles may himself be regarded as personifying an Initiate of the Mysteries. Interestingly, since Wisdom is not to be gained by the exercise of the normal process of reasoning, Heracles appropriately does not exactly know, as far as the points of the compass are concerned, in which direction he should proceed on his quest.

As does every sincere Aspirant and every member of the Ancient Mysteries, Heracles evidently knew whence the necessary information could be gained—namely, by transcending the limitations of the concrete mind (spatial direction) or allegorically going to Atlas who bore the space-transcending Vault of Heaven upon his shoulders. The decision was evidently correct; for Atlas was the father of the Hesperides who were orchardists taking care of the trees and the golden apples which grew upon them. Atlas himself — I further venture to suggest — may represent the physical plane and the physical substance of matter of which the earth is formed. He also portrays the physical body of man which carries upon its shoulders the instrument of thought — the brain — whereby and wherein the limitations of space may be transcended or fourth-dimensional consciousness attained as Atlas himself clearly had done.

When the goddess Hera, the owner of the apple trees, found that the daughters of Atlas were pilfering the apples, she appointed the dragon, Ladon, as guardian; not only of the golden apples, but symbolically of occult Wisdom, the author ventures to submit; for this action — of placing a serpentine creature as guardian — would seem to be a striking example of the intrusion by a sage into a possible fairy-tale both in order to arrest the attention of the reader and to reveal an aspect of the Wisdom Religion. Interpreted according to the Language of Allegory and Symbol, the golden apple tree itself, growing in the Garden of the Hesperides with its fruit unlike that of all other trees, is an age-old and universal symbol for the Wisdom-imbued Life-Force of the Universe — the Tree of Life.[1]

When this symbol of the Tree is thus used by allegorists, the serpent is frequently associated with it. The trunk of the tree anatomically represents the spinal column of man, whilst the serpent —*Ladon*—coiled round the tree indicates the presence within and around it of the Serpent Fire or *Kundalini Shakti*. This applies equally to all uprights around which snakes are twined, including, for example the pillar of the well of Cadmus.[2]

Unfortunately, as in the Garden of Eden and of the Hesperides, this presence of the serpent is not always a safeguard against the presumed misuse of the 'fruit' of the tree; for, as the Myth tells, Heracles obtained the golden apples by appealing directly to Atlas whose herds wandered over the pastures whereon the orchard of Hera

---

[1] See Appendix — The Sephiroth.
[2] See illustration of Cadmus, Chapter 9.

was situated. Thus, in communion and collaboration with a personification of abstract intelligence, aware in unconfined, unconditioned, immeasurable, limitlesss, sky-like space, (Atlas in one aspect. See later). Heracles killed Ladon with an arrow shot over the garden wall and so obtained that by which alone this Labour could be fulfilled—the golden apples, symbols of purest Wisdom in the most 'fruitful' form. The killing of Ladon by an arrow may permissibly be interpreted as a subjugation of the Serpent Fire brought under control by the power of the will—the arrow.

If this approach be accepted, we are presented with two ideas, one of which is Atlas with the celestial Vault permanently—if but symbolically—upon his shoulders and the other, Heracles similarly but temporarily also transcending the limitations of fixed space. One of the objectives before the advanced Aspirant to the stature of perfection or admission to Olympus—the goal before every Initiate and so of Heracles—is permanently to transcend in consciousness both past, present and future time and the limitations of the three dimensions of space.

In the description of Heracles' progress towards these achievements, he is first brought in touch and communion with Atlas who bore the Vault of Heaven on his shoulders, and second with himself for a sufficient time doing exactly the same thing. Allegorically, his head—meaning brain-consciousness—was brought into union with and made briefly to experience the timelessness and spacelessness of abstract awareness or Universal Consciousness. On the Pathway to Perfection one of the essential realisations or 'powers' is the ever ready experience of time-free, space-free limitlessness. We now see why Heracles had to be submitted to the difficult experience associated with the task of bringing back the Golden Apples of the Hesperides to Eurystheus. It was because, the author suggests, like all truly sage-inspired myths, this Labour reveals under the veil of allegory and symbol, some of the stresses and vicissitudes associated with the development of abstract awareness, of pure Wisdom and of superhuman perfection. The acquirement of the dimension-free state of awareness and its results upon the intelligence are personified by Atlas himself who, of course, was no real being but, amongst other possible interpretations, the symbol of abstract consciousness. This is not inaptly portrayed by the office which he is made to fulfil, namely to bear upon his shoulders (and so in contact with his brain-mind) universalised consciousness, immeasurable and timeless — veritably the Vault of Heaven.

The goddess Hera in this Labour may represent the Monad of man within which is contained the potentiality — together with other regions of abstract thought — of the eventual development by mankind of the purest Wisdom. Atlas, as stated, portrays a human being who had already thus attained. Allegorically, Hera, his Monad, entrusted him wih the guardianship of the golden apple-bearing trees — themselves symbols of the Source of perfect Wisdom — the attainment of which is made to be the underlying goal of this Myth.

The daughters of Atlas personify aspects of the very *human* nature of the individual who egoically may have achieved Wisdom. A valuable message, warning indeed, is herein offered to all aspirants to the spiritual heights, and even to those who have attained. Atlas himself tricked Heracles first. The guidance is that until full Adeptship is reached, attributes of the personal nature may fail fully to make manifest, and may even deny by false conduct, the state to which the aspirant has already attained. Even Atlas himself was tricked both by his own daughters and by Heracles. This danger resides in both the emotional and the mental nature of the personality, either of which — until Adeptship is reached — may be guilty of leading to **physical conduct and motives that are unworthy of, contradict indeed,** the high attainment of an advanced Inner spiritual Self or reincarnating Ego.

A most valuable guidance is thus offered to all who are treading the Pathway of hastened attainment: that the whole mortal nature must continually be guarded so that, as far as remaining human weaknesses permit, that which the Inner Self attains or seeks to attain will alone and strictly be manifest in personal life.

A further safeguard added to watchfulness is very truly presented by the action of Hera herself in placing the hundred-headed dragon, Ladon, with its body coiled round the trunk of the apple-tree; for herein is presented a still further symbolical presentation of the existence, nature and illuminating — and so guarding — power of the Serpent Fire which, when out of control, can produce one of the greatest dangers of all.[1] An example is included in this Myth under the concept of 'pilfering'. This kind of error is to take — without acknowledgement of source — golden (Wisdom-inspired) material (apples) from the works of others and both egoistically and falsely claim them to be one's own.

The emblem of the hundred heads aptly portrays the almost unlimited capacities for intellectual development and mental activities, and the freedom of their expression on all suitable occasions — divers tongues — made possible when the Serpent Fire is, with highest motives, successfully awakened and directed from personal to egoic consciousness. Indeed, when this is permissibly achieved, the possible intellectual developments are virtually without limit — Ladon had a hundred heads.

To accentuate the symbology, the myth says that Ladon was coiled round the trunk of the tree, exactly descriptive of the coiling position of *Kundalini Shakti* around and within the spinal cord of the developing yogi.

Although not directly one of the subjects chosen for study in this book, since Atlas plays a prominent part in the Eleventh Labour of Heracles, a reference to his place in Greek Mythology may here be both interesting and helpful in the present study.

Atlas joined the Titans in their unsuccessful war against the Olympian gods and although spared by Zeus, was condemned to support heaven on his shoulders for all eternity. He has held up the heavens ever since, except when Heracles temporarily relieved him of the task.

A possible reason for the fear which Ladon inspired in Atlas may well be that they represent exact opposites. Ladon, with a hundred heads and speech in divers tongues, clearly stands for the concrete mind and world. Atlas on the other hand, in the fulfilment of his Zeus-imposed punishment, represents the purest abstraction — the limitless but seriously misnamed 'Vault of Heaven'.

If, however, the highly evolved aspirant (Atlas) who had attained to the fulness and freedom of complete abstract or form-free and time-free awareness, permitted a 'descent' into the form-imprisoned state

---

[1] See *Ch.* 2, especially the digest and list of Kundalini and its dangers.

of the concrete mind, then the wondrous total liberation of 'abstractness' would immediately be lost and might even be very difficult to retain should such a recovery be possible.

To prevent such a self-imprisonment which was quite naturally feared or shrunk from, by Atlas, Heracles—who was not thus limited—destroyed Ladon or symbolically made such a 'fall' impossible. Thereafter, Atlas was able to obtain the "Wisdom-fruit' or enter Wisdom-consciousness without the danger of imprisonment in forma thought.

The incident thus viewed becomes an exposition of form-imprisoned and form-freed consciousness and the processes and problems associated with both the attainment of form-free-ness, and guidance against both hindrances and even total failures.

THE TWELFTH AND LAST LABOUR
To bring Cerberus from Hades

The Twelfth and last Labour of Heracles proved to be the most difficult of all. It took him down to the Underworld where he freed Theseus from the 'Chair of Forgetfulness', restoring his memory; for whoever sat on this Chair forgot everything. Heracles' task was to bring Cerberus, the serpent-maned, dragon-tailed, guardian dog up from Hades to his master, Eurystheus. Permission was given by Hades provided that Heracles employed no weapons to overcome Cerberus. The Hero could therefore only use his hands, but in spite of this limitation, he forced the terrible monster to submit to him and on his return from the Underworld, with Athena's assistance, he re-crossed the River Styx in safety and, half-dragging and half-carrying Cerberus up the chasm to its mouth, he brought the guardian dog all the way to the earth and on to Mycenae. Eurystheus was not unnaturally terrified by the sight of the awe-inspiring animal with serpents arising from its mane and, in consequence, took refuge in a jar. The king very wisely did not wish to keep the creature and made Heracles carry it back again, thus completing his twelfth and last Labour.

The Kingdom of the Dead was ruled by one of the twelve great Olympians, Hades, and is often called by his Greek name. It is said to lie beneath the secret places of the earth and to lead over the edge of the world across the ocean, various entrances passing through caverns and beside deep lakes. On guard before the gate sits Cerberus, the three-headed, serpent-maned, dragon-tailed, guardian dog, who, as does his master, Hades, permits all spirits to enter, but none to return.

HERACLES BRINGING THE GUARDIAN DOG CERBERUS FROM HADES TO KING EURYSTHEUS

Thus described, Cerberus is a complete and remarkable symbolical presentation of *Kundalini Shakti* in the form of a family pet—an excellent disguise! The dragon-tail and the serpentine mane provide a key, whilst the three heads indicate how the threefold Serpent Fire is triply manifest in man in three polarities, *Ida, Sushumna* and *Pingala*—negative, positive and neutral respectively. In this myth, these are objectively divided in the three-headed representative, whilst actually, though three-fold and different, they function together within and through the human head.

Cerberus could only be brought to the surface of the earth and to the King by one who achieves this mastery without weapons and solely by his own strength. Similarly, *Kundalini* can only be aroused into the head and into conscious activity by the individual's own successful awakening, upward-drawing, and complete control of the triple power. Appropriately, Heracles did this by his own might, thereby fulfilling his last mission or 'Labour'—meaning the highest attainment which may be described as direct personal discovery, knowledge and employment of the admittedly dangerous triple serpentine force. As suggested, throughout the story of his life Heracles personifies one in whom the Serpent Fire is aroused and mastered, as allegorically portrayed by the incident of his control of two serpents whilst in his cradle during early childhood. In his very great strength he also personifies the resultant power gained from the right use of *Kundalini Shakti*.

The sufferings of the Hero can in their turn be seen symbolically to refer to the effects of the misuse of the power of which these adversities are excellent examples even if but emblematically revealed. They clearly show the dangers of the aroused Fire and unmistakably indicate by Heracles' mistakes their serious consequences as portrayed in the mythological story of his life. In addition his very great strength demonstrates the effects upon the personal nature of active *Kundalini*.

As is related in the story of the Twelfth Labour,[1] his Director, King Eurystheus, was terrified by the sight of the awe-inspiring Creative Fire—symbolised by the serpents arising from the mane and the dragontail of Cerberus—and so took refuge in a jar. Eurystheus was not at all unnaturally self-protective and even made afraid by the sight of the actual awe-inspiring Creative Fire by which worlds and their contents are formed and which when duly prepared, human beings may bring to conscious function within themselves. He therefore both protected himself and ordered the return of Cerberus to the Underworld. This latter action may possibly also be regarded as a reference to the necessity for returning *Kundalini Shakti* to its source in the human sacrum after it had been raised along the spine into the head for the fulfilment of a spiritual and occult mission or 'labour'.

Since, however, King Eurystheus' position in general suggests considerable superiority—kingship and complete dominance of Heracles throughout the Twelve Labours, then an interpretation of him as a personification of a high Official in the Greater Mysteries would appear to be reasonably justified. This is especially so when one is dealing with

---

[1] The only one of the Twelve Labours mentioned by Homer.

myths and not with direct statements of fundamental Occult laws and descriptions of lofty ceremonial Officials.

Under this condition, Heracles-like high Initiates are naturally able to 'overcome' the fiery power, achieving this entirely without the slightest experience of the fear suffered by Eurystheus. Thus, in mythology hydras, dragons, snakes and other serpentine symbols of awakened *Kundalini Shakti* are all correctly made to be both dangerous and terrifying — this being also a possible form of 'guardianship' of the truth behind the myth.[1] Actually, however, every aspirant to Initiation and the higher life must become as a 'Heracles' and successfully perform dramatic 'Labours' or services for the protection and welfare of humanity.

Each character in an inspired myth personifies an aspect of *one person*, the whole performance being enacted by and within that one alone; for all are personifications of attributes, powers and experiences of one and the same person — Heracles himself in his Twelve Labours. Furthermore it is true that every person in the Myth represents an aspect of the sevenfold human being and therefore all characters are within the central figure, but also all events in their turn occur within the same person.

Cerberus, as a personification of *Kundalini*, is rightly not a prisoner in Hades but the guardian of occult knowledge and power to be gained by those who are able, symbolically, whilst awake or alive to explore the physical world (Hades) and penetrate its secret hidden depths — a dangerous process indeed.

Hades or Pluto, personifying Nature's Laws, insisted that the guardian dog be returned to Hades. Similarly, the *Kundalini*-powered and endowed occultist must always be able to cause the aroused Serpent Fire to be returned after use to its relatively quiescent position — Hades indeed — the human sacrum.

THE RESCUE OF THESEUS

As is not surprising. the totality of Greek mythology has not been preserved during the long period of time since these were 'invented' Apparently, one of the missing portions includes a direct record of the

---

[1] Greatly needed today when more widely diffused knowledge of *Kundalini* is leading to its unwise and potentially very harmful excitation and raising.

actions by Theseus for which Hades justifiably caused 'him to be seated on the Chair of Forgetfulness', from which he was unable to move, and upon which his mind became blank. One of these errors have been that Theseus undertook to carry off Helen, the future heroine of Troy (then a child) and when she was grown up, to marry her. Her brothers, Castor and Pollux, recovered her but did not find Theseus because he was then travelling to the Underworld. There, the Lord of Hades, frustrated him from the fulfilement of the purpose of his visit which, however, does not appear to be described in the myth. Hades invited Theseus to sit upon the seat called 'The Chair of Forgetfulness'. From this he could not arise, forgot everything and failed to move.

Although direct evidence does not seem to exist, one must assume that such a severe penalty was the consequence of a serious crime. Perhaps the nature of this misdeed could be conjectured as actions or an action which cruelly deprived another of his or her reason; for such misconduct could, perhaps, balance by its nature the Hades-given punishment.

If this be accepted, then either an ally or an enemy would appear to have been the victim possibly of assault so directed and so maintained as to have deprived the victim of his or her reason. If this were so — mythically or actually — then a similar experience would be justified under the Law of Cause and Effect. Indeed, in Virgil's *Aeneid*, Vol. 6, the 'Underworld' is made to be the place of just retribution for conduct to which the 'sinner' was submitted after death and consequent descent.

Evidently, however, the causative action was not so finally pain-producing as to create incurable madness and death. Hence the freedom exercised by Hades in permitting Heracles to rescue the Hero, Theseus. Unfortunately, the absence of an account of the causative action by Theseus prevents one from justly correlating this deed to the effect — 'The Chair of Forgetfulness' itself.

Another example of the operation of this law is suggested by the beneficent action of the goddess Athena who assisted Heracles to re-cross the River Styx in safety, bearing Cerberus to the chasm or mouth of the 'Tunnel' leading to Hades. The River Styx is elsewhere stated to be the River of No Return, for even though Heracles himself was guilty of many cruel deeds, his beneficent services — the Twelve

Labours, for example—justified the favourable action under karma[1] of the reigning goddess, Athena.

If it here be asked why such valuable knowledge be referred to in apparently misleading ways, an answer may be found by repetition here of the already quoted statement by S. De Guaita in his *Le Seuil du Mystere;* 'To enclose all truth in a spoken language, to express the highest occult mysteries in an abstract style, would not only be useless, dangerous and sacrilegious but also impossible. There are truths of a subtle, synthetic and divine order, to express which in all their inviolate completeness, human language is incapable. Only music can sometimes make the soul feel them, only ecstasy can show them in absolute vision, and only esoteric symbolism can reveal them to the spirit in a concrete way'.

As the author now completes the attempted interpretations of the Labours, he is increasingly—totally in fact—convinced that the individual who would make the mystic 'flight to Olympus'—Adeptship—must interiorly perform each of the Labours of Heracles, successfully complete the Voyage of the Argonauts and wholly fulfil the inspired missions of King Eurystheus.

ALLEGORY IN THE LIFE OF HERACLES

Since the events in the life of Heracles are so numerous and interpretations have been offered of many of them, the author ventures here to repeat the proffered explanations in abbreviated form of some of the more occultly significant episodes with the following summary.

1. *Event:* As a babe, at darkest midnight, two great snakes came crawling into the nursery and reared their heads above the crib. Heracles, only a child, sat up, grasped the snakes by the throat and although they turned and twisted and wound their coils round his body he held them fast, laughing as he did so, giving them to his father when they died.

Interpretation: Infancy indicates both purity of life and freedom from both egoism and demanding personal desire. The two snakes represent the twin currents of *Kundalini Shakti—Ida* and

---

[1] *Karma* (Sk.) The law of cause and effect. See *The Holy Bible: Matt.* v.18, vii.1,2 and 12.

Pingala—whilst their windings round his body portray the three Caduceus-like canals along which the *Kundalini* currents flow, the spinal cord being the central channel—*Sushumna*—around which they are entwined. Yogic mastery with ease of the correctly aroused Serpent Fire is indicated both by laughter and grasping the two snakes by the hands until they died, meaning they were controlled. Giving their deceased bodies to his father may suggest both the dispassion of the Yogi and the surrender of the resultant yogic powers or *Siddhis* to employment for the highest and so impersonal, purposes alone.

2. *Event:* Heracles was the strongest man on earth, with the accompanying supreme self-confidence and sense of equality with the gods, whom he helped in conquering the giants.

Interpretation: The faults, follies and crimes of Heracles belong rather to the built up, fairy-tale aspect of the Myth. Into this came—rightly intruded by one of the sages—his advanced yogic developments, his cooperativeness with the occult authorities and his supposed superhuman physical strength and courage; for these correctly, if allegorically, describe the qualities essential to the safe awakening, power to control and universalised application of *Kundalini Shakti*. All such attributes aptly and secretly portray the qualities of the advanced and 'enfired' high Yogi, who had aroused and mastered the Serpent Fire—a very dangerous force, hence the secrecy.

3. *Events:* With the consent of Apollo he forced the priestess, the Sibyl of Delphi, to deliver a response to his question.

Interpretation: The above is also supported by his association with Apollo who had conquered the python or dragon. The Sibyl personifies the resultant ability to communicate with his own divine self, whilst presence at the Centre at Delphi suggests, perhaps, Initiate Memberhip of the Greater Mysteries.

4. *Event:* Quality of omnipotence. Nothing that lived whether in air, on sea or on land ever defeated him.

Interpretation: The fully aroused, upraised, controlled and consciously employed *Kundalini*, endows every such yogi with the quality of undefeatableness in every adverse circumstance.

5. *Event:* He agreed humbly to any punishment it was proposed to inflict on him for an error or crime, never rebelling even against the almost impossible demands made upon him.

Interpretation: As a philosopher, he thoroughly understood the law of cause and effect and always adjusted his thought and conduct to the working of that law, at no matter what cost to himself, ever humbly bowing to its decrees even to the extreme extent of working as a female slave of Queen Omphales.

6. *Event:* Quality of ready repentence. He had complete courage based upon overwhelming strength, and his sorrow for wrong-doing and willingness to expiate fully showed greatness of Soul.

Interpretation: As developed by every high Yogi.

7. *Event:* Full grown at eighteen he killed when by himself the Thespian lion of the woods of Cithaeron, thereafter wearing its skin as a cloak, with the head forming a hood over his head.

Interpretation: As with Samson and other lion-conquerors, Heracles here showed the described qualities essential to the safe-arousing of *Kundalini,* and thereafter displayed the corresponding royal powers of the lion in deity, superman and man. The lion symbol—king of beasts—and the killing and possession of the hide also refer to the development of both rulership over oneself and the attainment of kingly qualities. A certain majesty characterises every Adept and most of those who are nearing that state, as both in his real nature, and in the occult additions to the fairy-tale, Heracles is made to portray; hence the lion itself and, the lion-skin worn as clothing with the lion's head as head-covering. This concept is supported by the idea of the Leontocephalic Lord of the Sun in Mithraism.

8. *Event:* Married Princess Megara who bore him three sons. Goddess Hera sent madness upon him and he then killed his children and Megara herself. His sanity afterwards returned in his blood-stained hall with the dead bodies of his sons and wife beside him and with no memory, causing complete bewilderment. Amphitryon told him of his deeds, and he then said, 'I myself am the murderer of my dearest. I will avenge upon myself these deaths'. But as he started to do so, his desperate purpose was changed and his life spared, the miracle having been performed by his friend Theseus — personifying the Adept Master—who clasped his blood-stained hands and took him home to Athens to live with him. Unable to forgive himself, he consulted the Sibyl at Delphi who sent him to his cousin Eurystheus, King of Mycenae, who ordered him to fulfil the famous Twelve Labours in

order to achieve complete self-purification.

Interpretation: The madness of Heracles may be regarded as fairy-tale material with little or no deeper significance, save that *Kundalini* aroused but uncontrolled can disturb mental balance and so lead to regrettable and unavoidable crimes, hence the universal enveiling.

The saving and recovery by a friend, Theseus, allegorically reveals the care of the Adept Master over his disciples, especially when in very deep distress and not wholly guilty.

FLAMING DEATH AND ASCENSION TO OLYMPUS

The general reader may not unnaturally regard the dramatic story of the death of Heracles as a literary triumph, a spectacular ending to a wonderful fairy-tale. Not so entirely for the student of occult science, however, since with its many magical elements the narrative contains deeply mystical episodes.

The account of the centaur, Nessus the ferryman, is one example of these. He was not only half-man, half-horse, but also, alas, a black magician. The half-man, half-horse *symbol* indicates a being who had not yet freed himself from 'animality' or animalistic desire. Nessus had, however, become possessed of magical knowledge and power and this he misused in the way described in the myth, from which valuable instruction may be gained.

As his assault of Deianira brought about his death from the well-aimed arrow of her husband, Heracles, Nessus employed both deceit and black magic in order to obtain revenge upon the human being — and Hero — who thwarted him; for, by illegally seeking to gratify his passion he brought about his own death. Whilst dying, Nessus resorted to black magic by charging his blood with fiery or "burn-producing' poison derived from the arrow of Heracles, so that when a garment soaked in it was worn, an agonising death was to be the result.

At this point, the Hero enters the story; for as he put it on, a fearful pain seized him, as though he were in a burning fire. Indeed, Heracles was in torture, but he lived through it and they brought him home. Long before Deianira had heard what her gift had done to Heracles, she had killed herself, and in the end Heracles did the same. He ordered those around him to build a great pyre on Mount Oeta and carry him to it. When at last he reached it, he knew that now he could die and he was glad. 'This is rest,' he said. 'This is the end.' As they lifted him to the pyre, he laid himself down upon it and asked his youthful follower, Philoctetes, who held the torch, to set the wood on fire. Then the flames rushed up and Heracles was seen no more on earth. He was taken to heaven—Olympus.

> 'After his mighty labours he has rest.
> His choicest prize eternal peace
> Within the homes of blessedness.'

If an occult interpretation be sought, particularly concerning the fiery end of the human life of Heracles and his translation to Olympus, then, the author suggests, it is his attainment of Adeptship which is thus being described; for he left his humanity behind or at least symbolically submitted it to blazing fire from within which he disappeared from view. Thus, Heracles symbolically reached the summit of human evolution by the aid and *control* of the element of fire.

In the language of myths, the determined possession of a body implies a still remaining high evaluation of existence as a personal being, of egoism and a strong desire to preserve the sense of self-identity. As Adeptship is approached, however, this mental concept declines in influence, especially in power to restrict the ability of the mind to comprehend formless truths and to enter the formless worlds of abstract thought. Eventually, the 'imprisoning' self-ness, or 'ego-centricity' ceases to control the mental attitude, and realisation of its restriction upon awareness brings about its complete renunciation.

Readiness to submit to the agony of death by burning, the resultant destruction of his body, and his achievement of freedom thereafter, may be regarded as a revelation that at least for Heracles, self-centredness and the desire for embodiment in dense form, with its enforced restriction of physical freedom, all these were finally outgrown. In consequence, preceding barriers to realised unity with the Divine Universal Life are transcended.

The flaming death and mental freedom in their turn suggest mastery of that fiery power by which all has been generated and created and by the right use of which the restrictions of dense physical bodies will be overcome. This is brought about by the conscious arousal and ascendance into the brain-mind of the illumination-producing Creative Fire. Heracles had displayed control of that Fire on

THE GODDESS ATHENA POURING A LIBATION FOR
HERCULES ON COMPLETION OF THE TWELVE LABOURS

several occasions—by killing the two dangerous serpents when a babe in the cradle; and by destroying the deadly Hydra of Lerna by the correct administration of the Fire of *Kundalini Shakti*, applied with the flaming brand to its neck, for example. He again victoriously employed the same cosmic and solar energy to overcome all human limitations and characteristics within himself.

The Hero, his death by Fire self-accomplished, thereafter ascended to Olympus or fulfilled the purpose for which he was born and had laboured so selflessly and successfully. Thus, by the conquest and transcendence of the human weakness of egoism, together with the other necessary developments, the attainment of Adeptic stature was finally brought about. Harmony with the goddess Hera (all Nature) had been achieved, and at last that peace became his for which he had yearned for so long a time.

Indeed, the epic narrative of the life of Heracles is profoundly occult; for every Adept—the perfected human being—has, one learns, similarly attained—actually, of course and not at all allegorically—or is received into Olympus, the abode of the gods, thereby becoming one of the Immortal Olympians.

CHAPTER 4

THE VOYAGE OF THE ARGONAUTS

This great adventure is said to have been undertaken as an endeavour by the Hero, Jason, to recover his royal position in Greece. Jason was the son of Aeson who was by rights a king in Greece but had his kingdom taken away from him by his nephew, a man named Pelias. The King's young son, Jason, the rightful heir to the throne, had been sent secretly away to a place of safety, and when he was grown he came boldly back to claim his kingship from the wicked cousin.

The usurper, Pelias, had been told by an oracle that he would die at the hands of kinsmen, and *that he should beware of anyone whom he saw shod with only a single sandal.*[1] In due time such a man came to the town. *One foot was bare,*[1] although in all other ways he was well-clad — a garment fitting close to his splendid limbs, and around his shoulders a leopard's skin to turn the showers.

Pelias came in hot haste at the tidings and when he saw the single sandal he was afraid. He hid his terror in his heart, however, and addressed the stranger: 'What country is your fatherland?' With gentle words Jason answered: 'I have come to my home to recover the ancient honour of my house, this land no longer ruled aright, which Zeus gave to my father. I am your cousin, and they call me by the name of Jason'.

Pelias gave him a soft answer. 'So shall it be. But one thing must first be done. The dead Phrixus[2] bids us bring back the Golden Fleece and thus bring back his spirit to his home. Do you go upon this quest, and I swear, with Zeus as witness, that I will give up the kingdom and the sovereign rule to you.'

---

[1] A most significant statement for all who are concerned with the Ancient Mysteries and their modern Representative, Freemasonry, as also Co-Freemasonry, a valid Masonic Order which admits women to its ranks. See my Book, *At The Sign of The Square And Compasses,* Ch.2, published by The Eastern Federation, International Co-Freemasonry, Adyar, Madras, 600020, India.

[2] Son of Nephele, the discarded wife of a Greek king named Athamas.

The idea of the great adventure thus presented to Jason delighted him and he called the young men of Greece to join him in meeting the great challenge to obtain—despite all dangers—the Golden Fleece at Colchis. They joyfully responded and amongst them were Heracles, whose story has already been considered: Orpheus, a mortal who so excelled in music that he almost equalled divine performers, having no real rival anywhere except the gods themselves. When he played and sang, no one and no thing could resist him.

Castor and Pollux, the very popular brothers, were said to live half their time on earth and half in heaven. This is hardly surprising since they were the sons of the Lord Zeus and Leda whom he visited—allegorically of course—in the form of a swan. They are represented as protectors of sailors and saviours of ships when endangered by storms and the ruthless sea. They were therefore potentially most useful members of the crew, and not only on this account but because of their divine origin; for their presence on board the Argo gave to the expedition an almost divine permission for the Quest and direct representation of the Lord Zeus himself through his two sons. The great Quest completed and fulfilled, the Golden Fleece was handed to Pelias, the members of the crew dispersed and in various ways entered upon their own more personal adventures.

One member, however, left the good ship before the fulfilment of the Quest. This was Heracles from whose misfortune much may be learned, for he went in search of his much loved servant, Hylas, who became a victim of the illusion of the importance of personal selfhood and in consequence was allegorically drawn under the waters by a nymph who fell in love with him, causing him to be lost to Heracles thereafter.

The error of both over-personal affection—Heracles' love for Hylas—and of excessive concern for and admiration of oneself—Hylas and his reflection in the stream—convey valuable warnings to those who would successfully fulfil the great Quest of attaining to full spiritual Wisdom—the Golden Fleece itself.

What, it may then be asked, *is* the story of the Golden Fleece and why was such an enterprise conceived, undertaken and described? Is it to be lightly regarded or even dismissed as composed of bizarre and chimerical fancies? Or is it a myth to be valued and read as the fascinating fairy tale of earlier peoples? Or is it a parable or allegory, both concealing and revealing mystical truths?

THE ARGONAUT ADVENTURE AS DESCRIPTIVE OF CREATIVE PROCEDURES

The great epic, like all other valid myths emanating from inspired mythographers, the sages of old, may permissibly be interpreted as descriptive by allegory and symbol of the voyage of pure Spirit across the waters of space through the resistances of matter to the accomplishment of the purpose of cosmic and solar manifestation. It may well be assumed that this was the objective for which the Argo was built and the voyage initiated, namely the attainment of the mystic Golden Fleece — intuitive insight and purest Wisdom. Similarly might be interpreted all 'voyages' of Solar Logoi aboard the 'ships' of the solar systems and of all component Monads within their vehicles — the Crew — through levels or 'deeps' of matter, from the opening of *Manvantaras*[1] to their close.

In addition, such stories apply equally especially indeed to the monadically-awakened human being — demigod or Hero — who is pursuing the greatest of all 'adventures'. This primarily consists of the over-riding of the limitations of both matter and chronology or normally-timed evolutionary schedules. For such Heroes, progress on this 'voyage' is marked by hastened passage through limiting phases of evolution — self-centredness, for example — and of concrete thought into the freedom of selflessness and abstract and spiritual awareness.

Such a 'voyage' is aided by admission to and passage through the successive Grades of the Greater Mysteries[2] — ever the field of thought of all great myths, whether scriptural or otherwise. Thus regarded the voyage is always interior. *All occurs within.*

The Argonaut Myth may thus be considered as a remarkable parable allegorically descriptive of the evolution of mankind through the phases depicted by the adventurous incidents to the attainment of the Golden Fleece — or the achievement whilst physically wide awake of full spiritual enlightenment. This highly abstract approach to the great epic can lead — the author ventures to suggest — to an understanding of some of the principles and procedures involved in the opening

---

[1] *Manvantara* (Sk.) See Glossary.
[2] See *Appendix* and *Matt.* 13:11.

and fulfilment of cosmic, solar, monadic and so human involutionary and evolutionary procedures. To help in this, the ancient story itself may usefully here be recorded. Jason was the son of Aeson, the rightful King of Iolcos, the town in Thessaly where the Argo was launched. The mother was Tyro and Jason was saved by her from his half-brother, Pelias, who attempted to take his life. The Hero was smuggled out of Iolcos and entrusted to the care of Cheiron, the centaur.

The Myth tells how when a young man, Jason returned to Iolcos and demanded his rightful kingdom. Pelias, who had stolen it in order to be rid of Jason, asked him to go to Colchis to fetch the Golden Fleece. This was the fleece of the ram on which Phrixus—the son of Athamas and Nephele—had escaped, having then given it to the king of Colchis. The Fleece was hanging on an oak tree in the grove of Ares and guarded day and night by a sleepless dragon, as Jason himself painfully discovered. The idea of the great adventure was delightful to Jason. He agreed and let it be known everywhere that this would be a voyage indeed. The young men of Greece joyfully met the challenge. They came, all the best and noblest, to join the company. Heracles, the greatest of all Heroes, was there; Orpheus, the master musician; Castor with his brother, Pollux, the inseparable twins who played notable parts in many myths—and who were worshipped as divine beings in Sparta, Zeus having set their image among the stars as Gemini; Achilles' father, Peleus; Theseus, and many another, some fifty in all. Jason commanded Argos, the Thespian, to build him a fifty-oared ship called the Argo. This ship was, however, miraculous in various ways, Athena herself, for example, having fitted an oracular beam into the prow.

After many adventures and misfortunes, each of occult significance for which interpretations will later be offered, they arrived at Colchis where Medea, daughter of the king, was celebrated for her skill in magic. She fell in love with Jason and charmed the dragon to sleep by singing a sweet magical song whilst Jason took down the Golden Fleece, and they fled together in the Argo.

If an interpretation based upon the procedures of successive manifestations of Cosmoi and Solar Logoi earlier referred to may be offered, indeed the voyage of the Argo may be regarded as allegorically descriptive of the procedures of the Creation and evolution of successive Cosmoi, Solar Systems and Monads of human beings. Abstract though these concepts admittedly are, the author ventures to offer them as possible underlying revelations which certain myths, including the present one, may have been designed to proffer to mankind. Such views concerning stories which are almost universally regarded as the fairy tales of primitive peoples may well be considered as either unacceptable or extreme. Nevertheless, the author ventures to proceed. The affairs at Iolcos and the activities of various beings belong to the preceding epoch, whilst the birth and nurture of Jason himself describes the 'conception' and the 'nativity' of a Cosmic Logos.

We will now consider each incident, the members of the crew, the boat itself, its dangers and successes and interpret them all as representing very faithfully phases and stages of human evolution. We begin with the birth of the idea and continue to the construction and unique power of the Argo, the position and meaning of Cheiron and of the experiences through which each Argonaut passes. These include failures, successes and the abandonment of the Quest. Should this seem to be extreme, the author has found that next to *The Labours of Heracles*, this myth is one of the most enlightening and so well worthy of close examination.

Cheiron, the wise Centaur who cared for and taught Jason, represents the transferred attributes and powers developed in the preceding *Manvantara*. One might reasonably wish to question the choice of Cheiron, the Centaur, as the teacher and guide of the Argonauts. Admittedly, Centaurs are half horses and half men, suggesting a portrayal of the evolution of life through the animal into the human kingdom with attributes of the former still not overcome. Cheiron was widely known, however, both for his goodness and his wisdom. Since he was immortal, may he not suggest one approaching the status of an Adept in whom the capacities and special powers of the two kingdoms—animal and human—have been developed to very great heights? In that case he would be employed by members of the Adept Brotherhood as Their representative, particularly as teacher to advancing aspirants.

Cheiron, though presented as an immortal, offered himself to die as a substitute for Prometheus, and Zeus would seem to have accepted him; for during a conflict, Heracles accidently wounded Cheiron and since the wound proved to be incurable, Zeus permitted him to die rather than live forever in pain. Total sacrifice of self for others is a known attribute of one approaching Adeptship as also is complete evolution beyond — dying to — both the animal and human kingdoms when realised immortality is discovered and superhumanity is attained.

THE COSMIC ARGO AND ARGONAUTS

If the great adventure may be interpreted not only from the human and superhuman points of view, but at far loftier levels, then Jason himself, as head of the expedition and captain of the Argo, personifies both a Cosmic and a Solar Logos, whilst the Argo, with its prow possessing the divinely bestowed[1] faculties of prophecy and speech, portrays the material and form-aspects of Cosmoi and Solar Systems. Thus viewed, each member of the crew represents a different power and force at work from the moment of First Emanation — the launching — and the Creative Hierarchies associated with each of these. The superhuman beings who participate in Cosmoi and Solar procedures of manifestation, are also personified, as may be seen when certain members of the crew are studied and interpreted.

The Golden Fleece itself — the objective — represents the highest possible degree of perfection of forms, of consciousness and of developing Monads attainable and attained in Cosmoi and Solar Systems. This includes that purest Wisdom which gives implicit insight into every first truth. The 'tree' upon which the Golden Fleece was nailed may be regarded as a symbol of the manifested Life-Principle — The Tree of Life — whilst the nails stand for the ultimate atoms by means of which the manifestation of Will-Thought as objective life and form becomes possible and actually occurs.

THE ARGONAUTS AS HUMAN BEINGS

In man, the microcosm, Jason is the Monad at varying and progressive stages of development, whilst the Argo itself portrays the vehicles in which it is incarnate. The goddess-endowed prow, the gift of Athena, represents the divine triplicity in man, spiritual Will, Wisdom and Intelligence, whilst the rest of the ship refers to the mortal vehicles. The wondrous voyage itself reveals many of the stages of

By the goddess Athena.

development and the experiences passed through before the prize—perfect or Adeptic Wisdom—is attained.

The guardian dragon represents the generative principle—the emanative, formative impulse—as a result of which creation begins and is carried through until the objective is attained. The terrible serpent is intimately present, being immediately close to, the Tree of Life on which the Fleece is nailed—the treasured prize, namely spiritual Wisdom sought by Jason with the help of Medea. One is here reminded of the Biblical presentation of these ideas. In the Book of Genesis one reads that Adam, Eve and the serpent were intimately associated with the Tree of Life.[1] The 'prize', in their cases, however, is the innate faculty and expression of the generative power, symbolised by the 'apple' by which Adam was tempted by Eve, the serpent encouraging them.

In man, the dragon is in large measure, but not quite entirely, the sex impulse, active *Kundalini* or Serpent Fire, the sheer energy which gives rise to the all-essential attribute—pressure even—of desire to create in the fullest meaning of the word.

The action of Medea in charming the dragon to sleep refers to the acquired post-Initiatory capacity to transcend sex-desire and sublimate the energy from physical to intellectual and spiritual modes of expression. The dragon (sex urge) symbolically sleeps—becomes physically inactive—and thereafter the 'Golden Fleece' of spiritual consciousness and self-establishment in union with the Solar Logos are obtained—hence one might presume the colour of the Fleece, gold representing divine Wisdom.

Useful, practical guidance in the control and transmutation of the sex impulse—the dragon—is revealed by the manner in which Medea reduced its potency. This was not by direct conflict or the actual slaughter of the dragon, but rather—very wise counsel—by 'charming' the dragon. This was achieved by powerfully re-directing the sensual impulse from physical pleasure to superphysical harmoniousness. Mystically, the creature was "charmed to sleep". Indeed, this is the secret of the fulfilment of this attainment; for when the individual has

---

[1] *Gen.* 3.

reached the necessary evolutionary stage, sex desire itself naturally declines and its transmutation is successfully achieved.

Before this had occurred and whilst Jason was being swallowed by the dragon, the goddess Athena—spiritual wisdom—intervened and forced the creature to disgorge him, as shown in the accompanying illustration in which also the Golden Fleece is seen to be hanging from the tree and the spear of the goddess *arises vertically through the neck of the Hero.*

In addition to these three approaches to the Myth—the dragon, the Tree of Life and the Golden Fleece—certain secrets pertaining to passage through the degrees of the Lesser and especially the Greater Mysteries[1] would seem to be referred to beneath the allegorical veil. Thus viewed, Cheiron under whose care Jason had been placed represents the Hierophant,[1] and Mt. Pelion upon which he lived and taught, the advanced Initiatory Degree attained and the resultant supra-mental levels of consciousness. The fall of Iole from the ram during the flight tells of dangers, and warns of possibilities of Icarus-like failures during the 'serial' (intuitional) flight.[2] The incident of Hylas, as has also been suggested, warns against surrender to illusion and desire. The successful passage between the clashing rocks—Scylla and Charybdis—tells of the necessity for balanced equipoise between all pairs of opposites. Fortunately, as symbolised by the dove, this had been attained by a sufficient number of the crew.

Thus, whilst the great voyage never actually occurred in its purely physical and historical form, it may well be regarded as an almost perfect allegory of the ever-continuing normal evolutionary journeyings undertaken by Logoi of Universes and their indwelling Monads, for indeed, many incidents may be permissibly, the author suggests, interpreted as descriptive of experiences and assistance granted to Monads and their human personalities. This particularly applies when as Initiates of the Lesser and Greater Mysteries[1] their spiritual unfoldment is being quickened. Under these conditions special guidance may not infrequently be needed. Fortunately, this is never withheld, since: ' The light from the one Master, the one unfading golden light of Spirit, shoots its effulgent beams on the disciple from the very first.'[3]

---

[1] See Appendix. *The Still Functioning Lesser and Greater Mysteries.*
[2] See *Introduction.*
[3] *The Voice of the Silence,* H.P. Blavatsky.

132 THE ARGONAUTS

JASON BEING DISGORGED BY THE DRAGON,
WITH THE AID OF THE GODDESS ATHENE

CHAPTER 5

THE HELIOS PRINCIPLE

The richness in occult wisdom of world mythology is nowhere more apparent than in accounts of the appearances of various personifications of the Supreme and Directive Deity of the Solar System. In early Greek mythology, after the Universe had appeared from Chaos, Gaea gave birth to Uranus whom she made her equal in grandeur. Uniting with him she produced the Earth and the first race of gods, the Titans.[1] One of them, Helios, was a nephew — and thereafter the human race. Uranus was reduced to impotence by Chronus (Time) — another deeply significant myth — under whose reign the work of creation continued, leading to the birth of Zeus as a son of Chronus and Rhea.

In the loftiest conceptions, the Lord Zeus was not only an individual Solar Logos, but also a personification of that same solar life-giving and life-preserving principle and power which is incarnate throughout all nature and positively active in every created being and thing. The nearest Hindu representation may perhaps be either the Trimurti, the Triune Divine Principle as a unity, consisting of Brahma, (Creator), Vishnu (Preserver) and Shiva (Destroyer or Transformer) or the Lord Vishnu alone in his special aspect of Preserver.

In Assyro-Babylonian mythology it is **Marduk**, the Head of the Creative Pantheon, who absorbed all other gods and took over all their functions and prerogatives, organised the Universe, assigned dwelling places to the gods and fixed the course of the heavenly bodies. In the mythology of ancient Persia, **Mazda** eclipsed all other divinities, achieved complete prominence as the God of gods, Master of the

---

[1] *Titans*. The *Uranidae*. The six sons and six daughters of Uranus and Gaea. Also, the divine or semi-divine beings who were descended from the Titans.

heavens and the Creator of all creatures. In Norse mythology, Odin was the God of spirirual life who decided man's fate, and ordained the laws which ruled human society. In Celtic mythology, it is the Tuatha De Danaan who watched over the whole of human activity, the most important Deity being Dagda, Lord of perfect knowledge, Father of all, progenitor of all the gods, omni-competent—a true Father-figure.

The student of occult science thus approaching a study of the powers manifested in a Solar System and all that it contains—and its almost infinitely varied manifestations—may naturally sooner or later seek to know whether indeed there does exist one Being, or unitary principle perhaps, responsible for the appearance and—throughout its existence—in charge of a single Solar System. Otherwise expressed, amidst the apparent multitude of Creative Intelligences of which during *Manvantara*[1] a Cosmos, is said to consist, is the God-concept itself a mere myth or is it a divine reality of mind-staggering immensity?

The body of ideas known as *Brahma Vidya* or Theosophia includes guiding principles proffered for the enlightenment of genuine seekers for both Truth itself and its happiness-giving applications to human life. Nowhere does it demand the acceptance of such views and in consequence it is hardly possible here to pronounce a dogmatic answer to this fundamental, spiritual and philosophic question: does there exist a single divine Being upon whom the titles the Supreme Deity, the Lord God of Hosts, may justly be bestowed? The Ancient Wisdom answers that emanating from the impersonal supreme and incognisable Principle of the Universe, the Absolute, there does exist such a Being as the Central Presiding Godhead of the Solar System,

OUR LORD THE SUN.

Furthermore, it is indicated, that when a certain evolutionary position has been attained—Initiation[2]—the existence of this Holy Presence may—does indeed—become actually known as a direct experience. Contrary to what might perhaps be expected, this recognition or discovery is not external alone—a central Sun in Space—but as an intensely brilliant and powerful Presence at the 'heart of the mind', as it were. Needless to say, this Divine Light and Power within

---

[1] *Manvantara* (Sk.) See Glossary.

[2] Initiation, see Glossary and second Appendix.

is in no slightest degree either individual or personal. Rather is the experience due to the opening out of the consciousness to awareness of a Universal Presiding Presence manifest as Source of Light, Life—as energy or power—of which no limits may ever be conceived; for THAT is impersonal in and to the highest degree.

'*The Sun is the heart of the Solar World (System) and its brain is hidden behind the (visible) Sun. Thence sensation is radiated into every nerve-centre of the great body, and the waves of the life essence flow into each artery and vein...The planets are its limbs and pulses.*" *The Secret Doctrine*, H.P. Blavatsky, Vol.2, p.264, Adyar Edition.

In Greek Mythology, Helios is to some extent such a Being, quite remote from the nature and restrictions of a human entity. In occult philosophy, however, the idea is found that as man evolves into superhumanity and beyond, the experience of existing as a separated individuality is increasingly reduced, this culminating in realised identity with the Cosmic Whole (what follows must therefore be read not as a contradiction of that Principle, but as a modification thereof, if the term be permitted.) Nevertheless, there is said to exist a Being who, however invisibly and mysteriously, directs the evolution of life and form within a Solar System and so upon all its component planets.

In their turn, groups of planets, physical and superphysical in the present Solar System, composing a Round[1] are said to be presided over by a *Manu*[2] or individual Official. Rounds grouped into the seven Chains[3] of globes are similarly said to be under the supervision of a Chain *Manu*. In some forms of the presentation of occult philosophy this culminates in the existence—I hesitate to use a more personalised word—of One Being who is referred to as the Solar Logos in Greek Mythology, Helios. If this system of philosophic thought be found acceptable, then the answer to the major question would seem to be in the affirmative. Yes, there does exist at the heart of a Solar System a Presiding Deity of evolutionary stature beyond all possible conception by average man. As the physical Sun functions on behalf of physical Nature, so this great Being is presumed similarly to preside over a Solar System as a whole—physical, superphysical and spiritual.

---

[1] Round—See Glossary.
[2] Manu—See Glossary.
[3] Chain—See Glossary.

Here, at once, an extremely important principle is met with by the student of Theosophy, one moreover that is not wholly in harmony with Greek mythology. This is that the Supreme Presiding Intelligence of a Solar System — strange as this may at first appear — is not only a separate entity. On the contrary, in a mystery beyond the comprehension of all save illumined mystics, the Godhead referred to *is also manifest within, is an essential part of everything and every being existent in the System under such 'Divine' direction.*

Thus, Greek mythology is totally erroneous in presenting the concept of an individual god riding across the sky by day in his golden chariot drawn by four winged horses of dazzling whiteness, their nostrils breathing forth flame.

As god of light to the Greeks, however, it is said that Helios 'saw everything and knew everything.' He was the son of the Titan Hyperion and Theia, a brother of Selene (the Moon) and Eos (the Dawn). He was worshipped as a god of light in many parts of Greece, especially on the island of Rhodes, where the famous Colossus represented him. Helios — nephew of the Titans — is said to be possessed of a palace which he left every day at the appointed time to travel in his four-horse golden chariot across the sky and so bring light to man.

Apollo, in his turn, was first of all a god of the light, a sun-god, without, however, being the sun itself, which was solely represented by a special divinity, Helios, himself. Of him it could be said what Pindar states of Apollo, 'He is the god who plumbs all hearts, the Infallible Whom neither mortals nor **immortals** can deceive either by action or in their inmost secret thought.' Apollo was also the god of light and because of his identification with the child, Horus — a Solar concept — he was worshipped as the Sun.[1]

Helios, the Sun-God, in his Solar Chariot also represents both the Solar Atma in the Universe and the Monad-Atma in man. In Greece, knowledge of this truth, was the vision splendid to which occultists aspired and sometimes attained. Thereafter, they were freed from bodily consciousness and caught up in a supra-mental state which allegorically could only be described as experience of unity with **Helios** and participation in his light-giving, chariot flight through

---

[1] See *The Greek Myths*, 1. p.82, par.3. Robert Graves.

HELIOS IN HIS CHARIOT

space. The observation of the movement by the Sun across the sky doubtless caused the ancient Greeks to represent Helios, the Solar Deity, as riding chariot-borne across the great vault of the heavens. Whilst natural, as suggested, this is indeed erroneous; for the Supreme Lord and Light-Bringer of the Solar System is also an essential part of all that upon which its radiance is shed.

Although to a certain extent a departure from the Greek concept of Helios as but *one* of the great gods, this philosophic view of Deity as universally omnipresent may perhaps usefully here be further considered. With all reverence, similarly, the Blessed Trinities of Christianity, including the Word of the Gospel of St. John, the Hindu Tri-Murti, the Egyptian god Atum, and even the Lords Zeus and Odin are in nowise to be regarded as beings however Divine, who are entirely separate from the Universe and worlds over which they are exoterically said to preside.

Indeed, in a mystery certainly beyond telling—though not beyond mystical experience—THAT PRINCIPLE which these Beings portray is said also to be THE SOURCE OF ALL WITH WHICH THEY ARE ASSOCIATED. In simpler terms and in all reverence, it may thus be said that the Deity is both the Source of all Creation and at the same time omnipresent within all that has been made. The study of Theosophia brings one to the affirmation that it is possible for human beings so to sensitise and develop body, brain and mind as to enable them to realise in an exalted state of consciousness, unity with THAT which is both the Source and the Hidden Life in all that exists, and *therefore within themselves*. Early Races might not normally have either known or understood this profound idea. Since an inviolable law exists that facts concerning Nature and the evolutionary procedures must continually be made available to mankind, these truths had of necessity to be stated in terms however simple and fairy-tale-like. World mythologies contain—indeed largely consist of—presentations of these truths in order that they may prove be 'portals' leading into the Temple of Wisdom and in due course to the very interior, the Holy of Holies. Hence, the author submits, the existence not only of the myths themselves, but also of the sage-provided authentic portions of them which allegorically present divine truths and lead to their personal discovery as both ideas and interior experiences.

The Solar Deity was named in Sanskrit by the Initiated sages and seers of ancient India—always with deepest reverence—Brahma[1], the spiritual energy-consciousness source of the Solar System. In one aspect, this Being was regarded as the Directive Agency responsible for the emanation, formation, preservation and evolution to the highest possible degrees of the Solar System. With its already known and as yet to be discovered planets manifested throughout the seven planes of Nature, the whole of this vast 'Empire', physical and super-physical, with all its evolving life and beings may thus be assumed to be within the care, responsibility and charge of an approximate approach to the Hindu concept of the Deity Brahma.

True, all the functions of Nature continue quite naturally and in that sense require no supervision. Nevertheless, one learns, certain over-all guardianships and directions are applied. 'Godship', if the author may coin the word, defines however imperfectly this 'over-seeing' of Nature's procedures. As indicated in the study of the Hephaestus Principle[2] and the suggested interpretation of such mythological ideas as the amours of Zeus and other semi-divine beings, an unfoldment-quickening influence is continually brought to bear on all that is evolving within the vast Universe which is Nature herself.

Whilst all humanly-written scriptures and myths personalise and overemphasise this Office of Godhead, even so, Theosophy teaches, naught in a Universe is left entirely to chance. The Divine Overlord does *not*, however, either directly lay down laws of human conduct or prescribe punishment for their infringements. An impersonal law of cause and effect[3] does exist and is operative whenever self-conscious beings deliberately perform self-chosen acts. This succession is entirely natural and in no sense ordained by a divine supervisor of a Universe or any of His collaborating Officials.

Then by whose directive, the reader may well ask. Whilst an effective answer is far beyond the range of the understanding, knowledge and adequate literary capacity of the author, a study of the writings of sages and seers—notably *Isis Unveiled, The Secret Doctrine,*[4] the

---

[1] From the root *brih* meaning expansion.
[2] Ch. 7.
[3] *Karma* (Sk.) See Glossary.
[4] *Isis Unveiled* and *The Secret Doctrine*, H.P. Blavatsky.

Hindu *Vedas* and proffered interpretations of the Hebrew *Kabbalah* in its mystical and occult presentations—evokes the following reply: Behind, above and within the *entire* Cosmos or Macrocosm there exists a Principle if not a Being Who timelessly presides over all Creation, and is always referred to with uttermost impersonality as That. In Greek mythology, the nearest approach only to this Principle or Being is the subject of our study in this Chapter and even throughout this book; for, in our interpretation Helios may be regarded as a personification of the First or 'Paternal' Logos, whilst the Sun itself—Apollo perhaps—could possibly represent the human Monad,[1] the Light-Bringer to mortal man.

At this point, as frequently in a study of world scriptures and myths, it is obvious that less educated, early human beings would hardly be able either to respond to, or even be aided by, such wholly abstract and impersonal conceptions concerning deity and deific functions. In consequence, to the existing fabricated, theocratic and even childish fairy-tale imaginings and folk stories—invented, changed and added to as from the beginning they have been—the sages introduced certain philosophic concepts which were reasonably within the range of normal human understanding. These were presented largely in the Language of Allegory and Symbol and referred however parabolically to the relatively impersonal agencies active with and throughout the Universe. Such teachings were made to apply to the nations, countries and landscapes of the recipients own more particular parts of the world. As earlier suggested, the result has been the most extraordinary compilation of the world's scriptural and mythological literature which has come down from ancient peoples and times.

The subject matter of this book is partly the product of the author's own efforts to distinguish between the allegorical, the emblematic and symbolic presiding deities and their agents on the one hand, and their actual existence on the other. Admittedly, these are often so intimately intermingled as to be almost impossible of separation one from the other. This is particularly the case when even a fairy-tale romance or drama may contain within itself vestiges of what may be described as the reality deliberately concealed amidst the unreal.

---

[1] Monad (Gk.) See Glossary.

THE SOLAR DEITY 141

Helios—to return more directly now to the subject of this chapter—was regarded by the Greeks as Ruler of the Day and source of all that the sun was known to bestow upon the planet earth. This included light, life-quickening processes as in plant growth, and all other forms of divinely donated energy attributable to the physical sun. Of course, neither *Surya*[1] nor Helios were driven in four-horse, two-wheeled golden chariots appearing in the East at dawn and journeying across the vault of the sky until their disappearance at sunset in the West; for as every schoolboy knows, it is not the sun but the earth which moves, revolving on its axis, thereby bringing area by area, land by land into the dawn, mid-day and sunset-light of the sun. These, as is well known, are produced with complete impersonality.

The extent of the journey was of course vast, and therefore to earlier peoples, horses, providing the motive power as they did, were necessary in order to make possible travel over such great distances. Naturally, no chariot is required, but protection and even rest might possibly be needed throughout the length of a day, and so a chariot became appropriately conceived.

CHAPTER 6
THE EROS PRINCIPLE

As readers of world mythology are aware, few of the supposedly divine and semi-divine characters ever really existed. On the contrary, they are personifications of generative forces in Nature and their continuing interactions. Eros, for example, represents the natural experiences evoked in the positive or male by the attractive negative or female, or in purely human terms—love. The sages who are believed by some to be responsible for such philosophical revelations could not possibly have presented them to the untrained minds of primitive people in their abstract and metaphysical forms. Since it ever was and still is the mission of the sages to reveal truths to mankind, they have continued to use an allegorical language in which gods, demigods, humans and semi-humans personify powers in both Nature and man and their innumerable inter-relationships.

THE COSMOGONICAL EROS

Eros, the young god of love may be studied from at least three differing but complementary and somewhat similar points of view. The first of these concerns the existence throughout the known Cosmos of the apparently immortal and eternal 'electric twins,' the pairs of opposites in Nature itself. Despite certain remarkable, rare absences or disfunctions, these magnetic pairs, as the omnipresent, perpetually operative powers, male and female, in biological creatures, make possible by their very nature the whole cosmo-generative procedure. Without these, Nature would be perpetually asleep, is so in fact during the periods of rest known as *Pralaya*. Eros himself shares in the repose of his then inactive Father and Mother whose English names are positive and negative. When, however, the parents awaken, so also simultaneously does Eros, the 'egg-born'. Hatched from the World-Egg, he is the first of the gods, none of whom could have been born without him. For Eros personifies the active interaction between spirit and matter which immediately operates when these two, and all other positives and negatives, awaken as the parents of all that comes into existence. Hence, one of his titles, the Egg-born. Then he as Cosmic Love allegorically fires his arrows not only into both of them — positve and negative — but also into the totality of their resultant offspring, *Manvantara*[1] — the active and continually generative Cosmos — itself.

Thus, as the mythographers allegorically revealed, the Trinity of Father, Mother and Love, positive, negative and their interactions, is universal, omnipresent and ever active throughout Cosmic Day, from their awakening at Dawn to their somnolence at Night. Since too abstract for the simple and untrained minds of primitive people, and since it is commanded that the Truth be made ever available, the sages conceived of Aphrodite-Venus, their love-awakening son, Eros-Cupid,[2] Angus or Mac Oc,[3] and his father — whether personified by Ares, Hermes or Zeus. This 'fairytale trinity' conveyed, and at the same time concealed, the immortal truth; for the real Father is, of course, the word[4] by Whom all things were made, and the real Mother is the hitherto Virgin Space[5] or Mare.

Adam and Eve personified the immortal Pair and the authors of the *Book of Genesis* gave the direct hint concerning the source of the erotic activity.[6] They chose the serpent, this being a very direct revelation of, and reference to, the Serpent Fire, irresistible as it proved to be for Adam and Eve, and ever proves to be until it is transmuted.

THE ELECTRO-MAGNETIC EROS

Throughout *Pralaya* all may be thought of as being equi-polar or neither active-positive nor active-negative. In consequence, Cosmos itself was asleep, *Pralaya* reigned and 'Darkness was upon the face of

---

[1] *Manvantara* (Sk.) Period of universal activity. See Glossary.
[2] Cupid — Roman.
[3] Angus or Mac Oc — Celtic
[4] St. *John*, 1:1 See Glossary under *Logos*
[5] *Mulaprakriti* (Sk.) See Glossary.
[6] *Gen.* 1:3-5.

the deep.'[1] Otherwise expressed, perhaps, Adam was then alone. At the appointed time, Eve was created from one of Adam's ribs, meaning to say that she had been present but bone-like or inactive until then.

One of the effects of the deeply mysterious utterances of the Word and the highly emblematic order then given, 'Let there be Light,'[2] is to awaken into activity the universal positives and negatives as a result of whose Eros-like activity, the total procedure of intra-solar attraction and repulsion became initiated. One might perhaps be tempted to say that the long-quiescent Heart of Nature awoke and the Cosmic and *Manvantaric* pulse-beat began. Thus viewed Eros may fittingly be regarded as a personification of this *manvantarically* perpetual attraction and repulsion or interchange within all the electrically-charged substances[3] of which Cosmos consists.

EROS AND NATURE'S CELL-BUILT STRUCTURES

Herein, the more familiar Eros begins to be perceivable. Procreative procedures occur in the plant kingdom of Nature in consequence of mutual attractions between positive and negative, however demi-semi-conscious or sub-conscious the experience nevertheless may be. Here, the processes of Nature — as also of all that has come into existence — undergo evolutionary changes or rather advances. However *unconscious* the responses to each other of oppositely polarised cells may have been in the beginning, the also universal development of increasingly conscious sensitivity and awareness may be assumed to be carrying the plant kingdom of Nature onward towards a future stage when some degree of Eros-like feeling may be experienced.[4]

Otherwise expressed, the Life-Principle unfolding in the plant kingdom may be assumed one day to become increasingly conscious or Eros-like in however remote a degree at first. The range of the targets for the arrows of Eros will however gradually extend both in

---

[1] *Gen.* 1:2.
[2] *Gen.* 1:1
[3] The ever-present electrical energy polarised into the positive and negative currents of terrestrial electricity. In Tibetan, *Fohat*, the Divine Energy.
[4] Later researches in this field support this concept.

depth towards the heart of Nature and in breadth towards the plant kingdom as a whole, His playfulness will then become less apparent and his fulfilments of his duties more purposeful; for, as suggested, he personifies the responses towards each other throughout Nature of oppositely polarised substances and creatures.

THE MIGHTY BOW

As the bow is a means of destruction, save when being used for defence, it might well be regarded, especially by humanitarians, as an evil weapon. Even the love-arousing and desire-awakening arrows shot by Eros, could in the ultimate be regarded as destructive of the calmness, peace of mind and serenity in possession of which *alone* true happiness may be both maintained and attained.

The bow, when in the hands of a hero, physical, intellectual spiritual or all of these, is used by mythographers as a means whereby both strength and skill are tested and demonstrated. Thus, the *Avatar*[1] Ramachandra, proved able not only to string a great bow but also and apparently with ease to break it. In consequence, he won the beautiful and divine princess Sita[2] for his bride, thereby demonstrating his possession of pure Wisdom. Odysseus on his return to Ithaca alone amongst those present was able to bend, and string his own unusually stiff bow and thereafter perform the feat of shooting an arrow through twelve rings, necessary for acceptance by Penelope.[3] Interpreted, this may possibly demonstrate his possession of the qualities symbolised by each of the parts of the weapons then in his hands. Heracles defeated all contestants for the hand of Iole, daughter of King Eurytus. When he arrived at the River Evenus, he gave his wife Deianira to the Centaur Nessus to carry across to the opposite bank. Halfway over, Nessus attempted to violate Deianira. Heracles saw this and at once struck him with an arrow.[4] The Hero also rewarded Poeas, father of Philoctates who lit his funeral pyre for him after all others had refused, by giving him his bow and arrows,[4] allegorically bestowing upon him wisdom and skill in its use. Other ancient writers similarly used archery as a means for the demonstration of superiority.

[1] *Avatar* (Sk.) Divine descent. See Glossary.
[2] *Sita*, daughter of the king of *Mithila*.
[3] cf. *The Greek Myths*, 2, p.37 Robert Graves.
[4] cf. *The Greek Myths*, Robert Graves.

The tradition of the Sakyas[1] for example, compelled their princesses to take as a husband only a true *Kshatriya* who could demonstrate his skill in all the accomplishments of his caste. A tournament was therefore, organised and the Prince Siddhârtha came first in all competitions of riding, fencing and wrestling. Moreover, he was the only one who could string and shoot with the sacred bow of enormous size — supreme Wisdom — bequeathed by his ancestors. Since so often used in mythology, we may here more fully consider some possible interpretations of the bow, the string and the arrow.

The bow when strung and in the hands of a skilled archer may possibly be regarded as a symbol of implicit insight, the essential agent for the accurate firing of the arrow or Atmic Will. The bow itself would in this interpretation symbolise the Higher Self or reincarnating Ego with its capacity for abstract Intelligence and so wise understanding of the unchanging principles upon which both Macrocosm and microcosm are formed, founded and evolved. Thus, the bow — compared with the string — is an enduring article, object or possession, as also is man's Wisdom-illumined higher intellect.

The string, in its turn, whilst essential to the functioning of the bow when 'firing' the arrow, is itself made of far less enduring substance and when in operation must be mobile and capable of being stretched to its limit. Valuable though these attributes are to the skilled archer, they can also be — and frequently are — reasons for inaccuracy. So also the concrete or formal human mind — bow-string like — whether turned towards comprehension of Nature in all her aspects or the attainment of chosen goals, can — especially in the hands of the inexperienced — lead to error and sometimes even to perilous mistakes.

How, then, are these errors to be avoided? How may the human mind become assured always of directing its purposes to the supposed centre of the target? Only one answer would seem to be available, though susceptible of varying applications. This answer is: by means of skill attained by regular practice. Granted, but how is the human archer to discover, to know, both the most desirable target (objective) and the centre or 'bull's eye' thereof?

---

[1] *Sakyas*, a tribe or clan ruled over by the *Gauthama* family into which the Lord Buddha was born.

Since even the most logical of arguments and reasons formulated by the lower mind can still be erroneous in determining important ultimate objectives—and still another facility is needed for these purposes—then may not that additional power consist of the faculty of direct intuitive perception, implicit insight into both fundamental and immediate purposes for the symbolic use of the arrow and the bow? Yes, indeed, I suggest; for the *perfect* archer in this sense is one in whom the intuition is both fully awakened and actively employed, especially in the conception and fulfilment of objectives, particularly the more serious ones. Only a highly developed archer (Prince Siddhârtha) could provide these necessities governing perfect archery, and so only could the most highly evolved archer who was present win the prize offered in Mythological contests.

If this view proves acceptable and is applied to man himself—though also to the Universe, of course—then string, bow, correct choice and perception of target and the arrow may be regarded as symbolising respectively: 1. The String—the formal or concrete mind essential to functioning but liable to imperfection and eventually wearing out and so must be replaced as similarly must the mortal mind at each reincarnation: 2. The Bow —the abstract mind, unrestricted by the demands of time, place and form, unchanging in its perception of truth—*the perfect choice of target*—the intuitive insight into truth itself, whether general or concerning some particular: 3. The Arrow —the swiftly-speeding, correctly directed decisiveness and utterly determined will power by which alone the desirable objective may be attained.

Admittedly other essentials have been omitted from this category of the necessities for success in archery. These include the eye, the hand and the desire to make the effort—also susceptible of application as further emblems of parts of the make-up of man. Eye and hand, as the principal physical agents, surely represent that particular vehicle, the physical body, with its vital principle, *prana*[1] or hand, without which no action is possible. The desire nature, or emotional purport, completes the sevenfold description of man himself.

---

[1] *Prana* (Sk.) Breath of Life or Solar Vital Energy, by which all living things, including man, are vitalised.

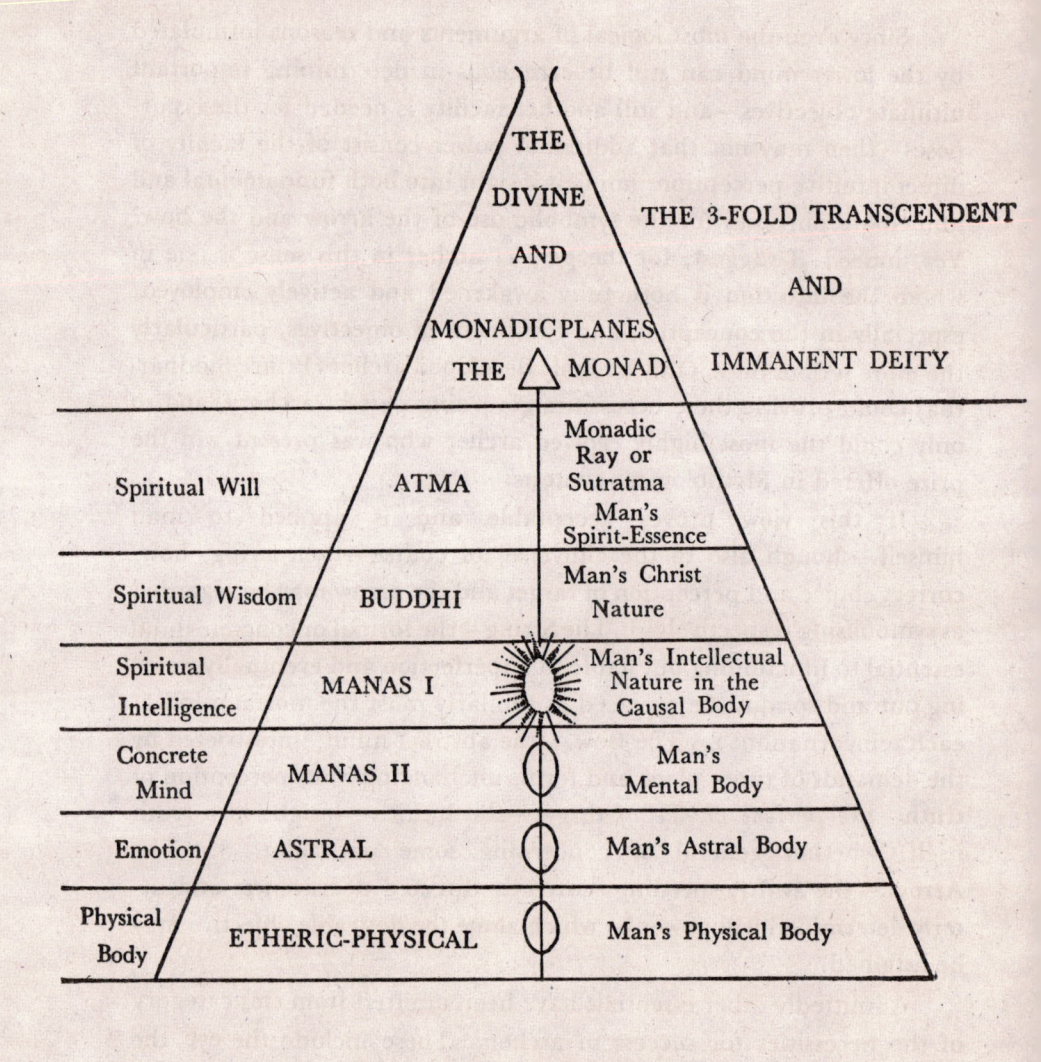

```
                    THE
                  DIVINE
                    AND                THE 3-FOLD TRANSCENDENT
              MONADIC PLANES                      AND
          THE  △  MONAD             IMMANENT DEITY
```

Spiritual Will	ATMA		Monadic Ray or Sutratma Man's Spirit-Essence
Spiritual Wisdom	BUDDHI		Man's Christ Nature
Spiritual Intelligence	MANAS I	☼	Man's Intellectual Nature in the Causal Body
Concrete Mind	MANAS II	◐	Man's Mental Body
Emotion	ASTRAL	◐	Man's Astral Body
Physical Body	ETHERIC-PHYSICAL	◐	Man's Physical Body

Eye.............................. physical body
Hand........................... vitality of etheric double.
Impulse to shoot, or
  Desire nature................ emotional body
String........................... formal mind of mental body
Bow.............................. Abstract intuitive Intelligence
                                of Causal Body
Perception of
  correct target................ Wisdom of *Buddhic* Body.
Arrow........................... Spiritual Will of *Atmic* body.

Archery and its implements may be seen as referring to and thereby revealing knowledge concerning the total constitution of man. Why, then, it may be asked, should the mythographers have placed so vitally important a symbol in the hands of an outwardly seeming, playful, mischievous and sometimes even naughty little boy? To preserve power-bestowing knowledge from profanations and evil applications, the author replies. These could include the directions of will-force to the attainment of personally desired objectives — especially those extremely harmful to others. Indeed, the author has become convinced that this is part of the reason for the age-old construction and use of the mythological system, the supposed 'Veil of Isis'[1].

The elevation of archery to a religious and even priestly function in certain Eastern countries may perhaps here usefully be mentioned and drawn upon as supporting at least a spiritual and esoteric significance to the classic art of archery and each of its component arms. In Japan, for example, archery is thus possibly regarded, is indeed, a highly occult system of self-discipline, demanding as it does *all* the attributes of yoga from posture to accurate and intimate focussing of attention and idealism upon the very centre of targets, symbolising the Universe and its spiritual Centre or Heart. Although, perhaps, not of precise association with interpretations of Eros and particularly his bow and arrows, a brief reference to certain concepts in Zen Buddhism may usefully here be made.

Archery is pursued today not only as a national sport in Japan; for archery in the traditional sense is esteemed not only as an art and honoured as a national heritage but, strange as this may sound at first, also a religious ritual. Consequently, by the 'art' of archery a Japanese does not mean the ability of the sportsman, which can be controlled, more or less by bodily exercises, but an ability whose origin is to be sought in spiritual exercises and whose aim consists in hitting a spiritual goal, so that fundamentally the marksman aims at himself and may even succeed in hitting himself.

The spiritual exercise of archery thus becomes an art, a mystical exercise. Accordingly, archery can not only mean accomplishing anything outwardly with bow and arrow, but inwardly, within oneself.

---

[1] See Introduction.

The aspirant learns to lose himself so effortlessly not only in the preceding breathing but — strange as this may sound — in being breathed.

'The bow is kept drawn until the moment of release while the archer remains completely relaxed in body. The yogi archer learns and achieves not only the relaxed drawing of the bow, himself relaxed, holding at the point of highest tension, loosing of the shot and cushioning of the recoil — all this serving the grand purpose of hitting the spiritual target. The teacher says, 'one must let go of oneself, leaving self and everything behind you so decisively that nothing more is left of you but a purposeless tension.'

'The archer, kneeling to one side and beginning to concentrate, rises to his feet, ceremoniously steps up to the target and, with deep obeisance, offers the bow and arrow like consecrated gifts, then cocks the arrow, raises the bow, draws it and waits in an attitude of supreme spiritual alertness....

'Archery thus becomes a ceremony which exemplifies the "Great Doctrine"'[1].

This Chapter closes with a brief resume of the proffered interpretations of the component parts of the bow and arrow. The arrow — the will; the bow — the abstract intelligence; correct aiming and striking — the formal or concrete intellect; yearning[2] to succeed — *Buddhic* longing to be unified with the Logos; the correct posture to the end of success — mento-physical exactitude; the burning desire to succeed — the astral nature reunified in ardent aspiration for realised identy with the one Supreme existence, the only reunified target.

All these components of every human being (see chart on p.148.) are thus mutually and occultly associated in the lofty art of archery, particularly as a form of yoga when aiming at, and leading to, the realised self-identity by the archer with the Spiritual Heart of the Universe — portrayed by the central point upon the target — the profoundly sacred bull's eye. Effective archery, whether purely physical or also yogically-occult, presents an almost perfect symbolical and allegorical portrayal of the mystical pathway from self-separateness to

---

[1] Extract from *Zen — in the Art of Archery*. Eugen Herrigel. Translated from the German by R.F.C. Hull. Foreword by Dr D.T. Suzuki, pages 14 to 57.

[2] The most spiritual form of love hence, perchance, the association of Eros with human love — as part of the Veil.

the most profound *Samadhi*,[1] and may even be practiced — whether physically, mentally or both — as part of one's *dharma*.[2] As is seen, the art includes all of the seven yogas from correct stance — Hatha Yoga — to highest excellence — Raja Yoga — leading to the mergence of the 'arrow-point' with the very centre of the 'target'. For these reasons, may it not be assumed, the bow — and of course the total instrument — so frequently finds a place in systems of allegorical revelation in general and of personal guidance in particular?

The Greek mythographer, Hesiod,[3] may be usefully and more fully quoted here.

'Eros, fairest of the deathless gods who gives good gifts to men.
'Small are his hands yet his arrows fly far as death
'Tiny his shaft, but it carries heaven high'.

EROS AND HIS BOW

'He whom love touches not walks in darkness.' Plato.

Despite such conflicting titles as 'Fairest of the deathless gods' (Hesiod), and his presentation as a mischievous boy, Eros may, the author suggests, also be regarded as a brilliantly conceived and accurate, if fabulous, personification of one of the most mysterious, deeply secret and loftiest attributes of sentient Nature. Indeed, he is thus very effectively presented and portrayed by the authors of Greek and Roman Mythology; for the highest and holiest passion of which a human being is capable consists of utterly pure (meaning selfless) devotional love for a beloved human being, for Deity Itself or for an *Avataric* visitation. The latter is perhaps best portrayed in the life-story of the Lord Shri Krishna, particularly in his allegorical relationship with his numerous 'devotees' *(Gopis)*[4] and with His beloved Radha and in the dedicated maternity fulfilled in the face of almost assured death by His mother, Devaki. This applies equally, of course, to the

---

[1] *Samadhi* (Sk.) Realised oneness with God.
[2] *Dharma* (Sk.) Doctrine and its dutiful expression in life.
[3] Hesiod. *Theogony.*
[4] *Gopis* (Sk.) 'Cowherdesses'

selfless devotees of other World Faiths, including the worshippers of the Lord Jesus Christ and His revered Mother, the Blessed Lady Mary.

Studied from various sources, Eros himself may severally be interpreted as an example of a beautiful winged youth whom some called Love, against whose arrows there is no defence; as a true and faithful lover of one human being, of all mankind even; and as a devotee or *Bhakta*[1] moved by divinely passionate dedication towards the Supreme Deity, the Universal Godhead, the spiritual Source of all that exists, personified in world scriptures. As this self-consecration becomes less and less directed to a personal deity, however, the spiritually-awakened devotee turns his or her burning love towards the totally impersonal Principle which is conceived as the single source of all that ever has been, is, and ever will be.

The author is fully aware that the mischievous boy, son of Aphrodite, who eagerly arouses the experience of sensual love in human beings by childishly piercing their bodies with one of his love-evoking arrows, would indeed seem to be very far from such a spiritually awakening influence. The purely mythical concept, the popular Cupid, may, however, permissibly be regarded as a means of directing attention towards the mystical Eros, deliberately concealed behind a chosen emblem or veil. Thus viewed, the author submits, the allegory becomes a revelation of the interior awakening by the God *within* a human being of Love — not emotionally for another person but, for the One Universal Interior Godhead. If this approach be accepted, then by means of the skillfully conceived allegory of a youthful, external god evoking personal love, a 'communication' — a call indeed — between the divine Inner Self and the human outer self of man, is portrayed, if a brief digression be here permitted.

Human beings are not alone in this responsiveness to subtle agencies. The plant kingdom of Nature, it has been found is susceptible to the 'arrows' of Eros. The eminent Indian physiologist, Sir Jagadish Chunder Bose, founder of the Bose Institute in Calcutta, demonstrated that plants have a perfectly good nervous system and a mechanism like a heart for pumping sap. With a galvanometer — as the author was privileged to observe — Bose discovered that plants go

---

[1] *Bhakta* (Sk.) Devotee, male or female.
[2] *Gopis* (Sk.) Shepherdesses.

through a death spasm similar to the death throes of animals. At the moment of death, intense excitation is produced in a plant together with a powerful discharge of electricity, the spasm itself being caused by contractions of the dying cells.

Luther Burbank, the New England geneticist and experimenter with plants who gave his name to Burbank, California, is reported to have said: "The secret of improved plant breeding, apart from scientific knowledge, is love. I now see humanity as one vast plant, needing for its highest fulfilment only love, the natural blessings of the great outdoors, and intelligent crossing and selection." This approach receives some support from Hesiod's *Theogony* in which the role of Eros, 'fairest of the deathless gods', was to coordinate the elements which constitute the Universe, to bring harmony and to permit life to develop.

The evolving life-principle in all Nature, including the mineral, the plant, the animal and the human kingdoms, may permissibly be regarded as responsive to the influence of human appreciation and a suitable form of affection. One result may well be an increase, a stimulation and so a quickening of the evolutionary processes occurring within the life evolving through the particular kingdom concerned. If this be so, as the author has become convinced as a result of research in other fields[1] then the love-evoking child, Eros, may be a personification of what might be termed the Eros Principle at work throughout all Nature.

Why, then, the concealment in such childish allegories? Because the average human mind is not normally aware of, (a) the presence of an Indwelling Life, (b) the evolutionary process in nature and (c) the operation of a quickening procedure therein. Thus informed, if taught in direct terms, the occultly uninstructed would be unable to understand the three orderly processes and would only be confused by and harmfully, even dangerously misapply the knowledge. More advanced minds are however, able to comprehend and be enlightened by the knowledge and in certain ways collaborate in the activity of increasing human knowledge and hastening human evolution, also avoiding conduct by which these could be delayed—selfishness, destructiveness and cruelty, for example.

---

[1] The Angelic Myth. See *The Kingdom of the Gods*, The Theosophical Publishing House, Adyar, Madras, India.

154   THE EROS PRINCIPLE

Spiritual unfoldment, including the acquirement of Wisdom, would seem also to be designated however allegorically by the action of Eros after the arrival of the Golden Fleece and its leader, Jason; for when Princess Medea first saw Jason — the leader of the Argonauts — on their arrival at Colchis, Eros shot an arrow deep into her heart. This awakened her great love for Jason whom she told how to use a special charm — her private ointment — thereby enabling him to overcome the terrible serpent which was guarding the Golden Fleece, or perhaps, to overcome psychological and mental conditions that hitherto had prevented the acquirement of Wisdom. Medea also kept her promise,

EROS WITH BOW

herself to charm the serpent to sleep, whereupon Jason swiftly lifted the Golden Fleece from the tree, hurried down to the ship within which the Argonauts immediately put out to sea, their Goal attained.[1]

Admittedly, thus viewed, Eros has little resemblance to the traditional winged child, the youngest of the gods whose caprices caused both happiness and suffering among men and gods. The latter may nevertheless, also be regarded as a deliberately concealed reference, a revelation indeed, of the awakening within responsive human beings—the conception and gradual development—of awareness of the divine Reality and an increasingly ardent aspiration to be forever at one therewith.

Plato, in his turn, wrote: 'Love-Eros makes his home in men's hearts, but not in every heart, for where there is hardness he departs. His greatest glory is that he cannot do wrong nor allow it; force never comes near him. For all men serve him of their own free will. And he whom Love touches not walks in darkness.' To this, with some presumption, might be added: 'He whom love touches becomes elevated beyond the limitations of the intellect and thereafter attains intuitive Wisdom—the Golden Fleece.'

ESOTERIC HINDUISM AND SYMBOLISM

The Archer in the Sacred Language is ever a symbol for the Logos in creative and procreative aspects. The bow, the string and the arrow constitute the trinity of creative forces: positive—the bow: negative—the arrow: the string—the force-conveying neutral element or factor. The arrow itself reproduces the whole symbolism since, by its construction, it is threefold, consisting of point, shaft and feathered end with nick to engage the string. Thus, the arrow resting on the string represents the inherent creative life-force of universal spirit-matter—the bow and the string respectively.

The act of stringing symbolises the establishment of the state of tension by the action of the one upon the other which is set up in hitherto quiescent, non-polarised, 'sleeping', primordial substance. The result of this 'Awakening' is a *Manvantara*, or a period of creative involutionary and evolutionary activity.

---

[1] See Ch.4

The act of shooting by the Divine Archer, primordial macrocosmic Logos, and the flashing forth of the arrow, represent partly the involutionary phase, partly the descent of the creative fire into the organic kingdoms of Nature, and partly the descent of the Monadic will into the highly evolved Ego-personality of an Initiate, both direct and at the hands of a Hierophant of the Greater Mysteries; for the Logic pro-creative, the Monadic spiritually creative or awakening, and the Hierophantic initiatory power are *one and the same*, though differently employed according to the evolutionary level of the Monad-Ego or Heavenly Archer in the microcosmic or human sense.

The first Logos 'born' as Universal Light from the parental pair primordial spirit-matter, is itself a triplicity as symbolised by the threefold arrow. Outwardly, objectively active, 'this 'mind'-born power enters, or flashes forth into, the awakened substance of the Universe-to-be in its third or creative aspect. The result is conception within, and pregnancy of, the now-spiritually impregnated 'Virgin Mother' or Sea of Space.

In occult terminology the Bow is *Purusha*, the String is *Prakriti* and the Arrow is *Fohat*. The Archer is the Universal Creative Intelligence—*Mahat*, and "His" Target is the differentiated area in *Prakriti* wherein 'He' will produce creatively the local Universe-to-be. The point of impact or creative penetration becomes the first creative Centre, the physical sun-to-be.

The whole symbology is strikingly cruciform, whether the arrow rests upon the bow, the shaft at right-angles to the string, or whether, penetrating the target after the shot. All phallic symbology is based upon the impact of the *Fohatic* Arrow—the vertical creative fire of Spirit upon the substance to be impregnated, whether universal space or 'ovum.' Significant is the fact that the spermatazoon is arrow-shaped. Thus, the *Fohatic* Hagar, Abraham, Ishmael becoming an Archer, is an allegory of the successful sublimation of the Creative force in Initiated man.

In Sagittarius the mind is both penetrative and accurate, hitting the mental mark. Sagittarians, when illumined, and even on ordinary occasions, perceive the essential verity, or to change the metaphor, 'hit the nail on the head.' They represent the Third Logos, as does the Archer, and their arrows, the flashing fire of the perceptive intellect, which both sees and fructifies, or enfires areas or regions which can be made intellectually fruitful. Inventiveness describes this aspect of human nature and of divine activity.

Herein is portrayed the Fohatic, creative fire, with the Arrow as the Monadic Atma, which descends creatively into the Universe of form and into the higher and lower nature of man, awakening and stimulating them both to creative and procreative activity respectively. The broken bow symbolizes both the victory over sensuality and desire, and the sublimation of the creative life-force from the levels of vehicles and form to their spiritual and universal expression.

CHAPTER 7

THE HEPHAESTUS PRINCIPLE

Hephaestus, the armourer and blacksmith of the gods and heroes is susceptible of interpretation as representing a particular Hierarchy of the Devas and their dual contributions to the 'shaping' of matter (the metals) in response to the divine impulse and quickening the evolution of the indwelling life. Hephaestus' lameness may be regarded as symbolising the effects upon him of the resistance of matter to his fulfilment of the divine order and to his own influence, thereby 'laming' him. His casting out from Olympus and 'fall' to earth represent the task of the Devic Hierarchy, notably the *Gandharvas*,[1] to convey the WORD from its spiritual Source, Olympus, throughout the lower material or form-built kingdoms of Nature. As the human blacksmith uses physical implements, so also do the Devas use the superphysical 'instruments' of sound and thought in their angelic 'forges' These aids assist them in their above-mentioned dual function of awakening responsiveness in the matter of the sub-Olympian Universe or space and quickening the evolution of the interior Life-Principle. Devas[2] are thus active as collaborators with the One Will in moulding substance according to the Divine idea and in stimulating the unfoldment of consciousness. Hephaestus mythically represents them as the divine 'blacksmith', the artisan-god, the *Demiurge*[3], *who created admirable works and taught men the mechanical arts.*

Since no forge can work without the essential element of fire, so from remotest times Hephaestus was also the personification of both terrestrial fire, of which volcanoes were the most terrifying manifestations, and also of the spiritual fiery force. As this element itself is of celestial origin, it is understandable that in the Greek mind

---

[1] *Gandharvas* (Sk.) The celestial Choristers. An Order of the *Devic* hosts.
[2] *Devas* (Sk.) Shining ones. The Angelic Hosts.
[3] *Demiurge* (Gk.) Artificer. The Supernal Power which built the Universe.

Hephaestus was a divine being, a god indeed. The fire which he represents is not, however, the destructive element, but rather the forge-like, beneficent one which permits mankind to work metals and so to foster civilisation. Thus, Hephaestus is mythically presented as both fire itself and the divine blacksmith, the artisan-god, the *Demiurge* who created admirable works and taught men mechanical arts.

The origin and history of Hephaestus may, perhaps, here usefully be considered. On many other occasions, Hephaestus assisted human evolutionary procedure; for example, as a skilled craftsman he was chosen allegorically to cut open the skull of Zeus in order that the goddess Athena might spring forth fully-formed and fully-armed; for only when the argumentative brain-mind (the skull) is inactive or stilled may the faculty of implicit insight or intuitive Wisdom (Athena) spring forth or be born in complete maturity.

Nothing was impossible to Hephaestus; for when Zeus, in order to punish mankind, decided to create the first woman, Pandora, it was to Hephaestus that he turned. He ordered him to mould the body of a woman with water and clay, to give it life and a human voice, and to form from it a virgin of ravishing beauty. To perfect his dual activity, to shape forms and quicken the life within them, Hephaestus encircled Pandora's brow with a golden crown which he himself had engraved—a direct reference, surely, to the 'opened' crown *chakram*[1] of an occultly awakened and developed human Initiate. The Lesser and the Greater Mysteries and their modern survivals are examples of the procedure of quickening the evolution of humanity, carried out by the combined ministrations of the sages—the Adepts of ancient days—and their Angelic cooperators. The god of fire, divine Master of Metals and of the art of their transformation into objects of beauty, may reasonably be interpreted—as is suggested in the opening paragraphs of this chapter—to be an Order of the Angelic Hosts and its special evolution-quickening functions.

This same procedure would seem to be—may legitimately be regarded as being referred to be—the 'very deceptive' glyph of Eros. All these stories of old, the author increasingly believes, have the same meaning

---

[1] *Chakram* (Sk.) A spinning, funnel-shaped force-centre.

the same message. These are, that a continuous procedure is in action upon this planet, consisting of the exertion by a very lofty Being, presumably the Solar Logos, and its Representatives, Superhuman and Initiate, Archangels and Angels, of evolution-quickening powers and influences. As a result, a spiritually-awakening power is projected into the consciousness and even matter of the bodies of sub-human and human beings. The effect of this ministration is the production of an awareness of the existence and presence of the Divine and yearning to be united therewith. One presumes that the intention is to arouse in the consciousness of all that exists, especially the responsive human minds and brains of people who are either approaching or are on the verge of the awakening of the capacity to respond with increasing self-consciousness, deepening devotion or highly spiritualised Love.

Thus, one may presume, the author suggests, that all direct accounts, allegories and myths of intimate inter-relationships between the Divine and the human are descriptive of and refer to the operation of this Universal, spiritually-awakening procedure. The author is fully aware that this concept of nature spirits as fulfilling a purpose on behalf of Nature herself—however unconciously—may reduce the almost world-wide view of all creatures which come under the heading of fairies, much of their appeal, glamour indeed, thereby taking away a large measure of their fascination, especially from children and those adults who may thus still cherish certain of their childhood memories.

The scientist of today has, however, been drawn to the same or very similar conclusion that an Intelligence is at work in every department, aspect and component of Nature. Hence the phrase: 'The Universe which thinks.' If this proves to be true, as the Ageless Wisdom has always taught, then not only the physically visible, intangible and measureable phenomena of Nature will be found to operate under the impulse of an inherent Intelligence, but the denizens of the etheric and superphysical levels of density of matter will in consequence themselves be subject to the same directive thought.

Occult scientists, without making the slightest claim to evolutionary seniority have already made this discovery: for them, not only the physical Universe, but its etheric counterpart and superphysical existences are in their turn all moved by Divine Thought. The application of this idea, then, to the apparently naive nature spirits is by no means a denial of the conceived idea of the existence and function of a directive Thought throughout Nature, but rather its fulfilment or at least acceptance as far as the members of the as yet undiscovered kingdoms of Nature are concerned.

May we now even more fully consider this most interesting Grecian Myth? Hephaestus, armourer and blacksmith of the gods and heroes represents, I have suggested, members of the *Devic* Hierarchy and their contributions to the process of quickening the evolution of the Life-Principle, particularly in metals and minerals, on the one hand and the shaping of matter in general in response to the Divine impulse on the other. His casting out from Olympus and "fall" to earth represents the physically effective activity of the Angelic Hosts, notably the *Gandharvas*, using sound as the implements in their forge wherewith to assist in the awakening of sensitivity in matter, forms and beings of the sub-Olympian worlds (the physical Universe or space). Such quickening of evolution is brought about by the increasing reaction to the Creative word of the inherent Life incarnate in all the Kingdoms of Nature, the Hephaestus Order of Devas being at work in each of them as collaborators with the One divine Will (Zeus). Thus, his expulsion from Olympus and fall to earth were in reality allegories descriptive of the more particular field of activity in which He and his Order (fellow 'blacksmiths') were ordained to serve—namely the shaping of the substances of the physical world and quickening the Life-Principle within them. So, also, perchance, were the 'expulsions' of Prometheus to the Caucasus and of Adam and Eve from the Garden of Eden, the last named being carried out by no less an appropriate Being than the Archangel Michael himself!

Why, it may not unnaturally here be asked, should this important and mind-illuminating truth be concealed under the veil of allegory and symbol? Because, the author ventures to answer, the sages will have wished both to reveal to the trustworthy and conceal from their opposites a veritably power-bestowing truth; for like all knowledge that can be harmfully misused, the full realisation of the significance of the Hephaestus Principle when in the possession of those ready to misuse knowledge for personal gain—and even at means of injury to others—must be guarded against. Hence, the Language of Allegory and Symbol.

We now return to the life-study of the subject of our study, Hephaestus himself. In retaliation for Zeus having brought forth

Athena from his own head and being ashamed of the ugliness of Hephaestus—her own parthenogenetic son. Hera the consort of Zeus, endeavoured to hide him from the Immortals—because he was lame. To achieve her purpose she threw him from the heights of Olympus down into the sea, where he was taken care of by the sea goddesses, Thetis and Eurynome. For nine years he remained concealed in their deep grotto, forging a thousand ingenious objects for the two nymphs. He excelled in the art of working metals and whilst on Olympus he built palaces for the gods and constructed for himself a sparkling dwelling of glittering and incorruptible bronze. This may possibly be interpreted as a reference to the function of the Hephaestus—Order of *Devas* in relation to the mineral kingdom of Nature and the Life-Principle evolving within it.

In this shining abode where he had his workshop he could be seen beside the flaming furnaces, bathed in sweat, bustling about his bellows, poking the fires under twenty crucibles at a time or hammering out the red-hot metal on an enormous anvil. Although Homer cites the workshop of Hephaestus on Olympus, the fire-god also haunted the earth—where he maintained various underground places of residence.

Hephaestus had never forgotten the welcome given him on the occasion of his fall from Olympus and, in gratitude, settled in a volcanic island. His presence there was attested by the flaming vapours which escaped from the Mount, to the accompanying sound of dull rumbling, supposedly produced by the divine blacksmith's hammers in the workshop he had set up in the bowels of the mountain wherein the giant Cyclopes assisted him.

The activity of Hephaestus was evidently prodigious and only equalled by his remarkable skill. He was ceaselessly employed on some work of great delicacy; for as well as the palaces on Olympus with their bronze trimmings, he fashioned Zeus' golden throne, sceptre and thunderbolts, the fearful aegis (shield), the winged chariot of Helios, the arrows of Apollo and Artemis, Demeter's sickle, Hercules' cuirass, the arms of Peleus, the armour of Achilles, the necklace which Harmonia, wife of Cadmus, wore for her nuptials, Ariadne's diadem, Agamemnon's sceptre and the invisible net in which he entrapped Ares and Aphrodite.

The 'skill' of Hephaestus, amounting to genius as it is allegorically said to have done, also suggests to the students of ancient myths and

CREATIVE FORCE 163

the wisdom they both conceal and reveal, may tend again to confirm their conviction that Hephaestus and his assistants personify the particular Order of *Devas* whose task it is to render matter ever increasingly responsive to the Divine Idea and the stimulation of the evolutionary pace of its indwelling Life. As far as the author's observations and interpretations of them have carried him, he concludes that on behalf of our planet earth and of everything and every creature upon it, there is occurring—even being pressed—a continual procedure designed to produce an evolutionary quickening.

According to the age-old teachings of Theosophia, this stimulating process is carried out upon the physical globes of each Round during these *Manvantaric* periods, wherein one such physical planet exists. Evolutionary quickening may possibly be accentuated at this time, because it presents the greatest degrees of density of substance upon which the seven planets of a Chain and Round are manifested.

On the sevenfold Pathway of Forthgoing and Return which is followed by the manifesting, evolving, incarnate Life Principles, the fourth cycle must always be the densest, therefore most spiritually unresponsive, the first and the seventh being the most refined, as indicated in the accompanying diagram.

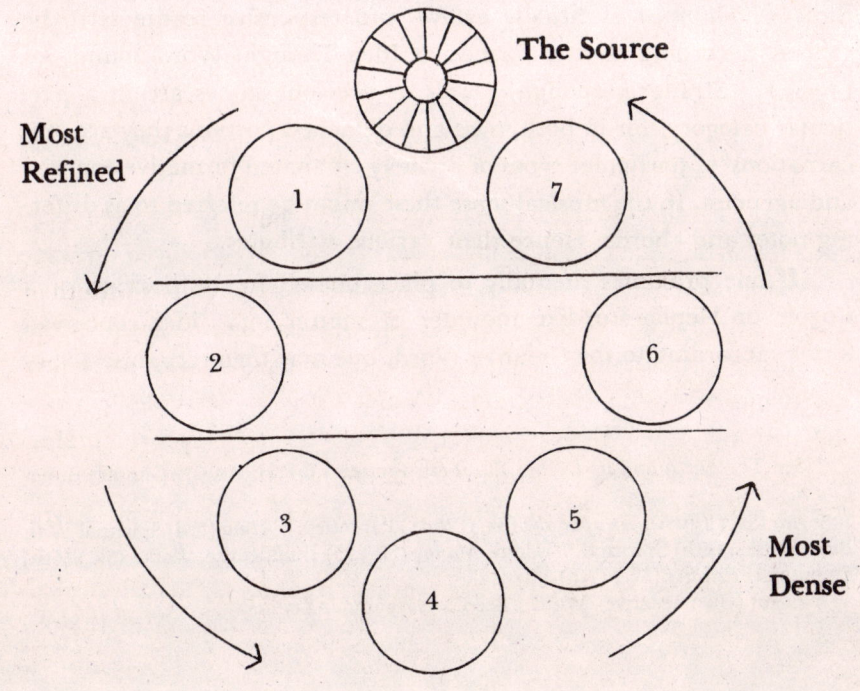

Just as spiritualising forces and influences are continually brought to bear upon all living creatures, from the interior levels of Universes, suns and planets, so also the substance itself of which these are constructed, perpetually undergoes a stimulating, rigidity-softening process by means of **Hephaestus** or **St. Michael**-like appropriate powers and their harmoniously associated Orders of *Devic* collaborators — projected into the atoms of which it is composed. This procedure has been, is still being, and will continue to be applied to physical matter throughout the whole of the present Fourth Chain.[1] In consequence, the substance of Universes and their contents — very particularly physical matter — receives perpetually into itself what might variously be described as softening, inertia-reducing or resistibility-reducing forces. These are directed from the heart of the Universe outwards through the seven planes[2] of Nature, and enter especially the matter of the four elements of earth, water, air and fire. The chief — and of necessity most needing — planet is, of course, the physical earth on behalf of which the objective is to bestow upon its substance the quality of malleability.

Philosophically, the rigidity of matter might be regarded as the great 'enemy' of Spirit. In no area, one assumes, is this more factual and apparent than in the densest mineral substances, particularly those which *must* eventually evolve into responsive readiness to be shaped according to the formative Idea-Thought-Word-Sound, or Logos.[3] Strangely enough, jewels or precious stones are in a particular category; for in both mass and detached portions they are 'incarnations' of particular types of divinely emanated formative energies and agencies. In the musical sense these might be referred to as differing notes and chords. Hence their various attributes.

If one presumes mentally to place oneself in the position of a Logoic or Hephaestus-like moulder of matter into 'idea-conceived forms' according to the Creative Word, one may then recognise a very

---

[1] See *The Earth and its Cycles*, Elizabeth Preston. T.P.H. Adyar. Glossary under *Chain*.

[2] *Adi* (Sk.) (First), *Anupadaka* (Sk.) (2nd) 'Parentless', *Atma* (3rd) Spiritual Will, *Buddhi* (Sk.) (4th) Spiritual Wisdom, *Manas* (Sk.) (5) Intelligence, *Kama* (Sk.) (6th) Emotional, *Prithivi* (Sk.) (7th) Physical.

[3] *Logos* (Gk.) Creative Word. See Glossary under *Logos*.

CREATIVE FORCE 165

great resistibility or *tamasic*[1] (inert) attribute of *all* metals, especially those which have not been named by man as precious. Lead, for example, is heavily resistant to Logoic thought, as also in varying degree are all the metallic and semi-metallic substances. Metals in the widest meaning of that word are also to be occultly regarded as perpetual recipients of Logoic malleability-producing forces directed into them by certain associated and appropriate Intelligences from nature spirits to *Devarajas*.[2]

Compared to time-ruled physical Nature, the Be-ness or ultimate actuality of the Logos is presumed to be time-less and time-free. Nevertheless, the processes of the conceiving and physically producing of Universes with their evolutionary changes and developments, *must* be regarded — surely are — as occurring within the limits of time, however *aeonic*. This, one assumes, is especially true from that 'moment' when the Logos begins to be incarnate at physical levels and so in the densest substances. Vast periods of time are indeed involved in the procedure of bringing matter to the state and form in which it becomes fully responsive to, and productive of, the Divine Idea and Word — Logos.

As far as the author's observations and interpretations have carried him, he concludes that on behalf of the planet earth and of everything and every creature upon it, as earlier suggested there is occurring — even being pressed — a continual procedure designed to produce an evolutionary quickening. This stimulating process is, the author therefore presumes, carried out upon the physical globes of each Round during these *Manvantaric* periods, wherein one such physical planet exists. Evolutionary quickening may possibly be accentuated at this time, since it presents the greatest degrees of density of substance upon which the seven planets of a chain and Round are manifested.

To assist in this process of rendering matter increasingly responsive to the Word, a particular divine power was established within the Hierarchies of Creative Intelligences in order to enable them to reduce the rigidity, and so increase the malleability of substances composing the element of earth. One Order of these Beings 'absorbed' this

---

[1] *Tamas* (Sk.) inertia — one of the three attributes or *gunas* of matter, the other two being *rajas* (activity) *sattva* (rhythm).
[2] *Devarajas* (Sk.) Archangels or kingly Devas.

divine intention. In consequence, members of this Order became ceaselessly occupied in the particular department of Nature concerned with the formation and evolution of Life-ensouled matter as an increasingly responsive and accurate embodiment of the Divine Idea. One division (only) of this Order has been named Landscape[1] Angels, referring particularly to those concerned with mountain-masses, their peaks, their ranges and the vegetation growing upon them.

If the process of the objective production of Universes and all their contents be regarded as a work of art — for such indeed it truly is — then musical, for example, instruments must be conceived, constructed, attuned, rendered increasingly sensitive and wider in range. These must continually be harmoniously combined in order that either individual or group performers may correctly play the heavenly symphony according to the Logoic 'Score'. The Angelic collectors of the materials of which such symphonies are made, their treatment, shaping and building into ever more suitable forms, somewhat corresponds — in terms of music — to the process of the composition and objective presentation of a Universe by the Divine Composer.

In Indian thinking, the order of Angels (Devas) conforming to these combined procedures is named Gandharvas, although these Beings are not restricted to the reproduction of sound alone; for *they*, particularly the younger members of their Hierarchies, are concerned with the process already described of reducing the inertia of matter itself. Indeed, the Universe in all its beauty is also describable — and very appropriately — in terms of each of the seven branches of the arts and not of music alone.

Such metaphysical expositions of the Macrocosmic and microcosmic procedures of the emanation, preservation and transformation of Cosmoi would, needless to say, be far beyond the comprehension of the average citizen and especially of the relatively illiterate and uninstructed inhabitants and members of early civilisations. In consequence, in obedience to the law under which certain knowledge must not only be witheld from unprepared humanity but, also contradictory though this may seem, those rightly prepared to receive it, the Ancient Wisdom was given in simplified and even purely

---

[1] Landscape Angels. See my Book, *The Kingdom of the Gods*, pp.58-59.

captivating and familiar fairy-tale forms which would nevertheless be understandable to sufficiently evolved recipients.

Yes, indeed, a very strange law both exists and is dominant concerning the relationship between the possessors of power-bestowing knowledge and those as yet uninformed. One might state that law in such terms as: *Mankind has the inalienable right to be informed. Truth must be taught and knowledge must be made available.*

Since information concerning subtler superphysical matter and the superphysical realms of Nature would not be comprehensible to those below the rank of Candidates for, and Initiates of, the Ancient Mysteries, world mythologies were therefore brought into existence by the sages or Adepts of those earlier days. Current folktales and myths were occasionally modified or received additional and more fascinating accounts of activities, adventures, heroism and even of domestic life. Thus, through the ages, the esoteric mythologies of Asia, Egypt, Crete, Greece, Rome and Celtic and Norse nations gradually arose and developed into their various traditional forms.

The task of clearly presenting these ideas in understandable ways has proved very difficult for the author, and may even be difficult to follow for some readers. The question therefore arises as to how it could be expected that earlier peoples would have responded to a purely literal statement of occult truths. Is this not still more pertinent when, moved by responsiveness, the sages of old endeavoured to present these occult and mystical concepts for the instruction of the humanity of their time? Seeking an answer is it not possible that existing and developing fairy tales were used as *media* into which in romantic legendary, and allegorical forms, these profound teachings could be interwoven, perceived and grasped by those individual sufficiently evolved to receive, comprehend and safely and usefully apply them?

How, then, was such a clearly esoteric doctrine as the Hephaestus Principle or a specialised and highly organised procedure of the rendering of the more inert substances increasingly responsive to the Divine Idea, to be even at least referred to in Greek Mythology? How did the sages of Ancient Greece introduce in mythological terms, knowledge of the existence and activity of a Hierarchy of Superhuman Beings and Their collaborators—certain Orders of the Angelic Hosts—to decrease the inertia of matter and so to increase its responsiveness to Divine Thought? One possible answer is, the author submits, by causing to arise in the minds of the original formulators of the fairy stories, the ideas of such an allegorical person as the lame god Hephaestus with his assistants who, at the command of the gods, shaped various metals into pre-designed forms including living beings (Pandora) and the armour of heroes and gods, and by himself made possible the 'birth' of Athena from the head of Zeus.

The concept of the gradually developing myths and especially that of Hephaestus, was brought strongly — with illumination indeed — to the author's mind as he investigated the appearance, nature and functions of certain Landscape Angels at the entrance of Whangarei Harbour, and at the active volcano, Mt Ngauruhti in the North Island of New Zealand.

At this point, the author offers in advance interpretations suggested later in this book of the person and activities of the god Hephaestus which deal with the functions of certain Orders of Beings (the Members of the Angelic Hosts) of whom I presume Hephaestus to be a representative. The first of two Principles concerning the existence of Universes and their components, is the unfoldment, development or growth of the inherent Life and Consciousness incarnate within them. The second is that this procedure is continuously aided by participants in this great Plan. Amongst these are members of the **Angelic Hosts who, by the injection of a fiery power and a consciousness-**quickening force, are perpetually active throughout the Universe. Those who are functioning throughout Nature herself, I have elsewhere named Landscape Angels, whilst other Orders similarly 'serve' in the realms of the sub-human and human kingdoms, including plants, animals (in the larger meaning of the term) and mankind.

In the following pages, I offer interpretations of the god Hephaestus and his functions as personifying the Intelligences who thus serve throughout Nature. Even whilst recognising parts of the story to be products of imaginative folklore, nevertheless, when interpreted in terms of the Sacred Language of Allegory and Symbol, the experiences and activities of the god Hephaestus would appear to support the preceding attribution to him of certain deeply occult associations. Thus, as previously suggested, within the admittedly fairy-tale-like and apparent folk-lore imaginings concerning the god

Hephaestus, there are to be found circumstances, actions, places and states of being that, the author submits, may very possibly have been inspired by the sages. If this be true, then the people themselves gradually built up the myths and the sages organised them into Wisdom-concealing and knowledge-bestowing allegories.

Indeed, this procedure of both concealing and revealing truth is said to have been one of the functions of the Greater Mysteries of which the sages themselves were high Initiates. In consequence, they were deeply informed concerning the nature and evolution of both Universe and man and especially with knowledge of their intimate inter-relationships. These enlightened ones may well have found in the developing myths, opportunities for placing before humanity in allegorical forms, truths of potentially great value to those who in their turn seek to find and tread the Pathway to *Theosophia,* as Ammonius Saccas[1] of Alexandria named the accumulated Wisdom of the ages.

Despite apparently contrary statements, the Hephaestus story could thus be found useable for the presentation of the existence of a perpetually-radiated, evolution-quickening, stimulating energy and the Order of Archangels to whom was, and is, apportioned the task of its application to every aspect of Nature. As suggested, this refers especially to the mineral kingdom of Nature in which at his forge—source of the Creative Fire—Hephaestus chiefly laboured. From the dawn of the period in the history of the planet earth at which its substance became solidified, towards and up to its present material condition, this evolution-quickening and inertia-reducing function has been continually carried out with maximum efficiency by the appropriate Order of Archangels and Angels. It is assumed, furthermore, that this will continue until the dual task is no longer needed, its animating, quickening purposes having been fulfilled according to the Divine Plan.

To sum up and re-state the principle ideas: By the pouring of the *Kundalini Shakti* into the sleeping life of minerals, this life is rendered more responsive to the general outpouring and inpouring of evolution-quickening power which landscape Angels and, when sufficiently evolved, the fairies throughout the world pour into its mineral and plant life. The inpouring energy is, as it were, also impressed or infiltrated

---

[1] Founder of the Neo-Platonic School in Alexandria between 2nd and 3rd centuries.

into and made to vibrate at the frequencies of the Divine Thought or the molecular combinations and the ultimate forms and shapes not only in the mineral, but also in the plant kingdom as well. The nature spirits of the four elements — gnomes, fairies, undines, sylphs — are far from being the supposed mere decorative and playful forms, but also unconsciously and instinctively play their part throughout time immemorial as agents of the One Source, the Solar Logos, Our Lord the Sun.

Thus, the outpoured and inpoured forces which the Nature-Devas more especially 'inject' into the planet's mineral and plant kingdoms, perform dual functions. One of these is to quicken the evolution of the indwelling Life, thereby also rendering it more responsive to Divine formative Thought. This causes that Life to be permeated by the Divine Thought and so to produce an effect instinctually to cause material substance to become more and more readily responsive to and so produce the world's or planet's myriad forms according to the Word. The second function was and still is to direct immensely powerful fiery *Kundalini* force into both the indwelling Life and the form, rendering both of them increasingly sensitive to Divine Thought, just as by heating and so softening iron, it is rendered more impressionable to the shaping process performed on the anvil by the hammers, according to the design in the blacksmith's mind. These two injected forces produce a continuous quickening of the evolutionary processes occurring within the Life incarnate in all mineral, plant, aerial and fluid substances; water, oil and sap, for example. Such, as far as the author's attempted researches have shown him, is a part — at any rate — of the process of the Devic quickening and rendering of the indwelling Life in all Nature more responsive than would be normal to the Divine Will-Thought (Zeus), the indwelling Life in all Nature.

The fact that Hephaestus brought about the birth of the personification of Wisdom (Athena) by opening the mind-brain of Zeus, her father, further supports the concept of Hephaestus as representing an activity of individualised members of the Deva Kingdom in Nature; for their work is to quicken[1] the evolution of consciousness, thereby bringing to birth in evolved humanity (Zeus) the fully-formed (armed), active spiritual Wisdom personified by Athena. Thus

---

[1] Quicken — not necessarily hasten.

interpreted, Hephaestus is found to be rightly presented as the "surgical" agent for the springing forth of Athena.

Homer and other responsible authors generated the quite fascinating fairy tale of the existence and experiences of Hephaestus. In the main, fairy-tale it is, and, with certain exceptions, may be so regarded—an enchanting and even humorous story, though tragic at times. However, certain references may cause one to consider that the authors were in certain matters inspired by one or other of the sages.

The mastery by Hephaestus over metals is shown by his ability not only to forge armour and other metallic objects, but also living beings such as his handmaidens and Pandora, 'the gift of all', with her box which she so tragically opened. These achievements may possibly be interpreted as referring to the fundamental processes of the evolution of the indwelling spiritual life up from mineral, through plant and animal and into humanity. In addition, people were formed by him out of the most precious metal—gold. The fact also that he was the offspring of Zeus and Hera, or perchance, of Hera alone, may refer to the source and nature of his being as personifying both the elemental kingdom itself and the nature-sprite, Deva and Devaraja stages of consciousness and attainment; for the Deva kingdom is a veritable projected part—offspring—of the Supreme Deity, a radiant member of the One Divine Family.

Hephaestus was endowed with the power to make gross metals so malleable that they could be hammered and moulded into desired shapes of great beauty and still more, as stated to bring out of the metal gold living human beings. These capacities indicate the ability to intrude effectively upon life and consciousness in those two kingdoms of Nature. Furthermore, he was miraculously able to bring the Life incarnate in grossest mineral to incarnation in gold and from thence into living human beings—demonstrating the faculty to *aid* in the evolution of that hidden Life.

The student of occult science may at once recall the function of a certain Order of Devas intimately associated with the evolution of life in form and thus engaged throughout the period of a *Manvantara* to quicken evolutionary progress. This suggests the power to hasten the attainment of freedom of the One Life from the imprisonment of one kingdom—minerals, for example—into the cellular organisms and composite materials of which the human body is built. Thus regarded,

Hephaestus personifies that Order of Devas—amongst many others—to which this *Manvantaric* task has been committed—to stimulate development, quicken evolutionary progress and hasten the advancement of Life from one stage to its successor.

As a result of attempted exploration of and even some association with members of the Angelic Hosts thus found to be ceaselessly at work, the author has become convinced that such an Order of beings does exist. For me, therefore, as I study his life and work, Hephaestus personifies that particular Order of the Angelic Hosts.

The fact that for untold ages its members must deal with the denser substances of the planet earth itself, especially minerals and plants—confirms this assumption. For such otherwise totally free beings this limitation may possibly be hinted at by the casting of Hephaestus out of Heaven, his ugliness and his lameness—symbols only, emblems only of such apparent accepted restrictions.

In my Book, *The Kingdom of the Gods,* I have described Devas who hve been thus engaged, some of them being displayed in certain of he illustrations in the midst of such activities—those of the mountain gods, for example, as also tree Devas.

The whole Hierarchy of the *Gandharvas,* the angels of music, who perpetually sound forth and re-sound from within the formless levels of Nature the uttered Creative Word may—and I feel sure do—continually exert an evolution-assisting influence upon the Life in all Nature and the inner and outer selves of human beings.

CHAPTER 8
THE UNICORN

The assumption that much of the mythology of ancient peoples, with its many glyphs and emblems, is Adept-inspired for the purpose of preserving for the race and of revealing, while yet concealing, power-bestowing knowledge, is supported by the remarkable aptness of the symbology.

THE UNICORN

The unicorn or horned horse as we have seen in one of its many possible meanings, is an appropriate symbol of the sublimated generative force in man. The horn, emerging from the brain, indicates that the expression of the creative power and desire then occurs through the will-inspired intellect and its cranical organ the physical brain and particularly the pituitary gland. The horn is thus occultly phallic whilst the horse is an oft-used symbol for man's purified lower quaternary—mind, emotion, etheric vehicle for vitality and flesh.

In Greek mythology this is represented by the winged—but not horned—horse, Pegasus, which the hero, Bellerophon, the Initiate-Ego, catches, controls and directs by means of a golden bridle. This harness is a symbol for the developed and wisely-used will-thought by means of which the personal nature of man (Pegasus) is guided.

The winged horse was caught near a fountain, typifying the source of Life. Mounting it, Bellerophon rose into the air and slew the Chimaera, a fire-breathing monster. Whilst riding on Pegasus, Bellerophon had no need to come anywhere near the creature whose breath was flame. He soared above her and killed her with his arrows at no risk to himself. The Chimaera was composed of a lion's head and four legs, a serpentine tail and a goat between the two. It is thus an impossible or unreal conception, a chimaera in the modern meaning of the word, an illusion, only to be 'seen through' (destroyed) when in a superior state of consciousness

Thereafter, the Initiate Ego, personified by Bellerophon, is no longer limited to the surface of the earth and the physical body; ascends as if winged, into the empyrean—the superphysical states of consciousness. Thus elevated, he is beyond the limitations of passionate desires (the fiery breath), the will to dominate (the lion portion) and sensual desires (he serpentine tail).

In the *Book of Job,* the change from the wild ass to the unicorn is also significant; for the ass is a symbol of stubbornness and in its wild state all its qualities are unharnessed. The Candidate for Initiation must tame the hitherto wild 'ass', so that thereafter, as symbol of a docile quaternary, it may bear the threefold spiritual Self onward to its goal, even as the Christ rode upon an ass in triumph to Jerusalem.

Egypt is a topographical symbol for the Sanctuary of the Greater Mysteries with their Halls of Initiation in one of which, it may be assumed, like every Initiate, Jesus was consecrated to His mighty task.

Jerusalem in its turn represents the immortal Self of man, the spiritual Triad — Will, Wisdom and Intelligence — in which the Initiate has been rendered fully conscious or has entered. This 'Jerusalem' state of awareness is achieved while wide awake in the body and throughout the often resistant quaternary — mind, emotion, vitality and flesh. Thus, as stated, the Christ triumphant (the Initiate) rides into Jerusalem (Egoic state) upon an obedient ass (the fourfold mortal personality).

The unicorn, be it remembered, is a fabulous animal whose spinal cord is presumed to extend beyond the *medulla oblongata*, through the pituitary gland and out between the eyes, after which it becomes hardened into a horn. Occultly interpreted, this refers less to the physical spinal cord than to the interior etheric canal which runs along its length and, as previously stated is called the *Sushumna nadi*. The equi-polarized creative fire, Serpent Fire or *Kundalini*, flows along this canal from sacrum to brain and in its progress in man, it is accompanied by the separate positive and negative currents which follow each their own pathways, known as Pingala and Ida respectively, intertwining the *Sushumna* as they flow.

The sublimation of the creative force — the ascent of the serpentine creative fire — occurs as a result of the transmutation of sex-force by means of the continued practice of yoga, aided by passage through valid rites of Initiation. Such knowledge was for a long period of time part of the closely guarded secrets of the Ancient Mysteries, and even now the technique whereby it is thus aroused is kept secret from the world. This reservation is designed not to withhold valuable information but to protect the profane and the unready from the danger and the strain inseparable from the premature awakening of *Kundalini*.

Many symbols are therefore employed to refer to this redeeming power in man, serpents, often intertwined, figuring largely in most of them. The stories of the transformation of the rods of Moses and Aaron into serpents to win freedom from bondage in Egypt (the body, the senses and abuse of power) for the Israelites (the spiritual Soul):[1] the glyph of Lacoon and his two sons: the brazen serpent on the cross held up by Moses: the Caduceus in the hands of Hermes, who frees the Soul (Persephone and Eurydice) from Hades (imprisonment in the physical body and world) — all these portray this redirection of the creative force

---

[1] See Ch.2

and the resultant liberation of consciousness from the restrictions of bodily life.

As stated — if some repetition be here permitted — the authors of the Book of Job used the round symbol of the wild ass and the unicorn[1] to indicate that Job had progressed through the wild, stubborn and sexual phases of human development. The horn of the unicorn is sometimes pictured as helical, which may be regarded as a suitable if veiled reference to the spirally intertwining forces of *Kundalini*, the power that moves in a serpentine path. In this sense the unicorn (conjoined mind, emotion, vitality and physical body of the man in whom the Serpent Fire is fully aroused and sublimated) is willing to serve him 'abide by thy crib',[2] can be bound and made to 'harrow the valleys'[3] (the three *nadis* or channels along which *Kundalini* ascends into the head.)

The unicorn may possibly also be regarded as a symbol of that early race of men in whom the pineal eye is said to have been at the surface of the head.[4] These were the so-called Lemurians, the Third Root Race in the succession of races upon earth, but the first to wear physical bodies and to renew human physical life on this planet. They were gigantic men, heavily built and clumsy, unskilled in the management of a physical form, but possessing still the psychic vision that was instinctually and naturally employed by the first two races on earth, which were astro-etheric. Their physical eyesight was limited, for the two eyes were still rudimentary. Their superphysical awareness was at first, however, remarkably clear. 'This Race developed the sense of sight, first using a single eye at the top of the head (now retreated as the pineal gland), and later two eyes.

'The one-eyed Cyclops, the giants fabled as the sons of *Coelus* and *Terra* — three in number, according to Hesiod — were the last three

---

[1] Who hath sent out the wild ass free? or who hath loosed the bands of the wild ass?
[2] Will the unicorn be willing to serve thee, or abide by thy crib?
[3] Canst thou bind the unicorn with his band in the furrow? or will he harrow the valleys after thee?
[4] See *The Earth and its Cycles*, E.W. Preston, p.66.

sub-races of the Lemurians, the one eye referring to the Wisdom-eye; for the two front eyes were fully developed as physical organs only in the beginning of the Fourth Race."[1]

---

[1] *The Secret Doctrine, IV*: 338. H.P. Blavatsky, Adyar Edition.

CHAPTER 9

PROMETHEUS; IMPRISONED BY ZEUS, FREED BY HERACLES

Prometheus stole some sparks of the Sun (physically natural creative fire, and so, faculty); gave it to humans and brought upon himself divine vengeance. He carried the sparks back to earth hidden inside a giant fennel—a pithy stalk—the central spinal canal? Zeus punished him by chaining him to a crag on Mt. Caucasus, where all day long an eagle tore at his liver which grew again during each night. Only after many generations did Heracles, with the consent of Zeus, slay the eagle and free Prometheus.

Prometheus (meaning fore-thought), the 'Fire and Light-Giver', was chained on Mt. Caucasus and condemned to suffer torture. He thus symbolises the Monad-Ego in man which—when in incarnation 'stole from heaven,'[1] actually possesses because of divine origin, contains within itself and conveys to the bodily man the Fire of Creation—and so of pro-creation—*Kundalini Shakti,* He thereby bestowed this capacity upon all human beings and upon all creatures that fecundate. As a punishment (actually as a natural consequence) he was symbolically chained on Mt. Caucasus (because incarnated in a physical body—a severe limitation upon the Monadic-Egoic Self, but also a means of evolutionary progress as far as the personality is concerned). All day long, an eagle tore at his liver (ever-renewed sex

---

[1] The price to be paid for the development of this deific power is heavy indeed. The Soul of man is encased in matter, wherein he temporarily becomes a prey to the delusion of self-separated individuality, to sex and to the dangers resulting from sexual over-indulgence. Self-degraded as a result, his condition is allegorically described in the Bible as being condemned by God and driven out of Eden. The story may also be interpreted as referring to the difficulty experienced by the aspirant to the higher consciousness in achieving the necessary transmutation of the procreative desire and energy to intellectual and intuitive creativeness. Symbolically, Prometheus is chained to earth.

desire) which grew whole again during the night, meaning that though satisfied, sex-expression never wholly dies away however frequently indulged in. It can therefore be the source of great suffering (unsatisfied sex-desire and diseases, for example) and, furthermore, for the spiritually unevolved, be very difficult to transmute — a torture indeed.

Whilst the experience of procreation is intentionally pleasurable in itself so that the various species of Nature may continue to exist and develop, it is nevertheless also a source of ever-continuing suffering, particularly when ill-used, misused or unable to be normally gratified. Allegorically, man is chained to a rock (the physical body) and the king of birds able to fly nearest the Sun (the source of the creative and sex-power) tears at his liver. Prometheus, as a personification of humanity exercising one of Nature's processes, thus sinned not at all; for humanity can become both a prisoner of insatiable sex-desire and a grave sufferer from heartaches emotionally and from diseases physically, this being a natural procedure. Eventually, therefore, he was set free.

When thus interpreted, the Myth does emblematically describe both the advantages and very serious disadvantages — a plague almost — resulting from the possession by man of the bodily faculty of procreation. Actually, however — as suggested — no sin was committed since the choice was not made by man as a race, but was and is a perfectly natural physical expression of the creative and formative power inherent in all Nature (stolen from Olympus), the abode of the gods (the god-Selves of men and super-men). Thus, no stealing occurred, and secondly, no one was adversely judged and punished deliberately by a presiding Deity. On the contrary, the myth records perfectly natural processes whilst revealing certain power-bestowing truths.

Prometheus personifies every human being, all of whom naturally inherit the creative fire inherent in Nature both favourably and very adversely functioning in and experienced by human beings. Man, being self-conscious, naturally misuses this pleasure-giving power and in this sense (though erroneously) 'falls' from heaven and is 'chained' to earth (temporarily loses conscious contact with his immortal Self). The story of Adam and Eve in the Garden of Eden is susceptible of a similar interpretation[1] (is aware of the physical body and world alone); for in both allegories no sin was committed. Suffering has in fact seriously come about for mankind, however, as a result of the exercise of the divine or heaven-born power to create.

The choice of the eagle, the king of birds, who of all feathered creatures can fly nearest to the Sun, as the producer of the pain (tearing at the liver of Prometheus each day) is also symbolically illuminating, suggesting as it does in its turn that the creative power is both royal and comes from on high—Mt. Caucasus indeed. The tearing at the liver by the eagle not inaptly describes suffering endured both from excessive and erroneous gratification of sex desire, and the continuing urge to its indulgence from which there appears to be no escape (the chains). The myth reveals both the existence and the nature of that relief. Heracles—conqueror of *Kundalini* from childhood—personifies the condition and the conduct to be followed in order to obtain the release from both 'chaining to rock' and 'tearing at the liver'.

Who, then, is Heracles? Does he not personify the individual who reaches the evolutionary stature at which both restriction to physical awareness and the sex craving have been overcome, thereby revealing a very great—if not in itself potentially dangerous because of possible misuse—truth of occult philosophy? Such a person must successfully ascend Mt. Caucasus (rise above the limitations of the physical body and world) and by awakened will-power have attained command over—and therefore indulgence in—sensual desire by which the sex-craving can be controlled and transmuted into intellectual and intuitive creativeness.

Thereby is attained command over indulgence in sensual desire, the sex force and craving having been controlled and transmuted into intellectual and intuitive creativeness. This achievement bestows on Heracles virtually irresistible power (physical omnipotence and the abilities to ascend in consciousness to the spiritual heights), enables him to climb Mt. Caucasus and, in addition, assist others in gaining similar freedom and spiritual realisation. Prometheus is allegorically freed from the rock on Mt. Caucasus and from subservience to and or

---

[1] *Gen.* 1-3. See also my book *The Hidden Wisdom in the Holy Bible*, Vol. 1 pp. 144-156.

enslavement by the sex desire, the eagle no longer tears at the liver, and Prometheus is freed from his chains.

Thus, the story of Prometheus both describes mythically the experience of almost all human beings in whom sex desire has become evident and expressed, and the way in which it may be transmuted, thereupon ceasing to become an imprisoning influence. This, the author venture to repeat, is attained firstly by rising in consciousness above physical limitations and desires (ascending Mt. Caucasus); secondly by conquering desire itself (destroying the eagle); and thirdly by universalising both the creative power within one and the activities of one's own life in the service of others (the ever-ministering Labours of Heracles).

CHAPTER 10

CADMUS, THE FOUNDER OF THEBES

Cadmus, whose highly complex life is here referred to in outline only, was famous as the founder of the citadel of Thebes, Athena having thereafter assigned to him its government. In these respects alone, Cadmus was a very important Personage, and for the fulfilment of his missions, the Oracle at Delphi advised him to follow a cow and to choose as the site for the capital city of Thebes the place on which the animal collapsed with fatigue. The district was later named the heifer's land or Boeotia.

When Cadmus arrived to found the city, a dragon, fathered by Ares, the god of war, denied his companions access to the stream and its well. Cadmus killed the creature and in consequence had to serve as Ares' slave for eight months. Thereafter, the gods married Cadmus to Harmonia, a daughter of Aphrodite, seven children being born to them. The marriage solemnity was honoured by the presence of all the Olympian gods.

After his victory, Athena advised Cadmus to sow the teeth of the dragon in the ground and—very strangely indeed—at once a crop of armed warriors sprang from the earth. These fought among themselves until only five of them survived, and ultimately became the ancestors of the noble Theban families. Towards the end of their lives Cadmus and Harmonia went to Illyria[1] where they were changed into serpents and thereafter elevated to the Elysian fields.[2]

As with nearly but not quite all of th named characters and creatures in Greek mythology, the story of the life of Cadmus is so humanly incredible that one may permissibly apply to its interpretation a universal form of that allegorical Rosetta stone which verbally

---

[1] The greater part of modern Albania.
[2] Elysium. Homer describes this as a happy land where is neither snow, nor cold nor rain. It was generally regarded as 'the abodes of the blessed'.

gave the clue to Egyptian Hieroglyphics. Indeed, certain proclaimed incidents together with their associated symbology, directly encourage this approach, amongst them being the cow that led Cadmus to the site for Thebes.

May we now examine this strange series of events in search of valid ideas in accordance wth the title of this book? Why, for example, did one of the most highly valued sources of inspiration—the Oracle at Delphi—advise Cadmus concerning the complete necessity for the fulfilment of his great mission, namely to follow so humble a creature as a cow?

Amongst available sources of information is *The Secret Doctrine* by H.P. Blavatsky. Therein, we discover the following references to the symbology of the cow.

'...The Cow was in every country the symbol of the passive generative power of nature, Isis, Vâch, Venus—the mother of the prolific God of Love, Cupid, but, at the same time, that of the Logos whose symbol, with the Egyptians and the Indians, became the Bull, as testified to by the Apis and the Hindu Bulls in the most ancient temples. In Esoteric Philosophy the Cow is the symbol of Creative Nature, and the Bull (her calf) the Spirit which vivifies her, or the "Holy Spirit", as Dr. Kenealy shows. Hence the symbol of the horns. These were sacred also with the Jews, who placed on the altar horns of shittim wood, by seizing which a criminal ensured his safety." (Adyar Ed., Vol.3, p.416, 2nd Footnote, line 5)

...lift a corner of the veil off those wondrous allegories that have been thrown over Vâch, the most mysterious of all the Brâhmanical Goddesses; she who is termed 'the melodious Cow who milked forth sustenance and Water' —the Earth with all her mystic powers; and again she 'who yields us nourishment and sustenance'—the physical earth. *Isis* is also mystic Nature and also earth; and her cow's horns identify her with Vâch, who, after being recognized in her highest form as *Parâ*, becomes, at the lower or material end of creation *Vaikharî*. Hence she is mystic, though physical, Nature, with all her magic ways and properties.' (Vol. 2, p.152.)

'...The ceremony of passing through the Holy of Holies—now symbolised by the Cow, but in the beginning through the temple *Hiranyagarbha*, the Radiant Egg, in itself a symbol of Universal Abstract Nature—meant spiritual conception and birth, or rather the *rebirth* of the individual and his regeneration." (Vol. 4, p.37)

...even now, the cow-symbol is one of the grandest and most philosophical among all others in its inner meaning." (Vol. 4, p.38)

If the Myth in its entirety is thus regarded as a heavily veiled revelation of occult truths and powers, then the story of the foundation of Thebes may possibly be regarded as an allegorical description of at least five important procedures: the creation, preservation and transformation of a Universe: the fecundating power by means of which these results are achieved: the receptive or "maternal" agency: the potentially dangerous creative fire present in every human being: and its arousal into full activity for the purpose of the illumination of the mind and soul of a successful aspirant.

The well that was guarded by the dragon, its teeth which gave birth to human beings, and the statement that Harmonia and Cadmus were changed into serpents and thereupon entered a place of blessedness called the Elysian Fields, all give support to the interpretation of this famous Myth. The symbols of the well and the cow—each being a source of necessities for the continuance of certain forms of life (water and milk)—are both appropriately included in an allegorical account of the birth, preservation and government of a new city and country, Thebes and Boeotia.

Concerning the symbol of water, H.P. Blavatsky writes as follows:-
'...These Waters (Chaos), called the streams of Elivagar, distilling in vivifying drops, fell down and created the earth and giant Ymir, who had only the "semblance of man" (The Heavenly Man), and the Cow, Audumla (the "Mother", Astral Light or Cosmic Soul), from whose udder flowed four streams of milk—four cardinal points;...' (*The Secret Doctrine*, Adyar Ed., Vol. 2, p.83)

The serpent or dragon—which figures so largely in various forms in both the illustrations and stories of which mythology consists—is throughout this book interpreted as a personification of a sevenfold, superphysical, generative force in Universe and man, functioning in the latter by means of a spiral or coiling action mainly in and around the spinal cord. This power called in Sanskrit the *Kundalini Shakti*, is portrayed in Hindu literature by a diagram indicating the three paths along which—when aroused into activity—the triple currents ascend the spinal column of illumined man. Interestingly—even arrestingly—the identical anatomical system is pictured by the Rod of Hermes, as illustrations of both of these clearly indicate.

Kundalini is also symbolised in Hinduism by the Serpent or *Naga*, doubtless on account of the winding pathways followed by two currents. It is found also to be depicted — if less exactly — in the Mythology of Egypt, particularly as the symbol of upper and Lower Egypt. *Kundalini* is present in all living creatures as the source of the generative and creative power by which reproduction — divine, human and sub-human — is achieved. When, in man, it is supernormally aroused and directed into the brain, the higher consciousness is then achieved whilst the physical body is wide awake. The yogic *Siddhis*[1] include the full realisation of one's divine, immortal Self which in Greek Mythology symbolically 'lives' on Mount Olympus or in Elysium.

The element of water is also essential to the continuance of life upon this planet. It is therefore not without possible significance, that the similar importance of *Kundalini Shakti* is revealed by placing the dragon at a well. As the creative force or *Kundalini* is the basis of the sex urge and so completely necessary for the succesion by parenthood of almost all species, and the element of water is also essential to the preservation of life upon this planet, it is not without possible significance — is symbolically apposite, in fact — that in this myth a dragon is associated with a well, is in fact placed as the guardian of a stream. The victory of Cadmus over this creature may be interpreted as the mastery of the Serpent Fire, meaning the arousal and conscious use of the power of *Kundalini*.

The illustration showing Cadmus slaying the dragon offers support for this view; for out of the top of the head of Cadmus an upright figure arises and from this radiations occur as is the case when fully aroused *Kundalini* flows upwards through the crown of the head. The dragon itself is also associated with an upright column suggesting the spinal cord of man along which the neutral current of the threefold *Kundalini* ascends — positive (*Pingala*), negative (*Ida*), and neutral (*Sushumna*).

The mysterious birth of human beings from the teeth of the dragon buried in 'Mother' Earth, whilst normally fabulous, indicates the generative function of *Kundalini* — the dragon. The 'Mother' Earth represents the female sex and the teeth the male, whilst the conflict amongst the armed men may refer to the dangers associated with the unwise arousal of the occult aspects of this universal, creative energy.

[1] *Siddhis* (Sk.) Main attainments of the successful Yogi.

CADMUS SLAYING THE DRAGON

A second serpent is less noticeably included in the picture, its body arranged in five curves suggesting the negative current of *Kundalini* which in Sanskrit is named *Ida* and arises through five main centres or *chakras*—whirling vortices at spleen, solar-plexus, heart, throat and brow—in the etheric or superphysical bodies of man. This view is supported by the translation of Cadmus and Harmonia into Elysium after their death, since as an experience in consciousness this is actually attained by the fully illuminied *Kundalini Yogi* whom Cadmus personifies.

In conclusion, the name of the wife, Harmonia, refers directly to the condition of consciousness necessary for the safe arousal of *Kundalini*. This alludes to both the attainment of psychological equipoise and particularly to the relationship between the two winding currents, namely complete balance or harmony.

Summing Up

As will doubtless have been realised, named places in mythologies do not necessarily refer to a geographical position. Rather are they used as mythical references to the world after death—Hades, Mount Olympus, the abode of the gods or Elysium, meaning the heaven worlds or the states of consciousness in which those conditions of the after life or the most exalted states of awareness and being are experienced. This especially would apply to the close of the story of Cadmus and Harmonia who, after being changed into serpents, entered the Elysian fields.

In occult science, the successive phases of development are passed through, beginning perhaps with the first acquirement of knowledge, in this case of the existence of the Serpent Fire. Developments then occur when that same energy becomes aroused and operative within an individual to produce, if only temporarily, highly uplifted states.

Eventually, the great fulfilment occurs when the individual, having passed through these stages, has become *totally* unified with a veritable embodiment of the particular potency and thereafter permanently resides in the corresponding state of consciousness. Indeed, every aspirant to Initiation and Adeptship in the Ancient but also ever-existent Mysteries, is first introduced to teachings on these subjects—how to elevate the mind and the hitherto dormant power within which makes this achievement possible, the Serpent Fire for example.

Eventually, as stated, the Initiate is no longer externally approaching, learning about and arousing into a measure of activity such forces; for the stage is reached at which individuality is as it were absorbed into the Truth itself—becomes that Truth in every aspect of his or her existence and experiences the operation of the energy or power to that extent at which they become veritable incarnations thereof. Indeed, this *is* the goal, namely no longer to study and accept a truth but to become a veritable living manifestation of it.

Similarly, power may be awakened to such an extent that the *whole being* becomes unified with it and its interior source—*becomes* that power and lives accordingly in every deed and thought throughout their whole nature. This is the ideal as affirmed by the Lord Jesus Christ, for example, in His words, "I and my Father are one"[1], or the yogi ultimately affirms: "Verily, I am that supreme *Brahman.*'

[1] *Jn.* 10:30

These ideals, if plainly stated in words, would be likely to be far beyond the conception and so acceptance of the occultly untutored and those who are as yet spiritually unawakened. Therefore, they are referred to in allegorical and symbolical ways, with the *dramatis personae* passing through stages of development as if in terms of geographical movements and visitations.

The time comes however when allegory and symbol are no longer needed—can be blinds in fact—whereupon the truth itself is both uttered and wholly passed into as a living experience. Hence, Cadmus and Harmonia are no longer confronted by a dragon as an external creature, but *become* that reptile, thereafter being an incarnation thereof in terms of both fully aroused and operative mind-illuminating power and states of consciousness. Thus, they are changed into serpents and thereafter forever abide in Elysium—the place of the Blessed.

The text of the Myth might, however, have been more carefully or more accurately translated as: 'Cadmus and Harmonia *became* the Serpent Fire', meaning "attained complete identity therewith." In consequence, they experienced its full and complete function in terms of spiritual and intellectual awareness. Thus, instead of 'being changed into serpents,' *'they became* serpents' and so attained the Yogic Goal[1]—the true objective, allegorically portrayed by—and often dramatically presented in—every sage-inspired world myth.

---

[1] Realised identity with the One Alone—the Spiritual Life—Essence of the Universe—Brahman.

EPILOGUE

FROM THE ANCIENT PAST THROUGH THE MIDDLE AGES TO PRESENT AND FUTURE TIMES

My presentation in this work of views concerning world mythologies are founded upon my conviction of the existence on earth of the Company of 'Just Men Made Perfect'[1] referred to by St. Paul. Among these, I firmly believe, are included the sages alluded to in Greek literature and the scriptures of the world, Who have arisen from the ranks of mankind through the acceptance and application to Their lives of procedures by means of which human evolution to perfection may be hastened. Having themselves attained to trans-human states They are moved amongst other purposes, to make available to their fellow residents of our planet a measure of the knowledge to which They have attained. This includes both the realities concerning the nature of man and the means whereby he may free himself from the limitations — and so the sufferings — that non-illumined beings generate for themselves.

The first, foremost and unchanging fact about man is that he is not the visible, mortal, bodily person *alone;* for the real individual is an immortal spiritual being, incarnate in the personality during the bodily lifetime.

In man highest spirit (Monad) and lowest matter (body) are united by intellect.

Man's spiritual Self perpetually unfolds potential capacities, this being the result of his existence.

This process culminates in the attainment of perfected manhood, Adeptship.

The method of human evolution is by means of successive and progressive physical lives, or rebirth.

---

[1] *Heb.* 12:23.

Human conditions and experiences are the results of human conduct under the law of cause and effect or *Karma*. Kindness brings health and happiness. Cruelty brings disease and misery.

The processes of evolution can be delayed by self-indulgence and cruelty, proceed normally, or be hastened by following a kindly helpful and self-controlled mode of life. The Kingdom of Heaven can be taken by storm. This calls especially for self-training, regular meditation and selfless service.

Perfected men and women, Adepts, do exist on earth.

Ages ago, and ever since, certain Adepts shared their discovered Wisdom and knowledge with humanity. This was and is named *Brahma Vidya* and *Theosophia*, Divine Wisdom.

Mankind's difficulties arise from the fact that at the present stage of human evolution on earth, except when inspired, the unfolding individual or Ego normally manifests physically only to a very limited degree. In consequence, people tend to seek and live only for bodily purposes, financial advantages, pleasures and what they mistakenly believe to be necessities—cruelly obtained animal food, for example.

The solution to all man's problems consists of the increasingly full—and so corrective—expression of the immortal Self in and through its outer personality. The purpose of religions, inspired portions of scriptures and mythologies is, the author submits, both to provide knowledge of these facts and to achieve an ever increasingly close inter-relationship between the Divine and the human in mankind.

In addition, special measures have been taken by the Adepts to bring about this solution by means of especial guidance to the mind, and a powerful evolution-quickening influence upon the body of those thought to be sufficiently responsive and stable to justify the experiment. In historical literature, this procedure is named the Mysteries, referring to observances kept secret from the profane and uninitiated.

If as author, I am here permitted to 'converse' briefly with the reader—whilst still continuing our study—may I give assurance that as I have dwelt upon and sought for the hidden wisdom within world scriptures and mythologies, and as in this book I share some of the results, I do not for a moment forget—indeed I have constantly reminded myself of—the danger, grievous mistake indeed, of erroneously attributing concealed Wisdom to a story that from beginning to end may be only a fairy tale. Bellerophon, mounted and flying upon his winged horse Pegasus, and thus elevated, destroying the Chimaera, might, for example, have begun as an imagined fable. The analogy of the necessity to rise above normal, mental attitudes before illusions may be entirely eliminated from one's mind is, however, so apt and so close to reality that it is reasonable to assume its revelation to have been the original intention of the author of the story whoever he or she may have been.

With deference to those for whom the scriptural passage provides an accurate account of the exploit, David may or may not actually have slain the giant Goliath by means of a stone thrown by his sling, and thereafter cut off his head;[1] for could not this in its turn possibly be a fabulous story of heroic adventure? Important and valuable guidance can however readily be received from a symbolic interpretation. The necessity for a certain simple directness of thought (David, the young shepherd boy) and the elimination of the argumentative, egoistic tendency of the human mind (decapitation of the arrogant Goliath) before wisdom may be attained, is so obviously true that it may well be regarded as the intended message of the narrative—granted the existence and use of the spiritually and philosophically revealing language of allegory and symbol. The simple weapon (the sling) and its missile (the stone)—a product of Nature recovered from the stream[2]—in the hands of a young shepherd and the procedure of decapitation, definitely present a profound underlying wisdom.

Since humanity is now moving through its Fifth Root Race and its Fifth Sub-Race, the concrete mind and its attributes are undergoing, however slowly, evolutionary development, and in consequence greatly but not entirely, control human thinking. Thought processes and their self-centred motives tend to accentuate such attributes as the desire to attain personal benefits and the satisfaction of egoism and pride. During the present thought period, these, with noble exceptions, most unfortunately rule human thought and so human conduct—the history of our times all too clearly portraying the tragic results.

Why, it may be asked, do such truths need thus to be concealed? Because they reveal not only valuable truths, but as earlier stated

---

[1] 1 *Sam.* 17:49—51.
[2] *Sam.* 17:40.

also the source of great personal power and the means whereby it may be attained — and therefore misused. As the history of the world records — especially since the discoveries of gunpowder and nuclear energy — power in wrong hands is dangerous in the extreme. To know that you are one with the Divine and are thereby Divine in your own nature can greatly inspire the mind and so bestow upon it many added faculties including sensitivity to spiritual and beneficent occult influences. Unfortunately, one could thereafter also be susceptible of being directed by dark powers[1] — intelligence giving over to evil.

Until Adeptship is attained, and so the possibility of error transcended, the strains and adversities inseparable from human life may bring about periods of Gethsemane-like darknesses with their perceived opportunities of manoeuvering for dishonest personal gains. These obscurities are able to eclipse the mind and cause a Judas-like betrayal even of the Master — the Divine One, Himself.[2] The Disciple Peter, temporarily overcome by craven fear, thrice denied his association with the Lord Jesus.[3] The murder by Cain[4] of his brother Abel and the sending by King David of the husband of Bathsheba — Uriah — to the front line of battle where he was killed[5], and the total glyph of power-endowed Satan in his every aspect — all these are Biblical examples of such 'falls'. In Egyptian mythology, Set murdered and dismembered his brother and senior, Osiris, whilst the life of the Lord Buddha was more than once endangered by the jealous relative, Devadatta.

In modern days, the leaders of every nation that embarks upon aggressive wars, and all the criminals who for their personal gain use special knowledge and opportunity in order to deprive others of possessions provide illustrations of the dangers associated with special power and the freedom to use or misuse it. Occult knowledge bestows the capacity to influence, to elevate — but unfortunately also to subdue — the minds of others and even to pervert them into the commission of evil deeds, the wrong use of hypnotism, hypontic oratory being

---

[1] See my *Basic Theosophy*.
[2] *Matt.* 26:14,47. See my *The Life of Christ From Nativity to Ascension*, pp.395-414-5.
[3] *Matt.* 26:69, and *The Life of Christ from Nativity to Ascension*, pp.406-7.
[4] *Gen.* 4:8 to 15.
[5] *2 Sam.* 11:12.

one example. Fellow human beings and even nations, as in more recent European history, can thus be controlled and led into evil ways by those possessed of sufficient will-force so to affect them. Since, however, the selfsame power rightly used is of the greatest value in purifying one's nature and hastening one's evolution—and therefore that of humanity as a whole—the Teachers of the race, with the necessary care (the use of the language of Allegory and Symbol) do not fail to make spiritual and occult wisdom available to mankind. *Isis Unveiled* and *The Secret Doctrine* by H.P. Blavatsky, amongst other works, may well be regarded as examples of such adeptic ministrations.

In what way then can and does the reception of inspiration turn some human beings to evil practices? In electrical terms, by making available extra potentials which thereafter render the individual more sensitive and so more susceptible to being influenced by their own spiritual natures and by highly elevated Beings, and unfortunately by both their own selfish characteristics and the Powers of Darkness—intelligent minds given over to 'evil'. The *Asuras*[1] (in their allegorically Satanic powers) and their human agents who attacked the Lord Shri Krishna, wishing to destroy Him as a hated superior in their midst, and the Kings Kamsa and Herod both of whom also feared the loss of their kingdoms, constitute emblematic scriptural examples of such hostile agencies. Not only by dark beings may a person by directly influenced, however—when over-sensitised by the premature discovery and use of occult knowledge and power—but also by other psychic forces that can lead mankind astray, adversely affecting mental and psychological stability and integrity. Furthermore, jealousy may be aroused towards seniors, who have been granted greater knowledge and power and so prestige than themselves.

Each additional faculty and all the energies associated with it, further arouse—and so add to—the activity and influence over a person of their already existing unfavourable attributes and tendencies. These could include dislike up to hatred, anger up to rage, jealousy up to

---

[1] *Asuras* (Sk.) Presented in Hindu thought as spiritual beings whose activity is associated with the demoniac or discordant side of evolution. Hence they are regarded as Satanic Powers as are the rebels of cosmic myths, the Titans of Greek mythology for example. They are, however, also considered as spiritual beings fulfilling both constructive and necessary destructive functions.

determination to destroy, pride because of the superiority over others not so endowed, and a general increase in the sense of egoism and so of most harmful separatedness from fellow men. As will readily be seen, all of these failures are especially adverse, even fatal, developments from the point of view of further occult and spiritual advancement.

Among simple examples or illustrations could be a school bully, a boy possessing and learning to use a catapult against fellow students, and one who is growing in muscular strength over fellow scholars and also in intelligence and learning capacity. All these successes could lead to the form of egoism that has been named 'snobbishness'. Thus, at *all* ages, the acquisition of that added power can lead to a tendency and habit of secretiveness which can develop very undesirably in a person's character. These dangers have been numerously exemplified in the history of man throughout the ages. Hence the Adeptic procedure of secrecy, enveiling and the careful guarding of faculty-bestowing knowledge. The unfailing dual safeguard — against falling into such errors — consists of being inspired by the single motive to gain knowledge and so to obtain power to be used wholly in the service of others, and without the slightest thought of personal reward.

Those human beings who are passing through the Sixth Root Race[1] phase of evolution will have naturally outgrown many of these weaknesses and by that time — as is already occurring to some extent — the restrictions will have begun to be reduced. Indeed, the knowledge will have become directly intuited and otherwise gained by that time. The Goliaths of the world will then be greatly reduced in number if not having entirely disappeared. Furthermore, the pituitary gland and associated areas of the brain will naturally have evolved into greater activity than at present as organs for the experience of implicit insight. In consequence, the small white stone from the stream[2] will not have to be slung through the forehead by the Davids of those future days, since the brow *chakra*[3] will already have become open.

The eternal, deific Cause, the One Source, (perchance Uranus) surrendered to the cruel restrictions of time (Cronus) which symbolically deprived it of its unrestricted and universal creative poten-

---

[1] See my *Basic Theosophy*
[2] 1 *Sam.* 17:49
[3] *Chakra.* (Sk.) *The Chakras*, C.W. Leadbeater.

cy—allegorically his genitals removed by means of a curved sickle—itself symbolic of cyclic manifestation. When Chaos gives place to Cosmos and everlasting Space becomes the Mother of a Universe in Time, Cosmic generative power is restricted thereto. From the hitherto still waters of the ocean of matter, then thrown into wave like or rhythmic motion, there is produced an embodiment of personification of creative desire—namely Aphrodite who is said to have been born from the resultant foam. Aphrodite means 'the foam risen', from *aphros* (Gk.) 'foam'. Again, the offensiveness associated with a literal reading of a myth is greatly reduced if not entirely removed when it is read as a dramatic and arresting allegory of procedures leading to the creation or emanation of Universes and certain of the effects brought about by this procedure. Macrocosm and microcosm are rightly made to meet in this glyph, which is also descriptive of the existence, activity and presence in both Universe and man of the inexhaustible, generative and reproductive power immanent throughout all Nature.

The unbroken continuance throughout successive epochs of the emanation and manifestation of the Logoic, formative power constitutes a fundamental principle underlying the creative processes of Nature—intellectual, cultural and physical. As already suggested, the curved sickle of Cronus[1] with which the fell deed[2] was performed upon Uranus, though itself not a full circle, implies the cyclic continuance of the creative procedure, as also the spiral pathway along which the hidden Life in all its manifestations and embodiments, ascends to ever greater evolutionary heights; for the doctrines of the continual development of the spiritual principle of Universes and the Monads evolving through the human and sub-human kingdoms of Nature is symbolically revealed. The parallel improvement of Nature's myriad forms or vehicles of Spirit was well known to the sages of old who imparted it directly to the Initiates of the Greater Mysteries and, by means of world mythologies and scriptures, to humanity at large.

In more modern times—not until the 19th century, indeed—does a Darwin[3] arise to discover and reveal, however partially, the selfsame

---

[1] Cronus—personification of Time.
[2] Castration.
[3] Author of *The Origin of Species*.

truth — physical evolution — and a Blavatsky[1] who reveals the extensions of this procedure into the superphysical worlds and the Monads therein. So, also, many other truths were secretly revealed and allegorically presented to the public until, in the course of time, a Gallileo[2], a Darwin and a Blavatsky should arise amongst men.

In order that this enlightenment should come about, the spiritual principle itself must become actively and discernably present within the minds of illumined human beings. This also continuously occurs as is told in the Myths of ancient Greece, which include accounts of the successive amours of Zeus consumated by various means — each profoundly symbolical — related in the form of sexual intercourse with unwilling and willing maidens. Other gods, goddesses and heroes are similarly presented as seeking and engaging in love-relationships. The improvements, illuminations and increased spiritual awareness are almost beyond the possibility of direct descriptions not only because of their nature but their variations according to the temperament and evolutionary stature of the recipient. Hence, the language of allegory and symbol in which world mythologies have from the remotest times been written. Even the task and the attempts correctly to interpret have their value since they in their turn demand and tend to awaken within the student the faculty of correct translation into normal, every day literature.

The author cannot but wish that his own ability in this field were more advanced. Nevertheless, whilst recognising considerable limitations, in this book he offers some of the results of his still-continuing endeavours, trusting that they may be both interesting and helpful to those who may read.

---

[1] Authoress of *Isis Unveiled* and *The Secret Doctrine*

[2] Gallileo (1564-1642). Italian scientist whose experimental- mathematical methods in the pursuit of scientific truth laid the foundations of modern science.

APPENDICES

KUNDALINI SHAKTI
The Cosmic Creative Fire in Universe and Man.

This is part of a theosophical teaching of great interest and great importance — the force which can illume, empower, and exalt a human being, the fire of God: the Cosmic creative fire in Universe and man.

It can be regarded in general as:

(1) The Power of Life.
(2) One of the forces of Nature, the occult electricity intimately associated with Azoth of the Alchemists.
(3) It is the creative principle in Nature and *Akasa* (sk.).
(4) The subtle, supersensuous, spiritual essence which pervades all space.
(5) The coiled-up universal Life Principle.
(6) A sevenfold, superphysical, occult power, in Universe and man, functioning in the latter by means of a spiral or coiling action, mainly in the spinal cord, but also throughout the nervous system.
(7) It is represented in Greek symbology by the Caduceus, the Rod of Hermes. The seven-layered creative power in nature, and the base of the spine of man.
(8) When supernormally aroused, this fiery force ascends into the brain by a serpentine path, hence its other name, the Serpent Fire.
(9) It is composed of three currents which flow along three canals in the spinal cord, named *Ida* (negative), *Pingala* (positive) and *Sushumna* (neutral). These names are sometimes applied (wrongly) to the currents themselves.

When, under expert guidance only, and with completely altruistic motives, *Kundalini* is awakened, it divides itself into the three currents. The positive current intertwines with the spinal cord and enters the pituitary gland, whilst the negative current oppositely entwines the spinal cord and enters the pineal gland. The neutral current ascends Sushumna, enters the third ventricle of the brain, and passes out at the crown of the head.

Dangers of Arousing Nature's Hidden Forces except under the Direction of a Master of the Wisdom

(1) Premature arousing of *Kundalini* with its disturbing effects.
(2) Sex excitation.
(3) Emotional disturbances due to incursions from the Astral plane of forces and beings through the solar plexus on to the sympathetic nervous system, which does not readily rationalize and so becomes confused. Those belonging to schools, classes or movements may already experience this.
(4) A sense of increased self-importance from which immoderate pride can develop.
(5) Enhancement of the powers of will and discovery of means of using will to influence others adversely.
(6) Whirling sensations in the brain, with consequent distress and fear of insanity.
(7) Physical sensations of various kinds, such as being touched, subjected to seemingly electrical energies, a crawling sensation on the skin, especially at the *chakras,* and a feeling of heat in the spinal cord, particularly at the sacrum.
(8) Partially seen and therefore misinterpreted clairvoyant visions of the Astral plane. These may increase any sense of self-importance which may have arisen.
(9) Eccentricities of conduct, personality and speech outside of the immediate control of the mind.
(10) Susceptibility to being influenced by superphysical beings, notably shells of deceased persons seeking renewals of their fading vitality and so *fastening* upon sensitive people, greatly to their detriment.

When arousing of the *Kundalini* and consequent development of the *Siddhis* would be deemed helpful to any person, a Spiritual

Teacher will *always* present himself and guide the neophyte through the dangers and difficulties likely to arise.

When the Pupil, is ready, the Master is ready also.

The ideal of Discipleship to a Master can be fulfilled. No one is overlooked.

Qualifications: to become a selfless, self-disciplined servant of humanity.

THE STILL FUNCTIONING LESSER AND GREATER MYSTERIES

Four theosophical ideas form the basis for a study of hastened human progress. These are: There is a natural evolution of life and form in our Solar System for all kingdoms, the *normal* rule being that one kingdom of Nature is passed through in each Chain; the possibility exists of enforced and speeded human evolution achieved by means of a scientifically planned procedure of self-quickening; provision has long been made on earth for special guidance by Adepts, and Their still human representatives, of those who embark upon this procedure, this schooling forming a part of the occult or inner, spiritual life of man upon our planet earth; the rules of the occult life are not man-made, but are natural laws indicating the kind of life to be lived by the aspirant who seeks the swift unfoldment of the deific powers within him or her, or hastened evolutionary progress.

From time immemorial, one form of Adeptic aid has been more especially suited to those who find themselves naturally drawn to an orderly and ceremonial way of life, long named 'The Lesser and Greater Mysteries' —(Gr. *Muo*—to close the mouth). What, as far as is known, were these Mysteries? They were, one learns, observances generally kept secret from the profane and uninitiated, in which were taught by dramatic representation and other methods, the origin of things, the nature of the human Spirit and its relation to the body, the method of personal purification and conscious restoration to a spiritual mode of life.

The purpose of the Lesser Mysteries was to introduce the mind to the concepts of philosophy and esotericism. The majority of the Initiates progressed no further, returning to their various pursuits inspired by a solemn pageantry, but not necessarily completely impelled to make philosophy a way of life. The more studious members, however, recognized in the symbols and tables of Initiation the outer vestments and trappings of a sublime science. Impelled from within to explore the world of learning, these natural idealists attached themselves to teachers of distinction, and prepared their minds for the tests and examinations demanded of those seeking admission to The Greater Mysteries.

Such, it is taught, were the chief spiritual purposes for the existence of the rituals of The Mysteries, and therefore of their continuing survivals—Freemasonry, ancient and modern, the ritual procedures of ecclesiastical services, the Orders of Chivalry and, it would seem, the coronation of monarchs. These were, and still are, the author submits, designed and performed in order to hasten the natural processes of spiritual, psychological and cultural unfoldment—to increase the speed of the evolution of Initiates.

The true or Greater Mysteries still exist, and Freemasonry is regarded by some as an unconscious witness to their existence in the past; for in its Rituals there are traces of the ancient Initiations and, if interested, the student may find these as he reads *The Egyptian Book of the Dead* and other early writings. Thus, as suggested, the purpose for which occult ceremonials are performed is to increase the speed of the evolution of Initiates, and this is achieved by the three processes of physical, moral and cultural preparations, successive Degrees of Initiation and the training by which these are accompanied.

What then was, and still is, the ultimate objective of the Mysteries? In terms of consciousness it is presumed to consist of the attainment of *realised oneness with the Divine Presence throughout all Nature and within both the spiritual nature and the bodily personality of every human being*. This is, however, the consummation of all endeavour, whether purely mystical, ceremonial, or an intelligent blend of both; for by these means this extremely lofty state of awareness may indeed be achieved. In truth, as the successful mystic discovers, man-Spirit and God-Spirit are one Spirit. In Hinduism, God *(Brahma)* is affirmed to be The Inner Ruler Immortal seated in the hearts of all beings. Because of its paramount importance, this affirmation is referred to as The Royal Secret, The Sovereign Truth, and in Freemasonry is named the Lost Word. In terms of transcendental consciousness, realization of this unity with the omnipresent, interior divinity is the summit of all human intellectual and spiritual achievement.

The sacred Mysteries were enacted in ancient Temples by the Hierophants and other ritual officials for the benefit and instruction of the Candidates. The actual word 'Mysteries' is, as stated, derived from the Greek *muo*, 'to close the mouth'. Complete secrecy was preserved and every symbol connected with them had a hidden meaning, or 'scintillated with significance'. The Ancient Mysteries existed in many countries, not only in Egypt and Greece, and consisted of a series of dramatic performances in which the Mysteries of Cosmogony, and Nature in general, were personified by the Hierophants and neophytes, who enacted the parts of various gods and goddesses — meaning superhuman and Archangelic officials associated with both the planet and the universe as a whole. They dramatically repeated supposed scenes from Their respective solar and planetary activities. In Egypt they were symbolically enrobed with ram, ibis, and culture head-dresses, and also wore the highly occult serpent symbol (*Ureus*, for example). The hidden meanings of this Regalia, and the associated dramatic actions, were explained to the Candidates for Initiation, and thereafter incorporated into philosophical doctrines.

The Greek Mysteries included the Dionysian or Bacchic, the Orphic, the Samothracian, the Aesculapian and the Eleusinian. Every September, for seven days or more, the citizens of Greece and of other countries gathered on the Athenian Acropolis and travelled — largely on foot and at leisure — both to the town of Agrae and in addition some fourteen miles to the City and Temples of Eleusis on the northern shore of the Saronic Gulf. Whilst all present were permitted to attend preliminary ceremonies, only a selected few who had proved themselves worthy were admitted to the sacred ceremony itself. Therein, Initiation into The Mysteries both brought about a spiritual birth, and regenerated and united the personal self with the divine Spirit. These experiences resulted in enlightened comprehension, intuitive insight, spiritual will-power and continually deepening realisation of oneness with the Life in all that exists.

The Eleusinian Mysteries were the most famous of these Ceremonial Orders. The Eleusinian Festival in honour of Demeter and Persephone was probably fully established in Athens by Pisistratus at the end of the sixth century B.C., and continued at least up to 200 A.D. It was named for the community in Attica where the sacred dramas were first presented and are generally believed to have been originally founded by Emolpos about fourteen hundred years before the birth of Christ. With their mystic interpretation of Nature's most precious secrets, they overshadowed the civilization of their time gradually absorbing many smaller schools and incorporating into their own system whatever valuable information these lesser institutions possessed.

Each year at Agrae the Festival of The Lesser Mysteries of Eleusinia was celebrated in the month of Boedromium or September, in honour of the Goddess Demeter and her daughter Persephone. At four year periods, a procession departed from the Acropolis of Athens to Eleusis, and those who were sufficiently qualified were initiated into the final Rite of the Mysteries. This was a most solemn and sacred event, for those who were to be admitted first came to the entrance to the sacred precinct, after which the doors of the outer Temple or *Telestrion* were closed behind them. There, in due course, permission was granted to them to enter the *Anaktreon,* the Holy of Holies, wherein the Sacred Rite itself was performed in deepest secrecy.

What, then, actually were the revelations made during the Initiatory Rite in the Mysteries of old that were revealed to the Initiates? Archeologists and historians with one voice confess—and it does honour to the men and women of ancient times—that the secret has been completely preserved; no one has ever recounted what occurred and what was revealed to the Initiate in the Eleusinian *Anaktreon*.

Cicero was able to write in his *De Legibus*, 11, 14:

> 'Though Athens brought forth numerous divine things, yet she never created anything nobler than those sublime Mysteries through which we have become gentler, and have advanced from a barbarous and rustic life to a civilized one, so that we not only live more joyfully, but also die with a better hope'

and the following Greek philosophers wrote:

Pindar: 'Happy is he who has seen the Mysteries before being buried underneath the earth; he knows the end of life and he knows its beginning given by Zeus'.

Sophocles: 'Thrice happy are the mortals who depart to the abode of Hades after having seen the Mysteries; they only will have life there; for the others there will be nothing but suffering'.

Plato: 'He who arrives in Hades without having been Initiated, and without having taken part in the Mysteries, will be plunged in the mire; but he who has been purified and Initiated will abide with the Gods'.

Plutarch: 'Those who are initiated into the great Mysteries perceive a wonderful light. Purer regions are reached, and fields where there is singing and dancing; sacred words and divine visions inspire a holy awe'.

An ancient record of Initiation (Hermes, *Promantres* 1.30) says:
'The sleep of the body becomes the awakening of the soul, and the closing of the eyes true vision, and silence becomes impregnated with God. This happened to me when I received the supreme authentic Word. I became God-inspired, I arrived at Truth. Wherefore I give from my soul and whole strength, blessing to the Father.'

Thus throughout all time the man who is perfected and initiated, free and able to move without constraint, celebrates the Mysteries. He lives among pure men and saints; he sees on earth the many who have not been initiated and purified buried in the mire and darkness and, through fear of death, clinging to their ills for want of belief in the happiness of the Beyond.

The Eleusinian Mysteries are said to have been founded by the goddess Demeter. According to the Homeric Hymn of the seventh century B.C., Hades, god of the underworld, asked Zeus' permission to marry Persephone and, as he received no downright refusal, was emboldened to carry off the maiden as she was gathering flowers. Demeter wandered the earth, sadly searching for her beloved daughter, until Helios, god of the sun, told her what Hades had done. She then shunned Olympus where she dwelt and wandered on earth, which she forbade to bring forth fruit. Zeus, when appealed to, finally told Demeter that her daughter might return, provided she had eaten nothing in the underworld, and he sent Hermes with his Caduceus to escort her back. Hades agreed to let Persephone go, but gave her a pomegranate to eat, and it was at last agreed that she should spend a third of the year with him in Hades, as Queen of the Underworld, and the rest of the year with Demeter, who once more allowed the earth to bear its fruit. In gratitude to the people of Eleusis who befriended her, the goddess Demeter founded the famous Eleusinian Mysteries.

Scriptural evidence exists and is confirmed by H.P. Blavatsky that—whether or not at this Institution—St. Paul was an Initiate. Occult tradition suggests that he was an Initiate of the Greater Mysteries, an idea which is supported by his use of certain terms from Mystery Rituals in his Epistles. Amongst these are:-

> "...as a wise masterbuilder, I have laid the foundation..." (I Cor. 3:10)
> "know ye not that ye are the temple of God, and that the Spirit of God dwelleth in you?" (I Cor. 3:16)
> "Let a man so account of us, as of the ministers of Christ, and stewards of the mysteries of God." (I Cor. 4:1)
>
> "Howbeit we speak wisdom among them that are perfect; yet not the wisdom of this world, nor of the princes of this world, that come to nought." (I Cor. 2:6)
>
> 'How that by revelation he made known unto me the mystery...' (Eph. 3:3)
>
> 'I knew a man in Christ above fourteen years ago, (whether in the body, I cannot tell; or whether out of the body, I cannot tell: God knoweth;) such an one caught up to the third heaven. And I knew such a man, (whether in the body, or out of the body, I cannot tell: God knoweth;) How that he was caught up into paradise, and heard unspeakable words, which it is not lawful for a man to utter.' (the Initiate's solemn vow of silence) (II Cor. 12:2-4)

The Lord Christ would at least seem to refer to the Mystery Tradition in His answer to the disciples' question:

> 'And the disciples came, and said unto him, why speakest thou unto them in parables? He answered and said unto them, Because it is given unto you to know the mysteries of the kingdom of heaven, but to them it is not given.' (Matt. 13:10-11)

These sacred procedures were carried out in many countries up to about the year 400 A.D., when the ancient ceremonials publicly came to a close. Only the ruins of the Temples now remain, as at Luxor, Karnak, Delphi, Corinth, Epidaurus and Eleusis, for example. The deeply occult procedure of Initiation has, however, continued until today, and will ever do so; for it is a law of the spiritual life that no single individual ever reaches the stage at which such Mystery ministrations could be helpful *without fully receiving them.*

The rise of Christianity and the cruel martyrdom of Hypatia in Alexandria in the fifth century — for holding opposing views — caused the Ancient Mysteries to cease to be publicly celebrated, as mentioned above. Nevertheless, it has been affirmed on good authority that the procedure of Initiation has continued and is now as active as it has ever been, even though concealed from a world that could neither understand nor benefit from its available activities. The opportunity for the individual Aspirant is, however, even greater than in olden days, **if only** because in certain aspects — though assuredly not in all — the grievous condition of humanity creates a very great need for the appearance and activity in the world of truly illumined and selflessly dedicated human beings — Initiates, in fact.

GLOSSARY

Absolute, The: The impersonal, supreme and incognisable Principle of the Universe. See Parabrahman.

Adept (Latin). *Adeptus*, 'He who has obtained'. An Initiate of the Fifth Degree in the Greater Mysteries, a Master in the science of esoteric philosophy, a perfected man, an exalted Being who has attained complete mastery over his purely human nature and possesses knowledge and power commensurate with lofty evolutionary stature. A fully Initiated Being who watches over and guides the progress of humanity.

Adi (Sk.): 'The first, the primeval'. The Foundation Plane, the first field of manifestation, 'the foundation of a universe, its support and the fount of its life.' For an exposition of the seven planes of Nature see *Through the Gateway of Death*, Geoffrey Hodson.

Akasa (Sk.): "The subtle, supersensuous, spiritual essence which pervades all space. The primordial substance erroneously identified with ether. But it is to ether what spirit is to matter. ... It is, in fact, the Eternal Space in which lies inherent the Ideation of the universe in its ever-changing aspects on the planes of matter and objectivity, and from which radiates the *First Logos* or expressed thought. This is why it is stated in the *Puranas* that *Akasa* has but one attribute, namely sound, for sound is but the translated symbol for *Logos*—'Speech' in its mystic sense. q.v. *The Theosophical Glossary*, H.P. Blavatsky.

Analogeticists: The Neo-Platonic School, founded in 191 A.D. by Ammonius Saccus, included Alexandrian philosophers who sought to interpret the Bible according to a system of allegory, analogy and symbol and were, in consequence, named Analogeticists.

Anupadaka (Sk.): 'Parentless', self-existing, born without progenitors, applied to both a plane of Nature—the second from above—and to those Great Beings who are in this sense parentless or 'self-born of the Divine Essence'.

Arhat (Sk.): 'The worthy'. Exoterically, 'one worthy of divine honours'. Esoterically, an Initiate of the Fourth Degree who has entered the highest Path and is thus emancipated from both self-separateness and enforced rebirth.

Astral: The region of the expression of all feelings and desires of the human soul. See also *Kama.*

Atma (Sk.): 'The Self'. The Universal Spirit, the seventh principle in the septenary constitution of man, the Supreme Soul. The Spirit-Essence of the universe. (Paramatman — 'the Self Beyond').

Avatara (Sk.): 'Descent'. The incarnation of a Deity, especially Vishnu, the Second Aspect of the Hindu *Trimurti.*

Brahma Vidya (Sk.): 'The wisdom of Brahma', the Supreme Deity.

Brahman (Sk.): The impersonal, supreme and incognisable Principle of the Universe, from the Essence of which all emanates and into which all returns. Extracted from *The Theosophical Glossary,* H. P. Blavatsky, and other sources.

Brahma's Day: 'A period of 2,160,000,000 (Earth) years during which Brahma having emerged out of his golden egg *(Hiranyagarbha),* creates and fashions the material world (being simply the fertilizing and creative force in Nature). After this period, the worlds being destroyed in turn by fire and water, he vanishes with objective nature, and then comes Brahma's Night.' q.v. *The Theosophical Glossary,* H.P. Blavatsky.

Brahma's Night: 'A period of equal duration, during which Brahma is said to be asleep. Upon awakening he recommences the process, and this goes on for an Age of Brahma composed of alternate 'Days', and 'Nights', and lasting 100 years [of 2,160,000,000 (Earth) years each]. It requires fifteen figures to express the duration of such an age; after the expiration of which the *Mahapralaya* or the Great Dissolution sets in, and lasts in its turn for the same space of fifteen figures." q.v. *The Theosophical Glossary,* H. P. Blavatsky.

Buddhi (Sk.): The sixth principle of man, that of intuitive wisdom, vehicle of the seventh, *Atma,* the supreme Soul in man. Universal Soul. The faculty which manifests as spiritual intuitiveness. The bliss Aspect of the Trinity.

Causal Body: The immortal body of the reincarnating Ego of man, built of matter of the 'higher' levels of the mental world. it is called Causal because it gathers up within it the results of all experiences, and these act as causes moulding future lives and influencing future conduct.

Chain: In occult philosophy a Solar System is said to consist of ten Planetary Schemes. Each Scheme, generally named according to its physically visible representative, is composed of seven Chains of Globes. In terms of time a Chain consists of the passage of the life-wave seven times around its seven Globes. Each such passage is called a Round, the completion of the seventh ending the life of the Chain. The Globes of a Round are both superphysical and physical and are arranged in a cyclic pattern, three being on a descending arc, three on an ascending arc and the middle, the fourth Globe, being the densest of all and the turning point. The active period of each of these units, from Solar System to Globe, called *Manvantara*, is succeeded by a passive period of equal duration, called *Pralaya*. The completion of the activity of the seventh Globe of the seventh Round of the seventh Chain brings to an end the activity of a Planetary Scheme. Our Earth Scheme is now in its fourth Round of its fourth Chain, and the life-wave is half-way through its period of activity on the fourth Globe, the physical Earth. Thus, the densest possible condition of substance is now occupied by Spirit and so by the Monads or spirits of men. The resistance of matter is at its greatest in this epoch, and this offers an explanation of the difficulties of human life at this period. The occupation of a physical planet by man consists of seven racial epochs and phases of evolutionary development. Throughout this work these are referred to as Root Races. According to that portion of occult philosophy which is concerned with the evolution of both the Immortal Soul and the mortal personality of man, an orderly progression is revealed. The basic rule is stated to be that the indwelling, conscious life in the mineral, plant, animal and human kingdoms of Nature advances to the kingdom above during a period of one Chain. Since each Chain is composed of seven Rounds, each Round is expected to be characterised by progress through subsidiary stages of the ultimate attainment for the Chain as a whole. Applied to man, the Monad has evolved Chain by Chain through mineral (first Chain), plant (second Chain) and animal (third Chain) into the individualised, self-conscious state characteristic of a human being of the fourth Chain. This is man's present position, and by the end of each of the remaining Rounds of this fourth Chain a certain degree of development will be attained. These stages chiefly concern the unfoldment of capacity for awareness and effective action — spiritual, intellectual, cultural and physical. Thus occult anthropology presents an orderly and systematic scheme of development for the life of all kingdoms of Nature.

At the end of the Seventh Root Race of this Fourth Round on earth the mass of humanity will have achieved the level now known as Initiateship or spiritual regeneration, characterised by Christ-consciousness, which includes both realisation of the unity of life and compassion for all living beings. At the end of the seventh Round the human race now evolving on earth is expected to achieve the stature of Adeptship or perfected manhood, 'the measure of the stature of the fulness of Christ'. (Eph. 4: 13). q.v. *The Solar System,* A.E. Powell, and *Lecture Notes of the School of the Wisdom,* Vol.I, Geoffrey Hodson.

Chakra (Sk.): A 'wheel' or 'disc'. A spinning, vortical, funnel-shaped force-centre with its opening on the surfaces of the etheric and subtler bodies of man and its stem leading to the superphysical counterparts of the spinal cord and of nerve centres or glands. There are seven main *chakras* associated severally with the sacrum, the spleen, the solar plexus, the heart, the throat and the pituitary and pineal glands. *Chakras* are both organs of superphysical consciousness and conveyors of the life-force between the superphysical and physical bodies. q.v. *The Chakras,* C.W. Leadbeater.

Creation: The emergence and subsequent development of a universe and its contents is regarded in occult philosophy as being less the result of an act of creation, followed by natural evolution, than a process of emanation guided by intelligent forces under immutable law. The creation or emergence of universes from nothing is not an acceptable concept, the Cosmos being regarded as emanating from an all-containing, sourceless Source, the Absolute.

Demiurgos (Gr.): The Demiurge or Artificer, the Supernal Power which built the Universe. Freemasons derive from this word their phrase 'Supreme Architect'. With the occultist it is the third manifested Logos, or Plato's second God, the second Logos being represented by him as the 'Father', the only Deity that he, as an Initiate of the Mysteries, dare mention. The demiurgic Mind is the same as the Universal Mind, named *Mahat* (Sk.) the first 'product' of Brahma.

Devas (Sk.): 'Shining ones', spiritual Beings, Planetary Logoi, and Hierarchies of Archangels and angels. The main stages of *devic* development have each their own name. Nature spirits, like animals and birds, are actuated by a group consciousness shared with others of the same genus. Gods, Sephiras, *devas* and angels have evolved out of group consciousness into separate individuality, as has man. Archangels, especially, have transcended the limitations of individuality and have entered into universal or cosmic consciousness, as has the Superman or Adept.

Ego: The threefold, immortal, unfolding spiritual Self of man in its vesture of light, the 'Robe of Glory' of the Gnostics and the *Karana Sharira* or Causal Body of Hindu philosophy. This higher Triad evolves to Adeptship by virtue of successive lives on Earth, all linked together because they are reincarnations of the same spiritual Self. Thus the Ego is an individualised manifestation of the Monad, which is the eternal Self of man, the Dweller in the Innermost, a unit of the Spirit-Essence of the Universe. The term is used throughout this work to denote the unfolding spiritual Self of man in which the attribute of individuality inheres. The adjective 'Egoic' refers to the Ego in this sense.

Elohim (Heb.): 'Gods'. A sevenfold power of Godhead, the male-female Hierarchies of creative Intelligences or Potencies through which the Divine produces the manifested Universe; the unity of the powers, the attributes and the creative activities of the Supreme Being. 'Elohim' is a plural name, the singular form of the word being 'Eloha', *i.e.* a 'god'.

Fohat (Tib.): 'Divine Energy'. The constructive force of cosmic electricity, polarised into the positive and negative currents of terrestrial electricity; the ever-present electrical energy; the universal, propellant, vital force.

God: In occult philosophy the term 'God' in its highest meaning refers to a Supreme, Eternal and Indefinable Reality. This Absolute is inconceivable, ineffable and unknowable. Its revealed existence is postulated in three terms: an absolute Existence, an absolute consciousness, and an absolute bliss. Infinite consiousness is regarded as inherent in the Supreme Being as a dynamic force that manifests the potentialities held in its own infinitude, and calls into being forms out of its own formless depths.

Group Soul: The pre-individualised manifestation of the human Monads when evolving through the mineral, the plant and the animal kingdoms of Nature. q.v. *A Study in Consciousness*, A. Besant.

Guna (Sk.): 'A string or cord'. The three qualities or attributes inherent in matter: *Rajas,* activity, desire; *Sattva,* harmony, rhythm; *Tamas,* inertia, stagnation. These correspond to the three Aspects of the Trinity — Father, Son and Holy Ghost — or Brahma, Vishnu and Shiva respectively.

Hierophant (Gr.): 'One who explains sacred things'. The discloser of sacred learning and the Chief of the Initiates. A title belonging to the highest Adepts in the temples of antiquity, who were teachers and expounders of the Mysteries and the Initiators into the final great Mysteries. q.v. *The Theosophical Glossary,* H. P. Blavatsky;

Initiate: From the Latin *Initiatus*. The designation of anyone who was received into and had revealed to him the mysteries and secrets of occult philosophy.

Initiation: A profound spiritual and psychological regeneration, as a result of which a new 'birth' a new beginning and a new life are entered upon. The word itself, from the Latin *Initia,* also implies the basic or first principles of any science, suggesting that Initiates are consciously united with their own First Principle, the Monad from which they emerged. Both the Lesser and the Greater Mysteries, ancient and modern, confer Initiations of various Degrees upon successful Candidates.

Kabbalah (Heb.): From QBLH, 'an unwritten or oral tradition'. The hidden wisdom of the Hebrew Rabbis derived from the secret doctrine of the early Hebrew peoples. q.v. *The Kingdom of the Gods,* Pt. III, Ch. IV, Geoffrey Hodson.

Kama (Sk.): 'Desire', feeling, emotion, See Astral.

Karma (Sk.): 'Action', connoting both the law of action and reaction, cause and effect, and the result of its operation upon nations and individuals. q.v. *Reincarnation, Fact or Fallacy?*, Geoffrey Hodson.

Kundalini (Sk.): 'The coiled up, universal Life Principle'. A sevenfold, superphysical occult power in Universe and man, functioning in the latter by means of a spiral or coiling action, mainly in the spinal cord but also throughout the nervous systems. It is represented in Greek symbology by the Caduceus. When supernormally aroused this fiery force ascends into the brain by a serpentine path, hence its other name, the 'Serpent Fire'. q.v. *The Hidden Wisdom in the Holy Bible*, Vol.I, Pt. III, Ch. I under "Serpents"; *Lecture Notes of the School of the Wisdom*, Vol.II, Ch.I, Sec. III, Geoffrey Hodson; *The Serpent Power*, Arthur Avalon (Sir John Woodroffe).

Kundalini Shakti (Sk.): The power of life; one of the forces of Nature. The occult electricity intimately associated with Azoth of the Alchemists, the creative principle in Nature, and *Akasa* (Sk.), the subtle, supersensuous, spiritual essence which pervades all space. The seven-layered power in the base of the spine of man, composed of three currents which flow along three canals in the spinal cord, named *Ida* (negative), *Pingala* (positive) and *Sushumna* (neutral). These names are sometimes also applied—erroneously—to the currents of force which flow in these canals. q.v. *The Kingdom of the Gods*, Geoffrey Hodson.

Logos (Gr.): "The Word", 'A divine, spiritual Entity'. The manifested Deity, the outward expression or effect of the ever-concealed Cause. Thus speech is the *Logos* of thought, and *Logos* is correctly translated into Latin as *Verbus* and into English as 'Word' in the metaphysical sense. See *Vach*.

Logos Doctrine: The universe is first conceived in divine thought, which is the governing power in creation. The creative 'Word' expressive of the idea is then 'spoken' and the hitherto quiescent seeds of living things germinate and appear from within the ocean of Space, the Great Deep. q.v. *Lecture Notes of the School of the Wisdom*, Vol.II, Pt.2, Sec. 2, Geoffrey Hodson.

Macrocosm (Gr.): Literally 'Great Universe' or Cosmos.

Manas (Sk.): 'Mind'. Generally used in reference to the planes of Nature built of mind-stuff, and to the mental faculties of man.

Manu (Sk.): "Thought' A generic term applied to Creators, Preservers and Fashioners. *Manvantara* means, literally, the period presided over by a *Manu*. According to their function and Office they are called Race, Seed, Round and Chain *Manus*, and so on up to the Solar Logos Himself. *Pralaya*, on the other hand, is a period of obscuration or repose, whether planetary or universal—the opposite of *Manvantara*—and is symbolised in *Genesis* and in all flood legends by their deluges.

Manvantara (Sk.): "Period between *Manus*'. Epoch of creative activity. A period of manifestation, as opposed to *Pralaya* (see preceding reference to *Manu* and also under Chain).

Microcosm (Gr.): "Little Universe'. The reflection in miniature of the Macrocosm. Thus the atom may be spoken of as the "microcosm" of the Solar System, its electrons moving under the same laws; and man may be termed the "microcosm" of the universe, since he has within himself all the elements of that universe.

Monad (Gr.): "Alone'. The divine Spirit in man, the 'Dweller in the Innermost,' which is said to evolve through the sub-human kingdoms of Nature into the human and thence to the stature of the Adept, beyond which extend unlimited evolutionary heights. The description of the destiny of man given by the Lord Christ supports this concept, for He said: ' Be ye (Ye shall be—R.V.) therefore perfect, even as your Father which is in heaven is perfect.' *(Matt.* 5:48—A.V.).

Mulaprakriti (Sk.): "Root matter," 'undifferentiated substance'. The abstract, deific, feminine principle, the *Parabrahmic* root. *Prakriti* (Sk.) Nature or matter as opposed to Spirit, the two primeval aspects of the One Unknown Deity.

Mysteries, The: From *Muo* (Gr.), 'to close the mouth,' *Teletai* (Gr.), "Celebrations of Initiation". The Sacred Mysteries were enacted in the ancient Temples by the initiated Hierophants for the benefit and instruction of the Candidates. A series of secret dramatic performances, in which the mysteries of cosmogony and Nature were personified by the priests and neophytes. These were explained in their hidden meaning to the Candidates for Initiation. q.v. *Eleusis and the Eleusinian Mysteries,* George E. Mysonas; *The Eleusinian and Bacchic Mysteries,* Thomas Taylor: *The Mysteries of Eleusis,* Georges Meautis, Professor at the University of Neuchatel.

Occultist: A student of the 'hidden' powers, forces and intelligences in Nature. Whilst necromancy may—very undesirably—be resorted to by such a student, the practice is frowned upon by all teachers of white or wholly altruistic occultism. These point out that the discovery of truth demands increasing self-control, and that any surrender of one's will to another leads to self-delusion and untruth.

All researches motived by the twin ideals of attaining knowledge and so of becoming more helpful to mankind are, in consequence, carried out whilst in command of mind and will. The power to produce occult phenomena is developed by self-training, but these are always the result of the will and thought of the operator employed in that full consciousness and complete self-command which are essential to success.

Occult Science: "The science of the secrets of nature—physical and psychic, mental and spiritual; called Hermetic and Esoteric Sciences. In the West, the Kabbalah may be named; in the East, mysticism, magic, and Yoga philosophy, which latter is often referred to by the Chelas in India as the *seventh* 'Darshana' (school of philosophy), there being only *six Darshanas* in India known to the world of the profane. These sciences are, and have been for ages, hidden from the vulgar for the very good reason that they would never be appreciated by the selfish educated classes, nor understood by the uneducated; whilst the former might misuse them for their own profit, and thus turn the divine science into *black magic*....' q.v. *The Theosophical Glossary,* H.P. Blavatsky.

Om or *Aum* (Sk.): The name of the triple Deity. A syllable of affirmation, invocation and divine benediction.

Parabrahma (Sk.): 'Beyond Brahma'. The Supreme, Infinite Brahma, the 'Absolute', attributeless, secondless Reality, the impersonal, nameless, universal and Eternal Principle. *Brahman* (Sk.): The impersonal, supreme and incognisable Principle of the

Universe, from the Essence of which all emanates and into which all returns. q.v. *The Theosophical Glossary*, H.P. Blavatsky, and other sources.

Prakriti (Sk.): Primarily original substance; the productive element from and out of which all material manifestations or appearances are evolved; Nature in general is the 'producer' of beings and things, with Spirit *(Purusha)* as the ever-active Creator; the veil of *Purusha*, the two in reality being one.

Pralaya: "Epoch of quiescence". A period of obscuration or repose, whether planetary or universal. q.v. *The Secret Doctrine*, p. 146 (Original Edition).

Sephira (Heb.): An emanation of Deity.

Shakti (Sk.): 'Ability', 'power,' capability, faculty, strength. The outgoing energy of a god is spoken of as his wife or *Shakti*. Thus, although a Deity or a central personage and his consort or wife are presented as two separate people, the latter (wife) actually personifies attributes or powers of the former (husband). In consequence, the supposed pair in reality represent one being.

Soul: When spelt with a capital 'S" this word refers to the unfolding, immortal, spiritual Self of man, the true individuality behind the bodily veil. When spelt with a small 's' it is used for the *psyche* or mental, emotional, vital and solid physical parts of the mortal man. Heb. *Nephesh Chaiah*, 'souls of life" or 'living soul'. *(Gen. 2:7)*.

Spirit: Not an entity but that which belongs directly to Universal Consciousness. The most tenuous, formless and immaterial spiritual substance, the divine Essence.

Sun: In occult philosophy the physical sun is regarded as the densest of the seven vehicles of the Solar Logos, the mighty Being in whom and by whom the Solar System exists. The other six vehicles are said to be constructed of superphysical matter of decreasing degrees of density, and to be sheaths and centres for the radiation of the power, life and consciousness of the Solar Logos.

Torah (Heb.): 'Law'. The *Pentateuch* or Law of Moses.

Vach: The mystic personification of speech. The female Logos, one with *Brahma*, who created 'Her' out of one half of 'His' body. Also called 'the Female Creator". Esoterically the subjective force emanating from the creative Deity.

Zohar: "The Book of Splendour", the basic work of Jewish Mysticism, the greatest exposition of the *Kabbalah*.

SCIENTISTS' AFFIRMATIONS

Prof. J.T. Robinson, Dr.Sc.
7326 Cedar Creek Trail, Madison, Wisconsin, 53717, U.S.A.

4 January 1981

'I was able to work very closely with Geoffrey Hodson for some months during the late fifties testing his clairvoyant powers on places of fossils of early man about two million years of age. Each session carried out in the field site from which the specimens came, was recorded on a tape recorder. No indication was given him what I thought of his information until after the series of tests were completed and analysed. Many of the questions put to him required answers which could be positively checked against known original specimens. The analysis showed that every statement made by him which was able to be positively checked against known specimens was absolutely accurate and most of what could not be positively checked was in close agreement with what was thought to be correct. At that time almost all of the known fossil material of those early hominids was in my laboratory and Geoffrey did not see of it until after the investigations were completed. I was impressed by the extreme care he took over being as accurate and clear as he could be in the observations he made, as well as his descriptions of them in such a way that his words were as precise as possible in offering the least possibility of misinterpretation. At each session a small number (2—4) of specimens were dealt with, and some were presented several times at more than one session without telling him this. He never handled the specimens himself; I placed them on his forehead while he was lying on his back with his eyes closed in a state of Yoga. Two different species of hominid were used mixed at random, only small specimens being used e.g. a single tooth. He never misidentified a specimen of gave conflicting statements about a specimen that had been presented more than once. As far as I could determine, his information was always accurate and he gave me a strong impression of complete reliability'

D.D. Lyness, M.B.CH.B., D.P.M., M.A.N.Z.C.P.,
295, Margaret Street, Toowoomba, Queenland 4350.

11 September 1981

'During the years 1956 to 1959 I was fortunate enough to work with Geoffrey Hodson. My contribution was to record his observations on the clairvoyant appearance of sub-atomic matter; I now have some forty hours on cassette tape giving a verbatim account of the experiments we performed. There is no doubt whatsoever in my mind that Geoffrey possesses quite remarkable powers of extra-sensory perception and invariably used these faculties with meticulous regard for accuracy in both observation and description. He frequently stressed the selective nature of clairvoyant observation and was fully aware of the pitfalls associated with the translation of what can be called "raw extrasensory data" through the brain-mind into words capable of conveying useful meaning to his hearers. Throughout these sessions he was a model of scientific caution, taking every possible care not to make statements that might be misleading'.

M.A. Stentiford M.Sc (Physics),
22 Kingston Heights Road, Wellington 2, New Zealand.

May 1982

'For many years, Geoffrey Hodson has co-operated with various scientifically qualified people in attempts to demonstrate the research potential of superphysical faculties of perception, with which he is evidently highly gifted. From 1978 to 1981 I was closely associated with him as assistant and technical adviser in two such pieces of research.

The first of these was an extensive series of observations of the superphysical effects of musical sounds and pieces. The record of his descriptions of these effects is extremely interesting from the artistic, acoustic, psychosomatic and other points of view.

The second main area, undertaken at the request of Dr E. Lester Smith of England, was an attempt to make further observations of matter at the atomic and subatomic levels with a view of testing recent hypotheses on the interpretation of the "Occult Chemistry" findings of C.W. Leadbeater and Annie Besant. This work has produced a number of tape recordings of Geoffrey Hodson's descriptions which are in the process of being transcribed and will be sent to England for analysis.

Having been present with him throughout the approximately 20 hour-long sessions in these two investigations, I feel able to offer some impressions of his attitude and approach to this work.

I have been repeatedly struck by his integrity and uncompromising desire to seek the truth in every situation, regardless of any risk of possible conflict with established findings of the scientific establishment or of earlier theosophical investigators. At the same time, he is clearly aware of the difficulties and limitations inherent in any process of observation, especially one involving inner levels of the psyche, and has a tremendously careful and indeed craftsmanlike attitude to the handling and direction of his extended perceptive abilities.

In my opinion, Geoffrey Hodson has amply succeeded in his goals of (a) indicating the potential of superphysical research methods, (b) producing material of great interest to the enquiring mind, and (c) providing a stimulus to others to follow his footsteps and expand and consolidate this work '.